MONSIGNOR WILLIAM BARRY MEMORIAL LIBRARY
BARRY UNIVERSITY
0 2211 0041256 0

D1565212

THE CHICAGO PUBLIC LIBRARY
FORM 19

A Frenchman, A Chaplain, A Rebel

THE WAR LETTERS OF
Pere Louis-Hippolyte Gache, S.J.

TRANSLATED BY CORNELIUS M. BUCKLEY, S.J.

LOYOLA UNIVERSITY PRESS

Chicago 60657

ISBN 8294-0376-0

ACKNOWLEDGMENTS

Special acknowledgment is made to:

Alderman Library, University of Virginia, Charlottesville, Virginia for material contained in the Z. Lee Gilmer Diary, referred to on page 76.

Bancroft Library, University of California, Berkeley, California for material from the Phoebe Apperson Hearst Papers referred to on page 140.

Howard-Tilton Memorial Library, Tulane University, New Orleans, Louisiana, for material from the papers of the Louisiana Historical Association Collection, referred to on pages 54, 227 and 228.

Swem Library, College of William and Mary, Williamsburg, Virginia, for material from the Ewell Papers, referred to on pages 80, 100, and 230.

Jacket photograph of Hippolyte Gache, S.J., obtained from Mme. Roselyne Laffont.

PREFACE

This book has been years in the making. I began working on the Gache manuscript while I was studying theology in France during the early 1960s. The letters were a therapeutic distraction from what I considered then—mistakenly I am sure—lethal class lectures.

Years later I began tracking down the people whose names were contained in the correspondence. This practice too began as a diversion. Then a whole new world opened up for me. Through Father Hippolyte Gache I met many delightful people who seemed pleased to accommodate the requests of a pesky stranger for help in identifying persons long since dead and forgotten. And thanks to the one-time Louisiana chaplain, I was introduced to many fascinating libraries and archival deposits. For such generosity extended I am indebted to many people and to many institutions. I can't mention them all, but there are some who must be singled out because they pursued me with their kindness. Among these are: Mrs. Lucille Mallon Connick, G.P.S. of Mobile, Alabama; Mrs. E. A. Broders of Baton Rouge, Louisiana; Mrs. Mary B. Oalmann, Military Historian, Jackson Barracks, New Orleans; Rev. Thomas F. Mulcrone, S.J., Loyola University, New Orleans; Dr. James H. Bailey, Historical Advisor, City of Petersburg, Virginia; Rev. Monsignor Richard C. Madden, Summerville, South Carolina; Mr. Eric Frank, Jones Memorial Library, Lynchburg, Virginia; Mrs. Anne W. Chapman, former Teaching Instructor, Department of History, and Mr. Jay Rader, former undergraduate, College of William and Mary, Williamsburg, Virginia; Mr. Stuart B. Campbell, Wytheville, Virginia; Rev. George J. Cleaveland, D.D., Register of the Diocese of Virginia; Mrs. Constance Stone McCulloch, Richmond, Virginia and Rev. Hervé P. Racivitch, S.J., New Orleans, La. I am also indebted to those families whose names are printed in the bibliography who have allowed me to make use of private papers and Bibles, and to the universities and archives, also named in the bibliography, who have permitted me to cite passages from manuscripts contained in their collections. I would also like to thank Jean Ertel who has saved me from making many a gaff and who has done a splendid editorial job.

Finally, readers will observe there are still a few persons not properly identified; that there are still some loose ends dangling. Although the book was composed leisurely, quite suddenly its publication has become urgent to coincide with the one hundred-and-fiftieth anniversary of Spring Hill College, Alabama.

Cornelius Buckley, S.J.
University of San Francisco
May 1, 1981

To the Jesuits of the South:

In esteem for the living;
in reverence for the dead.

Laudemus viros gloriosos
et parentes nostros in generatione sua.

CONTENTS

INTRODUCTION

During the American Civil War Louis-Hippolyte Gache, S.J., C.S.A., the chaplain of the Tenth Louisiana Volunteer Regiment, wrote in French, with relative frequency and easy familiarity, to his Jesuit confreres at Spring Hill College, near Mobile, Alabama. The extant pages of this correspondence were discovered by the editor-translator in the archives of the Paris Province of the Society of Jesus, Chantilly, France, and they are now on permanent loan to the Gleeson Library, University of San Francisco. Each letter serves notice that the author was more than a talented, educated, and sensitive observer of affairs; he was a participant in them, and even though these seventeen letters can be regarded collectively as one more account of a participant's experience in the *lost cause*, they focus on an aspect of the war which is different—the world of an urbane French-born chaplain in the Confederate Army.

The value of this correspondence—its charm one might say—has very little to do with the important considerations of the war. In his pursuit to inform his friends about the events he lived through and about the people he encountered, Chaplain Gache drew on the varied background of his own educational training in a most engaging way. That he frequently dwelt on platitudes and that the reader can anticipate most conclusions in his reconstructed conversations with a whole range of characters, makes little difference. Nor does it make much difference that sometimes he has intimations of goshawfulness. He has managed to get warmth, subtlety, compassion, humor, and—oh yes, much irony into his pages. He could be pompous, but not for too long. And he had a capacity for self-pity—for which he sometimes had reason—along with the knack of projecting it, but he also had the wonderful ability to mock himself at the very instant he was describing a real or supposed predicament.

He was born near the village of Beaulieu, Ardèche, France, on June 18, 1817, the oldest child of Paul-Fermin (1792-1872) and Marie Vauclaure (1794-1823) Gache, landowning peasants in a vine-producing area of the Languedoc. In 1826, three years after his mother's death, young Louis-Hypolite (for that is how he spelled his name then) journeyed some thirty tortuous miles down through the valleys of the Cévennes to Bourg-Saint-Andéol, an ancient town of tile roofs and honey-colored walls that clung to the right bank of the Rhône. Here he enrolled in the *petit sêminaire.* This establishment had been founded in 1713 by the bishop of Viviers as an alternative seminary for the "poor of the diocese who felt themselves called to the priestly state; here, between the ages of eight and ten, they were welcomed, lodged, fed and looked after without being obliged to pay for their keep, until the day of their ordination." During the Revolution the seminary was suppressed and the buildings sold, but in 1826 another bishop of Viviers repurchased part of the old building, and once again opened up the doors, under less generous terms, to boarding students from the back country of his diocese. Over the course of the next ten years the young seminarian distinguished himself in the classroom, winning the reputation of being an outstanding classical student, a lad of great promise. Then in 1836, at the age of nineteen, he made a momentous decision: he would shake the clay of Bourg-Saint-Andéol from his boots and begin his studies in rhetoric at the famous French Jesuit *collège-en-exile* at Chambéry, Savoy, in the Kingdom of Sardinia.[1] This was also the alma mater of Joseph de Maistre, the spokesman of the ultramontane position in Restoration France.

The Society of Jesus had been restored throughout the Roman Catholic world in 1814, and although still illegal in Restoration France, the Jesuits began, cautiously at first and then with recklessness, to open *collèges* throughout the length and breadth of the kingdom where they had been forever exiled in 1764. In less than fourteen years they had founded eight such institutions, all of which were now thriving. But this success had also given an incentive to their many enemies to free France once and for all from Jesuit influence, and so in 1828, submitting to mounting pressure, Charles X signed into law ordinances prohibiting members of the order from conducting schools in the lands of His Most Christian Majesty. The result was that the Jesuits once again packed up books and class notes and took to the roads that led to the frontiers. In neighboring lands, including Savoy, they set up a series of *collèges-en-exile* to accommodate parents intent that their sons receive an education which was radically French and unquestionably ultramontane, and also to provide seminary training for the large number of young men, like the nineteen-year-old seminarian from Bourg-Saint-Andéol, who were drawn to the priesthood in this post-Napoleonic era. Very probably at this period in his career, Hippolyte Gache indicated his desire to enter the Society of Jesus because he transferred, in 1837, to yet another Savoyard *collège*, at Mélan, where to defray expenses he acted as a disciplinarian to the younger boys while he pursued his philosophical studies and underwent the discerning scrutiny of older French Jesuits, who decided in 1840 that he was indeed ready to join the brotherhood.[2]

If many Jesuits had left France in 1828 to staff the *collèges-en-exile*, there were a number who stayed on, choosing to become itinerant missionaries in the rural areas of the country. Some of these now turned their attention to Ardèche, sacred in Jesuit history because of the almost legendary St. John Francis Regis (1597-1640) who had spent most of his life preaching in villages like Beaulieu before his death at La Louvesc. The guidebook of these new missionaries was everywhere the same, the *Spiritual Exercises* of their founder St. Ignatius Loyola (1491-1556), and in 1834 they took over the direction of a group of the Religious of the Cenacle, a local institute of nuns founded at La Louvesc to promulgate the *Spiritual Exercises.* Most probably the first Jesuit Gache had met was one of these traveling missionaries whose number had increased to such an extent that in 1836—the year he left for Chambéry—the General of the Order, Johann Roothaan (1785-1853), decided that the time had come to set up a new administrative district in France, separate from Paris, at Lyons. The "Province of Lyons" inherited a novitiate which had been established at Avignon in 1823. The history of this house of formation for aspirants to the Society of Jesus indicates how susceptible Jesuits were to the Bourbon government's vacillating policy and how insecure their legal status was in the neighboring sovereign states. Within a space of five years the novitiate had made five major moves between Switzerland and Savoy, but by September 8, 1840, when Hippolyte Gache was formally accepted as a novice to the Society of Jesus, the novitiate had settled down to unaccustomed tranquility beside the left bank of the fast flowing Rhône, some forty miles from Bourg-Saint-Andéol, at Avignon.[3]

At this date there were thirty-five scholastic novices in the community, besides nineteen priests and eleven lay brothers. Even though the Province of Lyons had been in existence a mere four years and had no corporate legal rights, it already numbered 281 Jesuits, fifty-seven of whom were studying for the priesthood.[4] Neither the restrained Latin prose nor the controlled handwritten script of the Province's lithographed *Litterae Annuae*, which were periodically published to describe the life of the novices for the benefit of Jesuit houses throughout the world, were able to muffle the loud and clear enthusiasm and unquestioned vision which were so characteristic of the Jesuits of Nineteenth-Century France. It was into this world of confident purpose that Hippolyte Gache was introduced, and after completing the customary two years of ascetical training, built around the *Spiritual Exercises*, he pronounced the perpetual vows of poverty, chastity and obedience in the Society of Jesus, and was sent to the hamlet of Vals, near Le Puy, Haute-Loire, to begin his study of scholastic theology. There is a road from Avignon to Vals which passes through Bourg-Saint-Andéol before climbing the mountains and twisting about conveniently near to Beaulieu. It is not recorded if the newly professed Jesuit scholastic took advantage of this appealing itinerary to visit his former teachers and his family, or if he emulated the model Jesuit missionary, St. Francis Xavier (1506-52), who, according to the popular belief of the time, gave his native village a wide berth under similar circumstances. Judging from Gache's wartime correspondence one might reasonably conclude that the future chaplain used every excuse, making certain that each one came somehow from the highest spiritual motives, to walk again through the cloisters of the *petit sêminaire* and to tarry a bit amid the parched rolling hills and scrawny vineyards of that corner of Ardèche which some unknown wit had baptized Beaulieu.

But if the route he followed in 1842 is unknown, certain is the fact that he met two men at Vals who had a considerable influence on his attitudes as a Confederate chaplain. The first of these men was the rector, John Baptist Les Maisounabe (1805-48). Maisounabe had been trained at Saint-Sulpice, Paris, and immediately after his ordination at the age of twenty-four, he was named Professor of Theology at the seminary in his native town of Bayonne. In October 1832 he gave up this position, and with it the certain guarantee of an episcopal appointment, in order to join the peripatetic Jesuit novitiate in the diaspora. While still a novice he returned to France in 1834 to fill the chair of Canon Law and Ecclesiastical History at Vals, the newly established theologate, where seven years later he was appointed rector. A Basque who wore a velvet glove over an iron fist, Maisounabe was a brilliant organizer, a man of energy and charm, a religious of the strictist observance whose own ambition to win spiritual conquests for the glory of God in Africa, Asia or America was easily disseminated to the Jesuit scholastics who had been sent to the theologate to complete their studies before ordination to the priesthood.

The teaching of theology at Vals at this date, although traditional in form and somewhat inclined to the defensive in consequence of past controversies, was solid and substantial. Those who left its cloister were educated men, but they were educated within the limits of a religious ideal. The ideal had not yet lost its vitality; that is to say, it had not lost the power of moving its devotees to sustained and successful action. Yet, sometimes the zeal of the scholastics was difficult to channel. There was so much to be done in so short a time. In the 1830s the Society of Jesus was a young man's order. The sap was still rising and the enthusiasms were undimmed, but the year Gache arrived at Vals a good number of the thirty-three students had already passed their thirtieth birthday, some being older than the rector himself. It was not easy for these and for others who were not as intellectually endowed nor as willfully integrated as Maisounabe to reconcile missionary enthusiasm with the sedentary life required to unravel the tangled threads of theological speculation. The spiritual director, François-Xavier Gautrelet (1807-86), had long considered this problem before the feast of his patron saint (December 3), 1844, when he assembled Hippolyte Gache and his fellow students together to suggest what he considered a practical way to reconcile the activity of the apostolic life with the forced immurement of Vals. His solution was the blueprint of what later became known as the worldwide organization, the Apostleship of Prayer. This plan was scarcely innovative, for it reflected the teachings of basic Christianity, drew copiously from the inspiration of the *Spiritual Exercises*, and borrowed from the affective piety of the so-called French School of Spirituality by stressing the humiliated states of Jesus in his incarnate and eucharistic life.

Gautrelet's method in establishing the Apostleship of Prayer was not revolutionary either, having for its model The Society for the Propagation of the Faith. He suggested forming a club, a union whose members would support the apostolic endeavours of the church throughout the world by their prayers and by the daily sufferings they experienced. Almost twenty-five years before Gautrelet's historic conference, a young Lyons woman, Pauline Jaricot (1799-1862) with the encouragement of Louis DuBourg (1766-1833), bishop first of Louisiana and the Floridas, and later of Louisiana, had founded the Society for the Propagation of the Faith. The members of this association agreed to donate the equivalent of five cents per month and to recite certain prayers for missionaries working throughout the world. It would be difficult to overestimate the importance of the Society for the Propagation of the Faith in the history of the antebellum Catholic church in the Gulf States. But equally difficult it would be to exaggerate the historic significance of Gautrelet's conference at Vals in December 1844. Even though his ideas and methodology were not novel, Gautrelet captured the enthusiasm of Gache and his fellow seminarians with the outline of the Apostleship of Prayer. Stressing the belief that although missionary success depended on activity and financial donations, it relied even more on prayer and mutual support. The Vals seminarians, the first members of the inchoate association, agreed to make an offering of themselves each day at mass at which time they would also offer all of their prayers, works and sufferings for the other members of the association, particularly for those working in the missions. An exchange of information was essential. From the time of Ignatius, Jesuits had been encouraged to correspond frequently with home base, and the *Lettres édifiantes et curieuses* and the *Relations des Jésuites* demonstrate how seriously French Jesuits before the Suppression took these recommendations. Following the practice of the Propagation of the Faith, Gautrelet reemphasized the practical apostolic advantage of exchanging information, a feature which explains to some extent the rationale behind Gache's correspondence with the Spring Hill Jesuits—who by prayers, works and sufferings in their less dramatic lives—were supporting him in his army apostolate.

Gautrelet published the basic features for his association in a booklet entitled *l'Apostolat de la prière* (1846) while Gache was still at Vals; and, until 1861, the confraternity slowly gained new members outside of Jesuit circles. The year that Gache enlisted in the Tenth Louisiana Regiment there was an explosive growth of the Apostleship of Prayer—thanks to one of the chaplain's fellow novices, whose own request to join the Louisiana Mission had been repeatedly thwarted. Henri Ramière (1821-84), a prolific writer and a man of unbounded energy, recast Gautrelet's plan into a more sophisticated mould, and by doing so structured and subordinated it to the ecclesiastical hierarchy. Its system became arterial—from Rome to the smallest village in some remote section of the world. Its periodicals were numerous, and although the worldwide expansion of the Apostleship of Prayer is a moving page in the spiritual history of France, it is not pertinent to the present work to note that by 1900 there were in the United States alone more than four million members of this Vals inspired movement. But what is pertinent is that Hippolyte Gache and his companions, who came to the South in 1847, brought with them many of the distinguishing characteristics which were, at a later date, destined to influence American Catholic popular spirituality and to contribute to its post Civil War vitality. True, the spirituality reflected in Hippolyte Gache's wartime letters to his peers is sketchy, spotty, alloyed with flexible good humor, and in itself of no lasting significance. After all, these letters were never meant for publication. But what little spirituality there is in his correspondence bears witness to the Vals synthesis, an aggregate of those religious principles and methods the author learned from such men as Maisounabe and Gautrelet. Moreover, some knowledge of this Vals spirituality enables today's reader of his war letters to appreciate better the manner the Confederate chaplain employed in directing and instructing others during the war years. For this reason some familiarity with the multiphased history of the Society of Jesus in France between 1814 and 1848 is significant for one aspect of the history of the American South. It also clarifies the reasons why the Jesuits of the restored Society returned to the South when they did.[5]

In June 1845, the smoldering anti-Jesuit sentiment broke out anew in the bourgeois monarchy, and for awhile it seemed as if the whole order, not merely the *collèges*, would be proscribed by Guizot's government. Roothaan recommended that the larger communities be dispersed, that all controversy be avoided and that the Society maintain a low corporate profile. Once again ministries were curtailed and the Avignon novitiate scurried across the border. Quite suddenly there was an excess of capable men without job opportunities to meet their talents and training. Such was the state of affairs in early 1846 when Reverend John Bazin (1796-1848), a former president of floundering Spring Hill College near Mobile, Alabama, appeared in Lyons. He had been sent to Europe by Mobile's first Catholic bishop, Michael Portier (1795-1859), to recruit qualified teachers to save the college from extinction. Portier, like Bazin a native of the Lyonnais, entertained great hopes for the seminary-college he had founded in 1830, less than a year after his Mobile appointment. But the short and turbulent history of Spring Hill, chartered in 1836, convinced him that if the institution was to perdure it had to have stability, continuity and a source of qualified manpower—contingencies which only a religious order could guarantee.[6]

The political climate both in France and in Alabama favored Bazin's argument that the Lyons Jesuits should assume responsibility for Spring Hill. Terms which transferred the properties and administration of the college from the bishop to the Society of Jesus were hurriedly concluded during the summer, by which time the twenty-nine year old Gache had acquired a peasant's ruggedness combined with a careful education, a refined taste and a splendid physique. He had been ordained a priest on March 28; and on October 27 he and five companions bid their *suprêmes adieux* to France at Le Havre where they boarded a ship bound for Guadeloupe. After a particularly difficult crossing the party reached its destination on December 8; and then, with more delays which kept the Jesuits in the West Indies until after Christmas, the haggard voyagers at last disembarked at Mobile, Alabama on January 17, 1847.[7] More than forty years later Hippolyte Gache wrote his soldier nephew who had expressed a preference "of living a bit longer and of leaving the inhabitants of Tonkin to take care of their own affairs," that "it was very true that while at Vals I myself asked our very reverend Father General permission to go preach the Gospel to barbarian peoples. But what I requested was the opposite to what I felt: I had a great fear both of crossing the ocean and of being killed. ... Alas, they sent me to America where I never dreamed of going." Good soldiers do not choose their battlefields.[8]

While yet in France one of the members of the group, Francis de Sales Gautrelet (b. Lampigni, Saône-et-Loire, France, June 27, 1814–d. New Orleans, Louisiana, December 20, 1894), the younger brother of François-Xavier, was appointed superior of the Jesuit community and president of the reorganized college. An irenic man, he had the reputation of being moderate and wise, but his experience had not prepared him to work with perfect equilibrium through the obstacles he encountered at Spring Hill. Even though one of his chief concerns had been partially resolved by the addition of more Jesuits, several of whom even spoke English, the possibility for opening the college in September seemed indeed remote in the spring of 1847. The fact that classes did begin on schedule is perhaps the most telling testimonial of all to the courage, determination and corporate vision of these immigrants from Lyons. Hippolyte Gache was not present for this momentous occasion even though his name appeared on the printed prospectus of faculty members. While still in

France he had been singled out to work in the diocese of New Orleans, and therefore early in 1847 he proceeded to take up his new assignment at St. Charles College, Grand Coteau, in St. Laundry Parish.[9] This institution had been founded by Jesuit Father Nicholas Point (1799-1868) in 1837. Point has been described by one Jesuit historian as a neurotic soul who was given to fits of melancholy and by another as a superior who suffered from being ahead of his times. Perhaps he was both. At any rate, he played a brief yet significant role in the reestablishment of the Jesuits in Louisiana, even though he is better known for his psychedelic-like art work and for his labors among the Indians of the Northwest.[10]

In April, 1847, Grand Coteau and the few Jesuit outposts and parishes in Louisiana were united with Spring Hill to become a mission dependent on the Province of Lyons. From this date until 1905, two years before Gache's death, all Jesuit institutions and personnel in the South were attached to the Province of Lyons, a fact which explains why Gache, a charter member of the mission, was transferred back and forth with such ease between Louisiana, Alabama and Florida before the Civil War. It also explains the commanding presence in Louisiana of a new arrival from Lyons, the regional superior. On the twenty-eighth of April the Lyons Provincial wrote to the rector at Grand Coteau: "Our rector at Vals, Father Maisounabe, has been given to Louisiana. He will arrive in August or as soon as we are able to let him go."[11]

Once given his assignment Maisounabe was difficult to harness. He put the old world behind him at an earlier date than had been planned, enlisting volunteers for the new mission from England, Ireland and France on his way to the land of promise. Once arrived, he made a whirlwind visit to the burgeoning Jesuit *collèges* in the Northeast and then descended upon New Orleans in mid-summer. Thoroughly convinced that a deficiency in the English language was a deterrent to Jesuits assigned to the mission, the scholar Maisounabe concentrated on perfecting his spoken English, and his efforts, unlike those of Gache, were crowned with the same laurels which had until now wreathed all of his undertakings. Next, he determined that existing and future Jesuit establishments in Louisiana be given full protection of the law, a luxury the *collèges* in France had never been able to achieve. Accordingly, he filed for a charter of incorporation under the laws of the state of Louisiana. On January 8, 1848, Governor Isaac Johnson (1796-1853) signed the Act of Incorporation for the "Catholic Society for the Difusion of Religious and Literary Education." Hippolyte Gache was one of the four trustees of this corporation formed "for the purpose of founding and directing colleges and other literary and scientific institutions . . . and other churches" within the state.[12] Accounts of the purchase of the New Orleans property on the corner of Common and Baronne Streets, and of the untimely death of Father Maisounabe have been given elsewhere.[13] Significant here is the fact that because Gache was a trustee of the corporation which planted the seedling out of which grew Loyola University and Jesuit High School, New Orleans, he can be considered a founder of these institutions, as well as a founder of the present Church of the Immaculate Conception on Baronne Street, and of Holy Name Church on St. Charles Avenue, also in New Orleans. But during 1847-48 Hippolyte Gache saw very little of the city. His responsibilities as director, or prefect of the students, and general manager (minister), of both St. Charles College and farm at Grand Coteau kept him ensconced in St. Laundry Parish with problems enough to distract him from the progress his order was making in New Orleans. The perennial problem at Saint Charles was, as it had been since 1837, the lack of qualified personnel. In February of that year, Point had written to Johann Roothaan begging for broad-shouldered brothers to work on the farm and for English-speaking fathers to teach in the classrooms, since "the price of negroes and professors is enormous."[14] In Gache's time the problems at the college were not very different from those encountered by Point. The hygienic conditions in the wooden cabins where the Jesuits were lodged were deplorable, as Maisounabe advised Roothaan. It was asserted that these lodgings had been constructed in such a way as to guarantee that the occupants would roast in the summer and freeze in the winter.[15] This fact must have added a heavy burden to Gache's administrative and managerial responsibilities during this period of his life, his first Louisiana summer.[16] On July 31, he began a preached retreat to the Religious of the Sacred Heart at Grand Coteau, and during the following eight days, as the house historian registered in the Convent Journal, "he stressed above all the spirit of obedience and death of self."[17] Could this have been Father Hippolyte preaching to Gache?

In the following winter he encountered a setback from an unexpected quarter. Some indignant parents had written to the Lyons-born bishop of New Orleans, Anthony Blanc (1792-1860), complaining that the newly arrived French priest was too strict, and that even though he spoke their language, Father Hippolyte's unbending severity in dealing with Louisiana boys was as offensive as it was foreign.

Blanc, ever sensitive to criticism, had to be reassured that the accusations against Gache were exaggerated.[18] But the young Jesuit had to learn by experience that Grand Coteau was not a *petit séminaire*, nor even a *collège-en-exile* exactly like Chambéry or Mélan, and that the Creoles were not "barbarian peoples," but that they were indeed different from the exiled French students he had disciplined in Savoy. In his wartime correspondence Gache still disparaged "*les têtes louisiannaises*," and at this time of his life he was described as one who, despite genteel manners, was unbending when it came to principles.[19] There is no way of knowing if the Frenchman's unpopularity with the Creoles and his inability to adapt to the rigorous living conditions at Grand Coteau were factors for his reassignment to Spring Hill in 1849. Probably they were, but his new post was more in line with his talents, and being with his friends once again must have made the spirit of obedience and death of self less trenchant an issue. During the past two years the Alabama college had been making steady progress and Gache, as spiritual director to the seminarians and lay students, was a welcome addition to the expanding faculty. He was also appointed "master of novices," the first to be formally designated in the mission. But no sooner had he settled down to instruct students in the way of Vals than he was ordered back to Louisiana.[20]

In 1847 Bishop Blanc had confided to the mission superior Father Maisounabe, that his ambition was to see a college established at Baton Rouge. Maisounabe in turn consulted with Gache about the feasibility of transferring Saint Charles College to the state capital. Hippolyte, arguing that the Grand Coteau college was serving the Catholic population of Louisiana where it was and that its future was promising, counseled against the move. Blanc decidedly concurred with this opinion and promised that he would help the Society found an additional college at Baton Rouge within a few years. Now, in 1849, the bishop prevailed upon Maisounabe's successor, John Cambiaso (b. Lyons, France, September 28, 1809–d. New Orleans, Louisiana, October 24, 1869) to see to it that the episcopal dream would become a brick and mortar reality. At this date there were twenty-eight priests, twenty-one scholastics and twenty-three lay brothers scattered about the mission. Besides the number of parishes and mission stations, there were three colleges—Spring Hill, Grand Coteau and New Orleans—all understaffed. It seemed sheer folly to establish yet another educational undertaking, but Cambiaso regarded Blanc's wish, his command. So, on June 29, 1849, he laid the cornerstone for the College of Saints Peter and Paul in Baton Rouge, an institution empowered to bestow all the degrees of a university. Hippolyte Gache was named its first president, and he was also designated pastor of the church and vice-rector to the six Jesuits whom Cambiaso managed to round up for this noble enterprise. The formal ceremonies completed, Cambiaso gave the unfledged president three dollars, his blessing, a promise of prayers and then returned to New Orleans. The next month Gache welcomed twenty-five boys into the two-story frame building that constituted the newest *collège-en-exile* staffed by the Lyons Province Jesuits. "Our position was not very pleasant," the president recalled many years later. "None of the upper rooms were plastered; there were no blinds on the windows; the door of my room was shut by a blanket suspended in front of it; the ceiling was still *in fieri*, and during the night, from my bed, I could contemplate the stars with great ease."[21]

The population of Baton Rouge, a mere five thousand, included some three thousand Catholics whose financial and political support for the new venture were less than encouraging. One Irish-born, French-trained Jesuit, who had preached a mission during Gache's tenure, complained to Blanc that the only consideration he was given for his efforts was a generous expression of congratulations for his pulpit eloquence, an eloquence which, however, had not inspired a single person to venture into the confessional box. The empty-handed, golden-throated orator concluded that "it is very hard to fleece anyone in Baton Rouge."[22] During Gache's tenure of office as president, the Jesuits also encountered the hostility of the town's Protestants, particularly the Methodists, who resented the presence of the College of Saints Peter and Paul. No sooner had four acres of property been purchased and intent given to erect the college than the Methodists made a petition to drive a new street, cynically named St. Hipolite, through the property and at right angles to the new foundations of the college buildings. This petition was immediately made into a resolution, supported by the cooperative mayor, and with lightening speed adopted by the Municipal Council, despite Catholic protests. The reality of the situation forced Gache to alter the building plans but not the determination of the Jesuits to remain. Threats and counterthreats were made; tempers flared. Cambiaso returned and threw himself into the fray at the very time when one of the protagonists warned that he had purchased "a revolver with five barrels," that could definitively settle the differences between the two Christian factions. The mission superior retorted that he was contemptuous of any man who had to depend on *five* barrels to perform a task that could be done with *one*. He too had a pistol, he bragged. It had only one barrel, but one was adequate; and he invited the Methodist to put one foot near the reconstructed fence of the college property to see whether or not this Frenchman was an idle boaster.[23]

Such opera buffa is embarrassing to Christians of a more ecumenical age, but it was recorded by Gache four decades later to make the addled heretics both believable and appalling. More importantly, the account sheds light on the rationale behind harsh statements he made about Protestant clergymen in his wartime letters. Of course, no Catholic chaplain during the war nurtured sympathy for, much less friendship with, his Protestant colleagues, and feelings of hostility and distrust were mutual. Yet Gache, for all his urbanity, was far less tolerant than others—in principle at least. He had come from a region in France where the Protestant population was visible and well established and where the smoldering resentment between the Catholic majority and the Protestant minority erupted, even in the nineteenth century, into violent conflicts. His French background and training, his accent and foreign ways, and his experience with hostile native-born Protestants in Baton Rouge and elsewhere were factors which conditioned him to regard the Protestant clergymen he encountered during the war with suspicion, fear and contempt.

Other events in Gache's Baton Rouge experience help put into perspective the sardonic asides one finds in his Virginia correspondence. Recounting some of them here will enable the reader of his letters to focus better on the personality of the man who so often wrote with amused malice about a number of people and events. By 1851 his energies were divided—

dissipated would be the more exact term—between constructing a church, administering the parish, teaching in the school, providing for the Jesuit community, and begging funds for a permanent brick building to accommodate the college. Added to this list of concerns was another worry which demanded his attention. The superior of the Convent of the Religious of the Sacred Heart at Baton Rouge, a formidable *grande dame* who wrote letters with the vigor, charm and constancy of Madame de Sévigné, was Madame Adine Guinand (b. near Lyons, France, November 15, 1816–d. St. Michel, Louisiana, August 28, 1880). On March 5, 1851, Madame Guinand fired off a complaint to Bishop Blanc about Gache who had just informed her that he could say no more than two masses a week at her convent, excusing himself with the claim that he had obligations elsewhere on the other days. In the president's defense it should be noted that the original number of priests had diminished as the school and parish expanded, so that at this time only one priest, besides Gache, was assigned to the community; the other Jesuits were not ordained. No matter; the valiant French woman informed Blanc that the Jesuit's unavailability had made it impossible to say "Amen," even though his decision had inspired her to pray, "let this chalice be removed from me." It is difficult to know with certainty whether Madame Guinand's chalice was a what or a who, but there was no ambiguity when she reminded the bishop that she had not left the Rhône valley to lisp an unconditional "so be it" by the banks of the Mississippi. "*Oui, c'est trop triste d'être supérieure,*" was the not too allusive conclusion of this brave woman who later spent herself caring for the plague-stricken at St. Michel. Five weeks after this letter Madame Guinand wrote again to Blanc about Gache.[24] This time it was to instruct him that one of her nuns, Madame Felicite Lavy-Brun (b. Dole, France, October 12, 1802–d. Armagh, Ireland, June 12, 1866) wanted to return to France because she could not tolerate the English-born visitrix to the Sacré-Coeur convents in Louisiana, Mother Elisa Maria Cutts (b. Loughborough, Leicester,

England April 12, 1811–d. Grand Coteau, Louisiana, October 24, 1854), a sickly woman and a convert from Protestantism, who had the reputation of making "use of her infirmities to advance in perfection." Madame Guinand had taken this latest convent crisis to Père Gache whose inability to offer an instant and acceptable solution was less than reassuring, and she wanted Blanc to know it.[25]

Witticisms about "convent piety" in letters from the chaplain of the Tenth Louisiana, however, should not obscure the genuine admiration Hippolyte Gache had for nuns. His own sister Marie-Thérèse was a Carmelite in France and his devotion to the Daughters of Charity, as his wartime letters testify, was boundless. In 1856 even Madame Guinand would have no one else give First Communion to the convent children, much to the exasperation of the new chaplain. Gache enjoyed the reputation as a competent director of the *Spiritual Exercises*, a good confessor and a prudent confessor to sisters in a number of states throughout the South. The one complaint the non-French speakers among them had was that his English was all but unintelligible, and so it remained long after the war.[26] Moreover, his flare for injecting irony and litotes into his correspondence was a trait which he displayed during the stormy Baton Rouge years. It was a feature of his personality which unquestionably gained him the reputation of being a wit, but in 1851 such a style could not have been tailored to inspire the bishop of New Orleans with unqualified confidence in the pastor of Sts. Peter and Paul's.

In the summer of 1852 Gache was fired from his Baton Rouge post. The decision was as sudden as it was unexpected. Work on the college was ahead of schedule; the classrooms were filled; the financial situation was encouraging. Long after the event there was still a note of perplexity in his account of what had taken place: "the three years of my vice-rectorship having expired, and my administration having failed to give the desired satisfaction, I was removed and sent to Spring Hill."[27] Some two years and three superiors later the College of Sts. Peter and Paul folded, its Jesuit faculty decimated by yellow fever. By then Gache, still in Alabama, had settled into the academic year routine: teaching and prefecting the boys during the week and supplying at one of the several mission stations on the weekends.[28] Summer months meant giving retreats and helping out in parishes along the Gulf Coast. In the summer of 1858 he pronounced his final vows as a Jesuit; but, other than this one event, his life in Mobile was uneventful. He was another teacher remembered by one student a half-century later as "learned."[29]

By the end of January 1861, Alabama and Louisiana had seceded from the Union; by April 12, when the bombardment of Fort Sumter had begun, excited, raw recruits from Alabama, Louisiana, Mississippi and Georgia jostled with native Floridians on the streets of Pensacola and nearby Warrington. A contemporary news correspondent wrote:

> The influx of troops into Pensacola the past week is unprecedented and astonishing. Although they remain only long enough to take a boat for the Navy Yard, they afford all patriotic citizens an opportunity for inspection by parading once or twice around the public square . . . Mississippi pours in her companies almost daily, Georgians from Augusta, Atlanta, and Columbus; Zouaves from New Orleans, with females habited *A la Fille du regiment* at their head.[30]

Into this pageant, decked out in a black frock coat, stepped Reverend Louis-Hippolyte Gache, S.J. offering his services to the participants in Mr. Lincoln's War. Modesty, a virtue upon which he placed such a studied premium, would have prevented him, no doubt, from parading about the public square, but from this date until his capture four years later, less than a week before Appomattox, he faithfully served the Confederate troops. Few chaplains in the Confederacy had served so continuously for so long a period, and few native Southerners were as passionately dedicated to the cause of Dixie as this French Jesuit from Ardèche.

Pensacola
[Philip de Carrière] May 15, 1861

Reverend and dear Father, Pax Christi

I have already written twice to Spring Hill: once to Father Gautrelet to whom at the same time I sent a draft of $40 for Mr. [Charles] LeBaron in payment of what he owed Father Coyle, and again to Father Jourdan asking him kindly to send me my Ordo which I forgot when I left, and which can be found in my prie-dieu. As yet I have received no answer and I don't know if my letters have reached their destination. During this period of general confusion it well might be that they were lost. I would, nevertheless, like to know, especially about the first letter because of the enclosed draft. I think the best way for making sure about this business is to write to you, Father, who, as everyone knows, is fidelity and exactitude personified. But be all that as it may; here are a few words from yours truly.

Not much startling news here. They say that President Davis and two or three other important persons have come to inspect the Warrington Naval Yard and General Bragg's position, but no matter what they say, I don't venture to think such is the case. The other day I made the mistake of believing on the word of the Pensacola newspapers and on a throng of so-called eye and ear witnesses that General Beauregard was coming to these parts, but instead he was sent, at least if you can believe the Montgomery newspapers, to Norfolk.

The troops are mustering at Pensacola and Warrington; new companies arrive each day. The dance will not be long a-starting, as the troops around here say. At the same time, it will not begin yet for a few days—at least not until the people from the North open fire first, as General Bragg has not yet made all the preparations which he aims to before sending Fort Pickens his first cordial salutation.

Meanwhile, we're clearing out the Navy Yard and we're transporting all kinds of provisions that were stored there to a place of safety so that if they demolish the Yard, which is quite probable, it will be only the buildings that will suffer. In order to make doubly sure that no warships come into the Bay, we plan on sinking the dry dock at the same spot where three barges were sent to the bottom; that is, at the narrows between Fort Pickens and Fort Barrancas. They say that this will be the signal for war, as it is not likely that the commander of Fort Pickens will let such an operation go by without offering any opposition. And if he fires, of course we'll reply. It is hard to say what the plan of the general-in-command here is; nevertheless, the common impression among both the officers and the soldiers whom I have talked with is that he'll bombard Fort Pickens and that he'll raid the Island of Santa Rosa. Then, as soon as he has made the breech, he'll try to keep our Fort from being attacked. Of course, whether he'll really do this or not, I couldn't say.

I'm still very pleased with my soldiers, as I said in my letter to Reverend Father President [Jourdan]. Every day some come to confession and to communion, and I assure you they do so with a good intention and not just because they are afraid. They'd come in larger numbers if they weren't so busy and if they could leave the camp with great facility. But they are worked hard and they can't leave the camp save for a few at a time and even then with considerable difficulty. Such precautions are necessary to avoid abuse.

Yesterday afternoon when I went into camp, Captain St. Paul [de Léchard] and Lieutenant Giradey presented me to the General Staff. These men greeted me most kindly and Major Bradford, realizing who I was, volunteered, with that discerning courtesy of a military man, to give me written permission to visit all of the military posts and to circulate freely wherever I chose.

Father Coyle has been called to Montgomery by Bishop Quinlan. He wrote me yesterday that the bishop wanted him to go along with him to Mobile, and that perhaps he wouldn't be back until next Sunday. God bless us all! Now there will not be a single mass at Warrington because the two which I am allowed to say have to be said at Pensacola. *Adieu, mon bien cher Père*; my best to all—particularly to poor, ailing Father Montagnan.

Yours truly in our Lord,
H. Gache, S.J.

COMMENTARY

Although Gache did not indicate to whom this first letter was addressed, the recipient was, as he reported in his second letter, Father Philip de Carrière (b. Toulouse, France, April 20, 1823–d. Macon, Georgia, January 27, 1913). Entering the Society of Jesus in 1844, de Carrière escaped from Vals when the Revolution of 1848 turned anti-clerical; then, disguised as a young roué seeking adventure in the New World, he booked passage on a sailing vessel bound for New Orleans. The vessel was ninety-six days at sea, long enough for him to shed his disguise, and when he arrived at the Crescent City in late December, de Carrière hurried over to Mobile. There he remained almost continuously for the next forty years preparing and teaching classes at the college. In 1888 he was given a new assignment—caring for a 39,000 square mile, fever-infested "parish" that included Hillsborough, Polk, Desota, Manatee, Osceola, Lee, Dade and Monroe counties in south Florida. With prodigious energy this volatile nobleman whom Gache sardonically described as "fidelity and exactitude personified," worked out of Tampa—first alone and later with limited assistance—until 1901, when he was seventy-eight years old. The next twelve years he spent at his final assignment in Macon, Georgia. It was during this period that he added Esperanto to the five languages in which he was fluent.[31]

Besides giving examples to prove the spiritual advantages of his new assignment, Gache also repeated in this first letter to de Carrière some of the rumors and camp gossip that contributed to sustaining excitement at Pensacola. President Davis' anticipated visit to the city did indeed take place, but not until the twenty-fourth, at which time he arrived on an inspection tour with a former Spring Hill student, now a member of his Cabinet, Secretary of the Navy Stephen Russell Mallory (1813-73). But General Pierre Gustave Toutant de Beauregard did not pay his expected visit to Pensacola. In fact, shortly before Gache wrote this letter the Napoleon in Gray had informed the president that he was not interested in the command at the Florida post because he did not consider Fort Pickens a worthwhile military objective. He would soon be on his way to Corinth. Meanwhile, the Catholic bishop of Mobile, John Quinlan (b. County Cork, Ireland, October 19, 1826–d. New Orleans, Louisiana, March 19, 1883), was continuing a "visitation" to Montgomery that conveniently coincided with the passage of legislation by the Provisional Government authorizing President Davis to appoint chaplains, and to assign them to those regiments, brigades and posts he deemed necessary. Since the troop build-up at Pensacola had made the pastor at St. Michael's a good resource person, it was logical that Quinlan should have summoned Reverend Patrick Francis Coyle to Montgomery, leaving Gache to care for the four churches then under Coyle's care: St. Michael's, Pensacola; St. John the Evangelist, Warrington; and two mission stations, one at Barrancas and the other at Perdido.

Quinlan and Coyle remained in Montgomery until after May 21, the day that Congress adjourned and also the day the Irish-born priest received his appointment (signed by Mallory) and his orders to report to General Braxton Bragg. Coyle appears to have been a popular and influential person in Pensacola, and at the outbreak of the war he was credited as a contributor "to equipping and supplying the families of two companies of twelve-month volunteers in the County of Escambra of the Confederate Army." In August, Bragg commissioned him to bring some Daughters of Charity from Mobile to care for the wounded at Warrington. On January 14, 1862, he resigned from the army, but there is a record of his having served as the chaplain at the army hospital directed by the Daughters of Charity at Corinth during the battle fought near there in the following April. After the war Coyle was appointed pastor of Mobile's largest and most affluent parish, but in 1868 he was transferred to Nashville, Tennessee, where he remained until 1870, after which he vanished, leaving not a trace of his subsequent history available to the researcher in diocesan archives.[32]

Not everyone mentioned by Gache in this first letter is as elusive as Coyle. Charles LeBaron (b. New Orleans, Louisiana, December 13, 1804–d. Mobile, Alabama, February 3, 1881) was the son of Charles (1761-1823), a former French naval officer who served under three flags in the Gulf States, and whose wife was Ann McVoy (1803-87), the ward of

Aaron Burr. Charles LeBaron II was a wealthy Mobile merchant with interests in Pensacola, where he had been the first American mayor under American rule. Captain Henry Saint-Paul de Léchard (b. Antwerp, Belgium, October 15, 1815–d. New Orleans, Louisiana, February 20, 1886) was a longtime acquaintance of Gache's, having been a member of the Louisiana State Convention of 1852 at Baton Rouge while the Jesuit was at Sts. Peter and Paul's. Previous to this political interlude, this son of one of Napoleon's officers had gained a certain amount of notoriety when, as a young lawyer, he defended Bishop Blanc in the Cathedral litigation of 1824. One of the by-products of this infamous controversy had been the appearance of the *Propagateur catholique*, the newspaper founded to "maintain the principles of catholicism in New Orleans and Louisiana" by Reverend Napoleon Perché (1805-83), who later became the city's archbishop. Early in 1861 St. Paul organized the *chasseurs-à-pied* and in March reported to President Davis at Montgomery. Davis ordered him to Pensacola where he remained until the *chasseurs* were transferred to Virginia. But Captain, later Major, St. Paul did not remain long on the Peninsula after the reorganization of his company, for he was back in Louisiana during the Teche campaign. Subsequently he was assigned to Mobile as quartermaster, and here he remained until he was paroled in May, 1865. After the war he founded the Mobile *Times*, and his son John (1867-1939), a justice of the Louisiana Supreme Court, was a founder of Loyola University School of Law in 1914.[33]

Another Frenchman Gache mentioned in this letter was Victor Jean-Baptiste Giradey (b. Lauw, Haut-Rhin, France, June 26, 1837–d. Fussell's Mill, Virginia, August 16, 1864), an officer destined for fame and whose untimely death robbed the Confederacy of a superior military tactician. Giradey was a 2d lieutenant in the Louisiana Guards at this date and, it seems, was known to de Carrière. But when could the two have met? Is it possible that St. Paul (also known to de Carrière, Giradey and other Louisianans) stayed with the Jesuits at Spring Hill on their way from Montgomery to Pensacola? And did they bring Gache with them to Florida? At any rate these two Louisiana officers, St. Paul and Giradey, introduced the chaplain to the General Staff at General Bragg's headquarters. Gache singled out another officer who showed him special consideration–Maj. Charles M. Bradford, who in April became a major in Strawbridge's First Louisiana Infantry. He resigned his commission July 23 and in September he was appointed lieutenant colonel of the Third Battalion of the Louisiana Infantry and transferred to the Peninsula where he became commanding officer of the Fifteenth Regiment. Court-martialed for disrespect to a superior officer and for conduct prejudicial to good order and military discipline, he resigned his commission and moved to Robertson County, Texas, where he was given permission by Maj. Gen. John Bankhead Magruder to raise a regiment. He was commissioned colonel in July 1864 of "Bradford's Regiment," which he had mustered into service and sent to the Galveston area. There it became known early in 1865 as "Mann's Regiment." After the war he returned to his law practice in New Orleans.[34]

In this first letter Gache named two Spring Hill Jesuits, and it would be difficult to find two people less alike. Anthony Jourdan (b. Lyons, France, November 9, 1809–d. New Orleans, Louisiana, November 4, 1886) incorporated into a complex personality many characteristics of the stage Jesuit in a nineteenth century anticlerical melodrama. His admirers praised him for a singleness of vision, which was indisputable, and for the kindness throughout his life toward the young, the sick, and the poor. He had been a professional army officer who showed mettle and intelligence against the Dutch during the seige of Antwerp in 1832, and afterwards he was appointed to the coveted position of headmaster at the government *lycée* in his native Lyons. Only four years a Jesuit, Jourdan was sent to the New Orleans Mission in 1847, ordained a priest the following year and put in charge of St. Charles College, Grand Coteau. In 1852 he was appointed mission superior, and one of the first things he did was to remove Gache from Sts. Peter and Paul's where he transferred his own headquarters. From this vantage point, almost single-handedly, he waged a two-year war against St. Charles, which he finally closed without the concurrence of Blanc and in the face of concerted Arcadian opposition. In 1854 he was recalled to France, enabling his successor to cover his retreat and to come to terms with the bishop and the Creoles. These terms were clear and simple: St. Charles was to be reopened and Sts. Peter and Paul's was to be closed. Predictably, Jourdan was criticized for not understanding American ways, but it is to Roothaan's credit that the mistakes of this competent leader did not keep him permanently *hors de combat*. In 1859 the Jesuit General named a more experienced Jourdan as the successor to Gautrelet at Spring Hill, and so for the second and last time he left his native France for the American South, where once again he became Hippolyte Gache's immediate superior.[35]

Gache showed concern in this letter for another Jesuit, the dying Joseph-Maria Montagnan (b. Haches, Hautes-Pyrénées, France, March 24, 1824–d. Spring Hill, Alabama, August 22, 1861), who had entered the Avignon novitiate two years after his own entrance and who, as a scholastic, arrived at Spring Hill in time to be inscribed on the 1847 faculty roster. A teacher of French and mathematics, Montagnan was described by a contemporary as "a man of all things capable, for all things ready, and to all men dear," a fact which might explain why he did not survive. At least it suggests an interpretation to Michael Kenny's judgment that "weighted with a multiplicity of duties beyond his strength" he died at the age of thirty-seven.[36]

One piece of camp gossip that the newly arrived chaplain picked up at the Naval Yard and reported to de Carrière was the plan for sinking the dry dock in the channel between Federal-held Fort Pickens and Fort Barrancas. This elaborate creation, "the most magnificent structure of its kind," was put to the torch on September 2 by the Federals, and Michael Nash (1825-95), the Jesuit chaplain to the Sixth New York Regiment on neighboring Santa Rosa Island has left a vivid description pertaining to its destruction. Nash, a witty, eloquent Irishman with a sense for the dramatic, has also immortalized the final hour of St. John the Evangelist Church. On the evening of November 23, he wrote, he was summoned by the commander of the water battery who advised him of the plans for the church where Gache had offered mass in May. " 'Now Father,' he said to me, 'though you will witness the ruin of the sacred edifice of your brethren across the bay, it will be worth your while to pass the night in my battery and view the awful conflagration.' Pending the proper moment for the commencement of these hostilities, supper was served . . ."[37]

J.M.J.

May 22, 1861

Rev. Father A. Cornette
Spring Hill, Alabama

Mon Cher Frère André,

Really you are too considerate once you put your mind to it. How can I thank you for such a letter? And even more important, how can I ever respond in kind? Whenever a man lends a sum of money to someone whom he knows is incapable of repaying him, he is reputed to have parted with his loan forever and to have abandoned all claim to it. Such is likewise the instance here, *mon cher petit Frère.* Nonetheless, I am happy to have found this principle which enables me to save myself from embarrassment and at the same time to set my conscience at rest. I am confident that Father Serra would not question either the principle or the application thereof. Let's agree then, that I'll be at quits with you after this wretched missive, however unworthy it may prove as a response to your own.

This morning I received a letter from good Father Philip [de Carrière], along with my Ordo, and for both of which I am not less pleased nor grateful. Last week—I don't know what day it was—I received besides your letter one from Father Jourdan containing only one copy of the *Propagateur catholique*; on the following day the medals arrived. I therefore have received everything, the one *Propagateur* excepted, which is to be sure no great loss. Thanks to everyone for everything pertaining to these affairs.

The work with the soldiers continues to jog along as I have indicated in my previous letters. Right now it's merely a question of attending to small items. Practically every day a few, but only a few, come to the 7:00 a.m. mass. The number at this mass never surpasses three or four, with the exception of last Sunday when there were six. A considerable number intend to come but their chores hold them up. On the other hand, all except the sentries were able to come to the last mass at 10:30. The Sunday congregation was so large that the church was more than filled. I would certainly like to have had some of the eloquence and a bit of the gift of tongues which were bestowed upon St. Peter and the other Apostles under similar circumstances. But the Holy Spirit doesn't communicate Himself in such wise to one and all, especially not to those who are so unworthy of His communications. Besides, I was able to do nothing more than repeat a few cliches on the Sunday Gospel, inasmuch as I was so exhausted from fasting, saying an early mass and preaching, and then having to sing a second mass and preach again at 10:30.

I should mention, however, that I had a very special consolation that day: the Good Lord let me see an old sinner at the Holy Table. I've been on this man's coat tails for nine years—that is, ever since the first time I came to Pensacola. He was more than forty-five years away from the Sacred Banquet. You can understand that this joy compensated quite a bit for my weariness.

I'm not going to give you any news about the war. I don't know anything about it except that it hasn't begun, that no one knows when it will begin, and that the soldiers are afraid that it will never begin. Besides, every day General Bragg urges silence on the part of those who know anything about what's happening, and nearly every day he has to look for new ways to prevent indiscretions. Speaking of soldiers, "we Frenchmen" have talked the subject over among ourselves in an off-handed manner, and I want you to know that we form a far more formidable and fierce army than I would have believed. True it is that there are a few youngsters of sixteen and seventeen, but in the whole group their number is insignificant. Besides, these lads are as scrappy as anyone else. They've got the reputation of being veritable grandsons of Mars and Bellum.

Adieu, mon bien cher Père. A thousand good wishes as pleasant as you are able to think them and say them yourself—on certain occasions, at least—to all of Ours and to Dr. Rohmer. Congratulate venerable Father Montagnan on the improvement of his health, and always believe me, as you pray for me, that I am your very own twin brother.

H. G.

COMMENTARY

In this second letter Hippolyte Gache boasted that, having taken stock of the situation, "we Frenchmen" were a pretty impressive group of warriors. Years later one of these *chasseurs-à-pied de la Louisianne* recalled that more than one third of the Frenchmen were in fact Irishmen. This was John L. Rapier (1842-1905), one of the scrappy "grandsons of Mars and Bellum" who had come with St. Paul and Giradey from New Orleans to Pensacola. After the war, in which he had participated with singular distinction, he married Henry Saint-Paul de Léchard's daughter and became the proprietor and editor of the Mobile daily *Register*. At the time of John's birth his father was a Spring Hill lay teacher, having a position like the two men among "Ours"—that is Jesuits—singled out by Gache in this letter. One of these men was the teacher of music and drawing, a bachelor who lived with the Jesuits since his arrival at the college in 1855, and who can not be traced after 1864. This was John Parada (b. Catalonia, Spain, 1830). The other was the college physician, Francis J.B. Rohmer (b. Rhinau, Bas-Rhin, France, August 14, 1812–d. Mobile, Alabama, July 2, 1904). Napoleon had knighted Rohmer's father on the field of Austerlitz and set up a fund for Francis' education, but the boy left France in 1832 for Louisiana, where, after a number of years crowded with hair-raising adventures along the Mississippi, he settled down to complete his medical studies and marry Ellena di Rosaldi Bell (1815-66) from the Trickfaw River country in St. Helena Parish, Louisiana. In 1849-51 the Rohmers were with Gache in Baton Rouge, and in 1856 they followed him to Spring Hill where the doctor was given the appointment of college physician which he held until his retirement in 1885.[38]

No sooner had the Rohmers settled down near the campus than another one of Gache's friends, the recipient of this second letter, joined the Jesuit community. This was Hippolyte's "*frère de lait*," or foster brother, the curious appellation for Andrew Cornette (b. Fleurey, Côte d'Or, France, March 5, 1818–d. Spring Hill, Alabama, March 21, 1872), which makes sense when it is known that both men entered the Society at Avignon at the same time. Cornette, an elected member of the prestigious *Académie des Sciences* in Paris, had been assigned in 1840 to the chair of science at the National University at Medellin, Nueva Granada (Colombia); but when the Jesuits were expelled from that South American country in 1849, he made his way, leisurely enough it appears, through Central America and Mexico to Alabama, arriving at Spring Hill in 1857. After the war he contributed a weekly column in Henry Saint-Paul de Léchard's Mobile *Times* on matters scientific, and he also published, on his own press, religious and scientific tracts. His laconic, orderly notations in what later became known as the "Vice-President's Diary" gave a skeletal, dispassionate view of Spring Hill during the war.

Self-effacing and stolid, the scientist Cornette stood in sharp contrast to John Baptist Serra (b. Castel del Sol, Catalonia, Spain, September 8, 1810–d. Spring Hill, Alabama, October 23, 1886), another Jesuit Gache mentioned in this letter. Exiled from Spain for his participation on the losing side in the Carlist Wars, the volatile, teaseable Serra entered the Avignon novitiate as a priest in 1854, and was dispatched two years later to Spring Hill where a Spanish teacher was needed for the younger students. Despite the fact that he was "unintelligible in four languages," his reputation as a missionary to the Catholics in the no-priest lands of the Gulf States gained in inverse proportion to his effectiveness in the classroom. Soon after this letter was written, Serra was removed altogether from the olive groves of Academe to trill his thick-warbled notes along the Dog River, the Fish River and on Mon Lui Island. Of course, no Spring Hill Jesuit remained the summer long on the campus, and even weekends emptied the Jesuit residence, seeing that all but the incapacitated—and their number was minimal—"took calls" at the mission stations around Mobile. Gache testified to this practice when he reminded Cornette that he had worked periodically in Pensacola ever since his Spring Hill assignment nine years earlier. This dedication to apostolic work may not have encouraged serious scholarship, although it is incredible how intellectually active these Jesuits remained, but it did keep alive a corporate enthusiasm and a sense of purpose. It also kept food on the tables because the college depended on the meager supplement such calls realized. But most of all, it was a Vals tradition.[39]

By the end of April Camp Moore had been set up at Tangipahoa on the Jackson Railroad Line, outside of New Orleans, to accommodate hundreds of volunteers eager to enlist in Louisiana companies for a twelve-month period. By the first of June the initial bureaucratic confusion had abated enough so that five regiments had been organized, mustered into service, and put on railroad cars bound for Virginia. Meanwhile, in Warrington the five Louisiana companies which formed a new battalion under the command of Lt. Col. Charles Dreux (1832-61) had also left for Virginia. On the first of the month, Maj. Gustave de Coppens (1802-72) herded his undisciplined, fun-loving Zouaves who had so amused President Davis, into railroad cars for the historic liquor-laced spree which began in Pensacola and ended in Richmond. St. Paul had also gone north with *les chasseurs*, and it is very probable that at this same time, less than two weeks after he had written to Cornette, Gache left Pensacola, returning briefly to Spring Hill, where he delighted his Jesuit brothers with stories that confirmed their belief that the coming conflict was, perhaps, the harbinger of a golden age.[40]

Among these French Jesuits there was an optimism, based on the conviction that the war, however deplorable, would somehow better the condition of the church in the South. This optimism, stimulated by a patriotic euphoria and by the holiday exhilaration of the spring of 1861, was captured in two letters to France which were published in the newly founded Jesuit review, *Etudes*. At the same time when Gache was preparing to leave for Pensacola one of his New Orleans confreres described the reaction the news of Fort Sumter had had on that city, and he explained why the position of the Jesuits in the North and South had not been compromised by the political questions which were at that time being contested on the battlefields. "With complete freedom," he stated, "we can offer each of the sides the benefits of our ministry." In the South the conditions had never been better for serving the needs of the neglected slaves, although it was the Irish, Germans, and Arcadians, this Jesuit correspondent explained, who demanded the immediate attention and leadership of the clergy. Catholics from different racial groups were joining the newly formed Louisiana regiments. Patriotism and religion had solidified and united them. "Some of our fathers are chaplains in the army," wrote the second Jesuit in his letter from Spring Hill, and he is clearly indebted to Gache for his observations. "Army generals and government officials, all of whom show profound respect and sincere admiration for the Catholic religion, have been asking for chaplains.... Jesuits in the army are so busy that they spend a greater part of the night in their tents hearing confessions. Religious sentiments among the troops are even stronger than these chaplains had dared to hope, and so is the effect of their special ministry to the troops. Blessed be God." It was a well-known fact in France that Americans on both sides of the line had never been properly exposed to Catholic teaching. But the war would change all that. It would be the catalyst that would speed up the work of pious associations founded in Lyons and Vals. There would be conversions, like that of the young Alabama captain who had presented himself to one of the Jesuits at Spring Hill hours before he left for Virginia so that he could be baptized a Catholic and "go to his death for his country and for his God with a clear conscience." Dreams dreamt by the shores of the Rhône and in the mountains of Velay were to be realized in the fields of far off Virginia. Blessed be God.[41]

Camp Magruder near Williamsburg
September 11, 1861
10th Reg. Vol., La G.C.S.A.

Rev. P. Phil. de Carrière
Spring Hill College

Reverend and dear Father, Pax Christi

A few days after I arrived in Richmond I wrote Father Jourdan a rather long letter in which I told him, for better or worse, about my journey here and about the various incidents which took place en route. I trust this letter was delivered even though I am somewhat wary since it appears that here in Virginia there is nothing so irregular as the mail, and nothing so easily taken for granted as its loss. And this is especially true in regard to letters written by the military. But be all this as it may, the poor old chaplain of the Tenth Louisiana Regiment once again sends his best to the *braves habitants* of Spring Hill, and at the same time he informs them of another change of address.

After a stay of sixteen days, I left Richmond on the twentieth of August. My regiment had embarked on the James River three days previously for where we were told would be our new assignment—Yorktown. The day the regiment broke camp was a Saturday, and since it would have to cover twelve miles on the march the next day, probably through rain and mud (and that's just what happened), and since I would have been deprived of the boon of saying Holy Mass, I yielded to the promptings of some prudent friends, not to mention the promptings of my own sound judgment, and postponed my departure until the following Monday. By this decision I avoided, as I had anticipated, walking twelve miles through drenching rain and sloppy clay, both of which render the march twice as difficult. I also avoided spending the night *sub jove*, soaked through and through and having no place to stretch my weary bones save some endless prairie. Yet if I missed this little military junket, I certainly had another which bade fair to compensate for it.

I'd intended to leave Richmond Monday morning but when Monday came round I wasn't yet ready. Among other items I lacked a permit which I should have picked up from the Quartermaster General, C.S.A. This would have enabled me to travel gratis (that is at the Government's expense) and to ride clear through to my destination. Consequently, it wasn't until Tuesday at 7:30 a.m. that I set out on the York River Railroad which goes as far as West Point, a little town where one can then get a river boat.

The weather was magnificent; the train coaches, first class; we ripped along at top speed. I couldn't have been more comfortable. Each time the conductors asked to see my ticket I produced my official Free Transportation Pass, which they immediately returned with a profound bow—impressed, no doubt, at seeing an officer in the Army of the Confederate States in a guise so humble and so indicative of another calling. But alas, such good fortune could not long endure. Ere we had gone fifteen miles, the train began to slow down. "What's the matter?" the people were asking the conductor. And the answer: under the heavy rains the track bed had given way in some places and hence it would be rash to bolt along at top speed. A few minutes later the train came to a dead stop. We all looked out to see what was happening. We could see about twenty Negroes clearing the track which had been covered over by a landslide during the night, but as the damage was not considerable we were delayed there only about a half-hour. Some forty-five minutes later the train stopped again, and again we all looked out. This time it was no mere landslide burying the rails, but now there was a chasm of about thirty feet deep and up to eight to ten yards long yawning right beneath the tracks themselves. It was sheer folly to dream of crossing over this gap; yet we could not wait for it to be filled in as this would have taken two or three days. We could have walked the rest of the way because it was no more than four miles to the station, but then there was our baggage. Happily there was a locomotive with a few attached flatcars some distance away on the other side of the chasm, and somebody suggested commandeering these cars for us and sending us on our way. There was little chance of refusal.

We should have arrived in West Point at 11:00 a.m. If we had, we could have caught a steamer immediately and been at Yorktown in time for lunch at 2:00 or 2:30. But we didn't arrive at West Point until 2:00, and there was no boat leaving until 3:00; furthermore, the boat at 3:00 was not a steamer but a schooner. This meant that we couldn't hope to arrive at Yorktown before 7:30 or 8:00 p.m.; consequently, the choice was between a dinner in West Point or no dinner at all. To forego the meal—that was the simplest, easiest, and most economical expedient, but it wasn't the most pleasant in view of the fact that my companions hadn't had breakfast at all, and that I myself had eaten very little. But the problem at this stage of the proceedings was, as Father Cornette would say, the *materia circa quam.* I assure you nothing is more difficult on this Peninsula than to find something to eat. True enough there was a hotel in town, but it was so far from the dock that if we went there we'd run the risk of missing the schooner. We didn't dare ask for hospitality at a private home as the Louisiana soldiers have gained such a reputation for pilfering and general loutishness that as soon as anyone sees them coming they bolt the doors and windows. Usually any affiliation at all with the Louisiana boys is enough to assure one a cold welcome no matter where he shows his face.

At any rate, a few minutes before the boat was to leave someone pointed out to us a little shack in the middle of the marshland not far from the port. Here they said we could get something to eat. It wasn't very inviting, but at this moment we, with our empty stomachs, were more encouraged at what we heard than discouraged at what we saw. So there we went, and there we found for our *maître* and *maîtress d'hôtel* an African version of Philemon and Baucis. I felt my heart sink at the thought of being a guest of this couple in a place where it seemed that cleanliness was not an hereditary virtue. But as I said above, if an empty belly has no ears neither need it have eyes. "Can you give us something to eat?" the young lieutenant asked the Black Patriarch of the Marsh.

"Yes Master," he answered, no doubt utterly transported with joy at seeing two such distinguished persons approaching his abode, "What do you want?"

"What do you have?"

"I have plenty things: eggs, fish, potatoes, corn . . ."

"Well, give us some of everything."

"Yes, Master."

And thanks to the diligence of the venerable Baucis, whose skinny form seemed to cheat old age of its sluggishness and to bestow upon it the agility of youth, the dinner was served in five minutes. I won't attempt to describe it for you; suffice it to say that in spite of my appetite I could only manage to swallow two eggs. I had to keep my eyes shut tight all of the time too, to make sure that I wouldn't have become ill—an event which surely would have occurred had I let my gaze rest on the *table du festin.* However, this was the last meal we had that day as we didn't arrive at Yorktown until eight o'clock at night.

We had considerable difficulty getting under way as the wind prevented the schooner from approaching the wharf, and we had to be picked up on a tiny skiff that danced across the wind-blown waves in between floating logs and jetting stones in a manner which gave little pleasure and less peace of mind. There was really some danger; however, the hope of finding a bite to eat and a place to sleep on shore carried us through. But alas! The first thing we learned when we disembarked was that both bed and board would be denied us.

During my sojourn in Richmond, I had made the acquaintance of an Alsacian who had been living there twenty-seven years, and who was certainly one of the finest men that I have ever met. His name was Miller. His son, a former Georgetown student and a boy certainly worthy of such a father, was in an artillery company stationed at Yorktown. Realizing that this place would be my destination, the father had given me a letter of introduction to the boy in the hope that he could be of some assistance to me. As matters turned out, this excellent young lad couldn't have been more accommodating, but unfortunately he had more goodwill than influence to put at our disposal. The only thing he could do for my young lieutenant and me was to invite us to share the floor of a humble chamber which resembled in its simplicity the room where Gaspar lived with his sons. This floor was our bed. It was likewise the bed for our host and six young men who, like him, worked in the commissariat. And as far as supper was concerned—well, we dined on dreams.

Yorktown is a place where there is absolutely no one who is not in uniform. All of the townspeople have left; consequently, it is impossible to find anything, even a store. This town is a camp; it's the headquarters for Major General Magruder, the commander-in-chief of the Peninsula Divisions. All supplies, of which there is every type imaginable, are for the troops, and all of the houses are occupied either by the General Staff or by the various employees of the different branches of military administration, or by the sick, as three of the largest houses have been converted into hospitals. The newcomer, therefore, can only obtain those provisions that his friends or acquaintances dole out, and since our friends were in the same predicament as we were, the conclusion was all too clear: bed without supper, internal rumblings notwithstanding.

But this was not the first time that I've gone to bed hungry, and it won't be the last either, although I always take advantage of the privilege we have for eating meat on Fridays and I always consider myself excused from fasting on ember days and vigils. In fact, I never fast or abstain except when compelled to do so by a simple lack of food. This does sometimes happen, as on the vigil of last St. Ignatius' Day (July 30) for example, when a modest breakfast taken at 6:30 had to suffice for the whole day, and on the feast itself I fared scarcely better. But let's get back to Yorktown.

After taking off our frock coats and making pillows of our knapsacks, my young lieutenant friend and I stretched out side by side on the floor. We moved as quietly as possible, without even kneeling to say our night prayers, as we were loathe to awaken those in the room who had already retired. My young companion slept middling well, which is more than I can say for myself. Being twenty-four years his senior, and therefore not having the same mattress-like quality in my old bones, I was acutely aware of the hardness of the floor. The night, however, passed quickly enough.

At daybreak, accompanied by young Miller, we hurried up to headquarters to find out where the Tenth Louisiana was billeted and to arrange for our transportation. We found out our camp was another eleven miles down the James, and that transportation would be available at four that afternoon.

I took advantage of my short stay at Yorktown to pay a visit to old acquaintances of Pensacola days: the Zouaves, the Louisiana Guards, and the Grivot Guards, who, I learned to my great joy, were camped in the area. I don't have to tell you how surprised they were to see me there; they thought that I had come from another world. For my part I was astonished at the change which had taken place in them since they left Florida. Poor fellows, how different they were from their old selves! These Zouaves, so happy-go-lucky and carefree at Warrington, who made the camp echo with their continuous singing and laughing, were now plunged into the most gloomy silence. Passing through their camp, one heard scarcely a word, but after seeing a few of those pale and emaciated faces, one understood well enough why they no longer raised their voices in laughter and song. Of the 600 who first arrived, there were now but about 250, and of this number fifty to eighty were hardly fit for regular service. The day I was there they had just buried a sergeant. One company of the Louisiana Guards had sixty men sick, and in another company there was only one lone officer fit for duty. Everywhere it's diarrhea, chills and fever. The other companies were in about the same condition, but they have since left Yorktown and their health has improved. Their complement, however, has been considerably reduced.

Anyway, I finally got an honest meal. After dining with good Captain [Samuel] Todd and other friends, the lieutenant and I left Yorktown for Camp Magruder where we arrived at 8:00 p.m. Everyone was already quartered, and by the following day, yes even we had a place to sleep. My tent is right in the middle of the line of tents occupied by the General Staff, at the far end of the main thoroughfare which separates the two batallions. Some obliging Irish boys have constructed an arcade of greenery at the entrance of my quarters. This construction serves as the church, and during the day it also becomes my retreat from the sun's too fervid beams. I say daily mass between 6:30 and 7:00—as soon as I can get a server which is not always an easy task. Up to now it's nearly always Captain [Eugene] Waggaman who serves my mass. He's the only officer who receives the sacraments regularly and, I might add, the only one who practices his religion at all.

Last Sunday [September 8] I said mass at nine o'clock and I gave a short sermon in English; the number of Frenchmen or Creoles in the congregation was very small. But it is better not to talk about religious practice in this regiment. It's too discouraging. For example, at mass Sunday morning there were two or three officers and about forty men, and yet in the regiment there are at least 600 Catholics of whom probably less than thirty frequent the sacraments.

In order to compensate for this sad fact I visit other camps and I attempt to do there what I can't succeed in doing in my own. Thus, at the invitation of Lt. Col. [Henry] Forno, about whom one sometimes heard hard criticism, I said mass on one occasion for the Fifth Regiment of the Second Louisiana. At that time there was even some suitable music during the Holy Sacrifice and after mass I heard about twenty confessions. Just about the whole predominantly Protestant regiment was present, with Lieutenant Colonel Forno and the Protestant chaplain right up in front. They also stayed for the short sermon which I dared to give in English since the congregation was made up wholly of Americans or Irish. Afterwards I was assured that the sermon was well received, and the Protestant preacher and the colonel vied with one another in making me welcome. Each of them extended to me an invitation to dinner; I accepted the colonel's request, as was only proper. Even though I didn't go over to say mass in the camp of the Second Louisiana Regiment nor in the Fifteenth Virginia, as these camps were near enough to our own, I did give the Catholics in both regiments the opportunity to attend mass. About thirty took advantage of this opportunity.

I have paid many visits to the hospitals in Williamsburg, a town which is about five miles from here, but I have found only one individual, a Zouave, who had need of my service. The other patients are either non-Catholics or they are not seriously ill. Williamsburg, like Yorktown, is one of the oldest cities in this part of the country, yet Williamsburg is considerably larger and more beautiful. I am told that the oldest college or university that was built in the English colonies is located here. One of the buildings of this institution now serves as a hospital. Two or three years ago it was ravaged by a fire; however it was rebuilt in the same style and according to the original dimensions, and parts of the old walls which could be salvaged were incorporated into the new building. It is really nothing very extraordinary.

Last week I said mass at Yorktown for the Eighth Alabama Regiment (Colonel [John] Winston), which contains a company that is solidly Catholic. One of the members of this company is Captain [Patrick] Loughry who knew me, even though I did not know him. I had planned to remain only two days with these good people, but the same little malady which incapacitated me at Spring Hill on my return from Pensacola obliged me to tarry two days more. I was, nevertheless, able twice to offer mass for this company. Some thirty men came either out of supererogation or, more likely, out of strict fulfillment of precept. I have nothing but praise for the excellent Captain Loughry, not only because he proved himself a devoted and zealous Catholic, but also because he has given me so many eloquent testimonials of his sincere respect and deep affection. I promised him I'd return for a visit every fortnight; and he, for his part, assured me that on each of these occasions that he would have a number of men present for confession and Holy Communion. I ran into the youngest of those Mobile Lyonses whom we had as students at Spring Hill. He's in the same regiment, and he hasn't changed one iota. He is one of those rare few who thrive physically as well as morally on camp life.

The commander of the Dreux Batallion invited me to spend two or three days in his camp so that I could say mass for the many Catholics in his group. I'm going to stay with this batallion Thursday, Friday, and Saturday of this week; some of my oldest and best friends are in this camp, which is some eight miles from Yorktown. Next week, unless I return to Richmond to go to confession myself and to renew my supply of hosts, I'll visit several other camps near Bethel, another six or eight miles further away.

I had the opportunity of seeing Major General Magruder and of talking with him about the needs of the Catholic troops and about what I'm hoping to do for them. He immediately gave me permission to visit all of the camps under his command as well as an order addressed to the Quartermaster requesting that, whenever possible, transportation should be put at my disposal. This is a great privilege, one which would never have been accorded to any Protestant minister; nevertheless, I'm still not satisfied. I'm hoping for an even greater privilege, but I don't want to tell you about it now. I will only say that should I receive what I desire, I will be able to accomplish more in one week than I have up till now in a whole month. During the past month, by the way, I've heard ninety-two confessions and I have distributed ninety-six Communions, of which a very, very small percentage were merely Communions of devotion.

They talk a great deal around here about [Major] General Magruder and what they say is not always complimentary. As far as I am concerned, however, he is a very unpretentious and likeable gentleman. During our little visit his houseboy brought him a bowl of peaches. Since it was a little after 12:00, I wouldn't be surprised if he had ordered this for his lunch.

"Here, have a peach," he said, offering me the bowl, and I, who have made it a rule never to refuse what I am offered, chose the least prepossessing of the lot. "You, sir, are not a good peach-picker," he said, taking the most succulent and thrusting it into my hand, adding: "Here, take this one."

Then as he began eating he asked me: "To what denomination do you belong?"

"To the Catholic denomination."

"Oh, I know that. But to what—er, order—do you belong within the Catholic denomination?"

"I am a Jesuit."

"I thought so. You Jesuits are everywhere . . ."

"Yes sir, doing all sorts of good works."

"Oh yes, that's exactly what I understand."

'Tis curious how much more esteem educated and intelligent men have for Catholicism than they seem to have for the Protestant sects. This is particularly evident where there are two chaplains, one Catholic and the other Protestant in the same camp—the Catholic receives all the attention and respect and the poor Protestant is forgotten. This in my opinion is a sign that a great harvest is ripening in America: *Oremus enim Dominum messis, ut mittat operarios in messem suam.* ["Therefore ask the harvest master to send workers to his harvest." *Luke 10:2*]

Well, Father, this letter gives you some idea of the life I'm living. It is a life of a wanderer, *n'est-ce pas? Eh bien*, it's bound to become even more gypsy-like than before, but it has not had a bad effect on my spiritual life. The rather low moral standards of the camp instead of making me more lax have had, rather, the opposite effect. It has been almost as if I were making a retreat. The more I see God offended the more I am determined not to offend Him myself; and the more I see Him served, the more determined I am to serve him more faithfully. Finding myself in a place where so few honor Him, and where, on the contrary, so many insult Him, it seems to me that I am bound in some way to love Him for those who do not love Him and to offer to Him even more than I owe Him, if such were possible, in order to make amends for what others refuse Him. Another thing which gives me consolation is the thought that, probably, never before in this land where we now tread has true worship been offered to the true God, and that I and a few Catholics may be the first people in the Old Dominion who know God truly and who worship Him according to His Holy Will. It is this thought that makes me welcome the opportunity to say Holy Mass in various places, and that makes me say my mass on an old packing crate in my tent with greater devotion than I have ever said it on the altar of any church or convent chapel. It is this thought, moreover, that encourages me to say my prayers, my office and my beads, in the forests, along the roads, and in the fields. I say to myself that at least Almighty God can gather up a few acts of adoration and a few prayers of praise from this land that has been, perhaps, up till now so sterile for Him. Help me, Father, by your good prayers to become that which I should be: *caritas Christi urget nos.* ["The love of Christ impels us," *2 Cor. 5:14*] Pray that Christ will make me feel this charity more ardently.

In union with our Holy Masses and through the Sacred Hearts of Jesus and Mary, I am, Reverend and dear Father, your Reverence's servant.

H. Gache, S.J.
Chap., 10th La. V

P.S. Nineteen days have passed since I began this wordy, and perhaps even inane letter. Today is the thirtieth of September, and we have moved camp twice since I began to write—a fact which was not important enough to mention in the letter. At the present time we are camped at Lee's Mill, six miles southwest of Yorktown. It was from this camp that I made my last visit to Yorktown. Address my letters to Rev. H. Gache, Chap., 10th La. Vol. Reg,

Yorktown, Va. My best to all the Jesuits. Tell Father Yenni that when I passed through Richmond President Davis was loaded down with work and was rather ill; consequently I was not able to deliver the message. Right now you are at Grand Coteau. Have a nice vacation. There is no news at all here on the Peninsula. I don't know—in fact nobody knows—what's happening elsewhere. Don't be surprised therefore, if I fail to send you news. Since I left New Orleans I haven't had a meal even equal to Spring Hill's most ordinary fare: no bread, no soup, no wine—need I say more about the food? Then there is always miserable diarrhea. Oh well, all of these things don't go for developing a pottle belly, anyway. I keep busy all of the time, and I find the days go by very fast—much faster, sometimes, than the nights. *Adieu encore.*

COMMENTARY

Before regiments were formed in Louisiana, as in all states of the Confederacy, officers and men in the constituting companies elected their chaplain. When their choice was a Catholic priest Louisiana troops addressed a petition to the archbishop of New Orleans, John Mary Odin (1800-70). Short of priests under his own jurisdiction, the archbishop sought the assistance of various religious orders for help. And so, Hippolyte Gache, ordered to New Orleans by his provincial, received his chaplain's appointment on the nineteenth of July; then, on the twenty-second, when the 10th was mustered into service at Camp Moore for the duration of the war, the Spring Hill Jesuit was assigned to its commanding officer, Col. Antoine-Jacques-Philippe de Mandeville de Marigny (b. New Orleans, Louisiana, November 2, 1811–d. New Orleans, Louisiana, June 3, 1888). At this date Mandeville de Marigny was "One of the best specimens of the French Creole in physique, general appearance and manners that (Louisiana) has produced." Son of the legendary Bernard de Marigny (1785-1868), the tutor of Louis Philippe, and Mathilde Morales (1789-1859), he was the son-in-law of Louisiana's first American governor, William C.C. Claiborne (1775-1817), and the grandson of one of her last Spanish intendants. Despite the fact that he represented the fourth generation of the Marigny family born on American soil, he was an officer in the French cavalry, having been educated with the Duke of Orleans at the Saumur military college. There is no reason to suspect, however, that he had requested the French-born Jesuit as chaplain to his regiment. Rather, the inchoate regiment had opted for a priest and Odin offered Gache. More than seventy percent of the 845 men that made up Marigny's newly formed regiment were Catholic, at least in name, and although they represented seventeen different countries, the Irish-born—according to available statistics—accounted for more than fifty percent of the total number of the six companies.[42]

A lieutenant in the *Tirailleurs d'Orléans*, which became Company I when the regiment was formed, kept a journal which was eventually published. It covers with a wealth of information the time from July 22, 1861 until April 21, 1865, when the remnant of the regiment "left Fortress Monroe at two o'clock on our way home." This was Henry D. Monier (b. Assumption Parish, October 23, 1836), destined before the end of the war to be appointed lieutenant colonel of the decimated regiment. According to Monier, the 10th left New Orleans on July 29; and "after a fatiguing journey," arrived in Richmond on August 3, where it was enthusiastically received by the local populace and by the Confederate authorities. The troops then proceeded to the Fair Grounds where they bivouacked until they were ordered to the Peninsula on Sunday, August 18. Then, on the twenty-third, they made the first of many marches from Williamsburg to Eutopia Bluff along the James River. The captain of Company F, John Legett (b. Scotland, 1835–d. Manassas, Virginia, May 3, 1863), whose death at Second Manassas had enabled Monier to assume command of the regiment, also began a journal of sorts on the blank pages of a manual he carried with him, *Exercises et Manoeuvres de l'Infanterie.* This New Orleans lawyer had recruited eighty-three men as early as June 10 into a company called the Louisiana Rebels, and in his account of events he noted that the 10th left Camp Moore for Richmond on the thirtieth, and on Saturday, July 17, they broke camp at Richmond—arriving at Jamestown the same evening on the *Northampton.* On Sunday they made the long march from Jamestown to Camp Magruder, Eutopia Bluff, where they arrived late at night. In his letter Gache gave an account which tallied better with Legett's version than it did with Monier's.[43]

It is unfortunate that Gache did not give the name of his travelling companion from Richmond to Yorktown, but the description of this lieutenant from the 10th, twenty-four years his junior and unknown to the Spring Hill Jesuits, reduces the possibility to three. At this date Henry Clay Marks, Jr. (b. New Orleans, Louisiana 1840–d. Malvern Hill,

Virginia, July 1, 1862) was a 2d lieutenant in Company B, known as the Derbigny Guards. In January he was promoted to company captain, and was one of the four Derbigny Guards mortally wounded at Malvern Hill. His father, Isaac Newton Marks (1817-96), a New Orleans businessman and philanthropist, was one of the members of the convention which passed the ordinance of secession.

A second possibility is Thomas N. Powell, Jr. (b. Donaldsonville, Louisiana, 1840–d. near Petersburg, Virginia, April 1, 1865), whose death Henry Monier describes in his Journal: "During the quiet days of the occupation of Petersburg, the officers and men had been accustomed to attend church service on Sunday. The last battle about Petersburg occurred on Sunday, and at about 10:30 a.m. Colonel Waggaman, who had frequently attended on these occasions with Powell . . . by way of inquiring what was the hour, jocularly asked if they would yet have time to get to church. 'Hardly,' said Powell, consulting his watch, 'unless we leave quickly.' He had scarcely finished speaking before a bullet came along which caused his instantaneous death. . ." Powell had considered himself major and was recognized as such, after the death of Legett. A student of medicine before he enlisted in the Hewitt Guards, later Company C, he was regarded as an outstanding officer, popular with the troops.

The final possible candidate to qualify as Gache's companion on this trip is Auguste Edouard Seton (b. Opelousas, Louisiana, August 28, 1840–d. Fort Delaware, Delaware, February 11, 1865), a 2d lieutenant in the Confederate State Rangers, Company K. Promoted to 1st lieutenant in the Hewitt Guards in February, he was captured at the Battle of the Wilderness, May 5, 1864, and died in prison. Most likely the unnamed lieutenant was a Catholic, judging from the fact that he and the chaplain considered kneeling down together for evening prayers in the room that reminded Gache of where "Gaspar lived with his sons," refraining at the last minute out of consideration for the sleepers. It is doubtful that Gache would have performed such an exercise of piety with a Protestant. Or if he had, he certainly would have mentioned the fact. Marks was an Episcopalian; Seton, although a Catholic, was not officially commissioned lieutenant until November, and efforts to determine conclusively Powell's religious affiliation have not been successful.

The reference the chaplain made to Gaspar and sons has also been unverifiable. It is possible that the Jesuit had in mind the Gaspar of Charles Dickens' recently published and immensely popular *A Tale of Two Cities*. But the reference may also have conjured up a picture of the room on the Spring Hill campus that Gaspar Balland (b. Saarlouis, Saar, France 1797) shared with his son Stanislaus (b. Saarlouis, Saar, France 1840). At any rate, both the fictional and the factual Gaspar had but one son.[44]

But if the identities of Gaspar and the young lieutenant of the 10th have not been satisfactorily established, there is no question about the identity of their Yorktown host, Henry J. Miller, Jr. (b. Richmond, Virginia, August 1, 1838–d. Richmond, Virginia, November 3, 1866). This young soldier, a member of the Georgetown University class of 1853, enlisted on April 2, 1861 to serve for a year in Captain Standard's Company, Third Howitzer Battalion, Virginia Artillery. Never married, he died in the Richmond cholera epidemic during the early days of Reconstruction. His father, Henry, Sr. (b. Saarlouis, Saar, France, 1804–d. Richmond, Virginia, July 22, 1883) was at this date a tailor and merchant. After the fall of Richmond he was appointed to the City Council by the Military Government and here he showed himself to be "one of the most valuable members of that body, always looking to the interests of the city."[45]

Other military personnel, whom Gache named in his first letter from Virginia, can also be better identified. The commanding officer of the Louisiana Fifth was Lt. Col. Henry Forno (b. Charleston, South Carolina, 1789–d. Amite City, Louisiana, February 1, 1866). A former police chief in New Orleans, he was also a veteran of the Mexican War. As commander of the First Louisiana Brigade, he was critically wounded at Second Manassas, and in 1863 he was detached to Mobile to serve as a recruiting officer. Returning to New Orleans after the war, he was killed in a railroad accident.

The chaplain of the 5th was Livias H. Baldwin (b. Newark, New Jersey, October 20, 1831). It was not until July 30, 1862, ten months after he had vied with Forno to make Gache welcome at the 5th's campsite, that Baldwin received his appointment. On October 13, 1862, he requested a permit from Gen. George B. McClellan to cross the lines in order to attend to the wounded and to visit his parents in Newark. Although both of his parents had died in 1856, other of his family members were still alive in Newark, the city founded by Baldwin's direct ancestors. On November 10, he returned to the Louisiana Fifth, and twelve days later, for reasons which have not been recorded, he was relieved as chaplain to the regiment. Probably he was not an ordained minister, for his name does not appear in any church directory; nevertheless in May 1863 he was a post chaplain at Monroe, Louisiana, and there is a record of his having been a post chaplain the following May at Galveston, Texas. This is the last date his name appeared on the rolls, and presumably he left the military at this time. He was dead before the turn of the century.[46]

Two outfits for which Gache always admitted a special predilection were camped alongside of the Fifth Battalion at Yorktown. These were Major de Coppens' Zouaves, who were primarily responsible for the bad reputation Louisiana troops had acquired among the citizens of Virginia, and Dreux's, now Rightor's, First Special Battalion.[47] These two battalions, or what was left of them after disease and fever had taken their toll, were soon to become part of Forno's Second Brigade.

The unnamed sergeant who was buried the day Gache visited the Zouave camp was Charles Monbar, the 1st sergeant of Captain de Bordenave's Company B. Captain Samuel Manning Todd (b. Ithaca, New York, September 2, 1815–d. New Orleans, Louisiana, February 1, 1905) was the commanding officer of the Shreveport Grays, now Company D, Rightor's Battalion, and since the Jesuit had known the "good Captain" in Pensacola, and perhaps even in Mobile, he identified him by name. But such was not the case with the battalion's new commanding officer, Nicholas H. Rightor (b. Donaldsonville, Louisiana, March 16, 1832-d. New Orleans, Louisiana, August 11, 1900), who was, unlike Todd, a Catholic. Judging from his correspondence, Father Hippolyte never seemed impressed by this man destined to become one of Louisiana's most distinguished jurists, nor is there any evidence that he was struck by Mandeville de Marigny, but for reasons apparent in this letter, and in those that follow, he had the highest respect for his daily mass server, Captain Eugene Waggaman (b. New Orleans, Louisiana, September 25, 1826-d. New Orleans, Louisiana, April 24, 1897), the captain of the *Tirailleurs d'Orléans*, now Company I of the 10th. This aristocratic planter, among whose ancestors were some of the most distinguished men in Maryland and Louisiana history, would attend church services regularly, in 1865, with Thomas N. Powell, Jr.[48]

In this letter Gache advised de Carrière that he had also visited the Eighth Alabama while he was at Yorktown. This regiment was under the command of Col. John Anthony Winston (b. Madison County, Alabama–d. Mobile, Alabama, December 31, 1879), one of that state's best known citizens. Twice governor, in 1835 and in 1855, he was a stern disciplinarian and an unpopular officer, who nevertheless commanded respect from all under his charge. One officer on his staff that Gache singled out was the captain of the famous Emerald Guards, Company I, Patrick Loughry (b. County Mayo, Ireland, 1817–d. near Richmond, Virginia, June 1, 1862). Another member of the 8th that he met was a former Spring Hill student—the "youngest of the Mobile Lyons." This was Cornelius (b. Mobile, Alabama, September 16, 1843-d. Spotsylvania, Virginia, May 11, 1864), whose older brother John (b. Mobile, Alabama, April 28, 1839–d. near Atlanta, Georgia, July 22, 1864) was in Company D Alabama State Artillery. They were the sons of John Lyons, Sr., a wealthy merchant, and his wife Ellen McCormack Lyons, who accompanied Alabama's famous nurse-journalist, Kate Cumming, to Corinth, in the spring of 1862, to nurse at the hospital where Patrick Coyle was serving as chaplain.[49]

The only Jesuit whose name appeared for the first time in this correspondence was Dominic Yenni (b. Rankeil, Varalburg, Austria, January 1, 1810–d. Spring Hill, Alabama, July 7, 1888), a sweet, harmonious, swan-like soul, an accomplished musician who had brought a rare Cremona violin with him when he came to Spring Hill in 1847. This gentle man of refined taste and broad culture had begun teaching Greek and Latin grammar in 1837, and for the next fifty-two years, forty at Spring Hill, he dedicated himself to this same exacting task. He was also the author of a Greek and a Latin grammar, texts which were *de rigeur* in all American Jesuit schools until recent times. It appears that Yenni had been acquainted with President Davis, for Gache attempted to deliver his message to Davis. The fact that the chaplain of the Louisiana Tenth was not granted an interview with the president is not surprising, but the fact that the Jesuit was not shy about making such a request indicated that he regarded Yenni's request a proper one. Furthermore, Gache's interview with Major General John B. Magruder (b. Port Royal, Virginia, May 1, 1807–d. Houston, Texas, February 18, 1871) is one more example of the cordiality manifested by the commanding officers of the Confederate Army toward the Catholic chaplain. Gache had already experienced similar hospitality and encouragement from General Bragg. He remained coyly silent about the one further privilege that Magruder might have granted him to make his satisfaction complete, but it is clear from future letters that the object of so ardent a desire was a horse.[50]

J.M.J.

Camp Lee's Mill
November 22, 1861

Rev. Father D. Yenni, S.J.
Spring Hill

Reverend and very dear Father, Pax Christi

In the last letter which I received from Spring Hill, somewhat more than three weeks ago, I was assured that Father de Carrière admitted he owed me a letter and promised he would write soon. I will not presume to judge; I do not know whether he has kept his word. But this I do know: since that time I've received no further letters from Spring Hill, either from him or from anyone else. Possibly the distractions of vacation have prevented Father de Carrière from putting his generous intentions into an envelope. But be that as it may, I've decided to write this time to your worthy Reverence. My letter may serve to remind you of the fact of my existence, and perhaps even to acquaint you with some of the more recent events in my insignificant life. I will not write further to Father de Carrière again lest I crush him with the burden of yet another debt. I strongly suspect that you too will fail to answer me, but it matters not. One must be munificent.

It has been about two months since I have sent you any news. During this time I've moved about quite a bit. At the beginning of October—before going to Richmond to renew my supply of hosts and to go to confession—I decided to stop over in Norfolk to see Fathers Prachensky and Hubert. I had hoped to get some of their ideas on the apostolate, and to enjoy simply the pleasure of talking with them. Having gone so long without any stimulating conversation whatsoever (you have no idea what sheer misery this can be), I was intellectually stale.

I met Father Hubert on the road to Norfolk. He was traveling with the pastor of Lynchburg [Oscar Sears] on the way to Manassas, in western Virginia, to attend some social function. I almost had to be told who it was that I had met. Imagine, if you will, a young dandy: his hair elegant, his beard splendid; gold-braid festooned upon his blue kepi and embroidered upon the sleeves of his high-collared frock coat; the golden buttons of his waistcoat emblazened with the Louisiana pelican; his gold-filleted trousers falling neatly into a pair of comely boots. This dazzling sight was none other than Father Hubert himself! Can you blame me for scarcely recognizing him?

I was a bit vexed to learn that he had just left the very place where I had expected to visit him, but our plans made it impossible for either of us to stop at this point; so each of us went his own way, I toward Norfolk via Petersburg, and he toward Manassas by way of Lynchburg. I decided to spend the night at Petersburg so as to avoid night travel and to be assured of a place to say mass the following morning. I would not say that Petersburg is a pretty town, but although it has nothing in particular to offer travelers, it is, nevertheless, much bigger than I expected. It is almost as large as Mobile. The pastor, Father Thomas Mulvey, impressed me as being a fine and truly priestly man. I had already known about him through Father [David] Whelan, his successor as chaplain at the Petersburg convent, but even though Father Whelan had spoken highly of him, I found the man himself more impressive than I had anticipated. I took advantage of his hospitality two nights and one day. On the second evening of my stay we visited the home of one of the most interesting young couples that I have ever had the pleasure of meeting, a certain Mr. and Mrs. [William E.] Hinton. They are both converts. Mrs. Hinton became a Catholic while she was still a student in a convent of the Sacred Heart; Mr. Hinton, I believe, made his studies in a

Protestant institution, but he is certainly no less well-instructed on that account. He is of a serious temperament and has a remarkable library, especially of religious books, among which one can find all the recognized French authors of theology and asceticism. I should also mention, of course, that Mr. and Mrs. Hinton not only understand French, but even manage—considering that they are foreigners—to speak it very well. Seeing these young people who were so religious and at the same time so cheerful and wholesome, I could not help but wonder why their example hadn't opened the eyes of their Protestant neighbors and convinced them that the religion which could form such a couple could hardly be a false one.

After my Petersburg sojourn I pushed on to Norfolk where I spent four days, and where I was able, as you might suspect, to renew many old acquaintances and to make some new ones. No sooner had I stepped off the wagon than I found myself face to face with John Burns of Mobile. You know him well. We recognized one another in a flash, and spontaneously he took a hold of my baggage and escorted me up to the rectory where he delivered me safely into the hands of Father Prachensky. In my books this young fellow is a real gentleman.

According to Father de Carrière, Father Prachensky has already informed you of his assumed title of "major." I had heard rumors about this nonsense myself, but knowing that Confederate chaplains are chaplains and nothing else, and that they enjoy no legal title to any rank whatsoever, I regarded the whole business as a joke. But I was wrong. Father Prachensky is dead serious when he puts on that he is a *major*, and the proof of it is that he wears a uniform with all of the accessories, including a moustache and a little tuft of chin-whiskers in the style of Frank, the carpenter at Spring Hill; or, should you prefer, *à la Napoléon III.* He is so set on wearing this uniform that no amount of reasoning will make him give it up. I scoffed at his pretensions and informed him everyone else did the same—and that's scarcely an exaggeration. I told him that the bishop of Richmond, [John McGill] as well as all of the diocesan priests, found it passing strange that a Catholic chaplain should dress up in an officer's uniform. And I told him also that General Blanchard himself, in my very presence, had asked by what right it was that this Father Prachensky had put on a uniform. Nor did I fail to add that the general had found such airs rather amusing.

But to all of this Father Prachensky merely answered: "I'm wearing this uniform and I'm going to continue to wear it. I couldn't care less for those who criticize me for it." This is exactly the same answer that Father Hubert had given to these same objections. Ah, the desire to pose as an officer! Would you ever suspect that such a sentiment could find its way into the hearts of Jesuits? For my part, I cannot claim to have gained any merit for resisting such a temptation, since the desire to wear a uniform has never crossed my mind; however I am disappointed that Fathers Hubert and Prachensky not only were tempted but yielded so easily. I regard it as only natural that Protestant ministers should disguise themselves in such a get-up, but that two Jesuits should do it—well, I have a hard time believing it, much less approving of it! Fortunately for them the justification of their conduct doesn't depend on my understanding or approbation. But the fact remains, to my knowledge they are the first and only Catholic chaplains to wear a military uniform. But on to other matters.

You've heard, I'm sure, about the beautiful church at Norfolk—a marvel which deserves all the praise that one can give it. It will suffice for me to say that Father Cambiaso greatly admires it, and even though it is built in a different style from his own, he admits that it is in no way inferior. It owes its entire existence to Father [Michael] O'Keefe, an outstanding young man who was appointed pastor immediately after his ordination when he was only twenty-two years old. He began the actual building two years after his appointment, and the church was paid for almost exclusively from the alms the young pastor collected on weekly calls to New York, Philadelphia or Baltimore. Every Saturday he would go up to one of these cities and hear confessions all day long, and every Sunday after his two masses, he would return to Norfolk with the money he had collected. Then on Monday morning he would pay the laborers for the work they had done on the church the previous week. The following Saturday the cycle would commence again. It took him six years to finish the construction. But what an amazing man he is! What a worker—though he never gives the impression of being rushed; and what a saintly priest—though were you to see him, you would think that there was nothing at all extraordinary about him. If Father [Robert] Kelly were still at Spring Hill, I would tell him that I find the Irish from the North quite a different breed from those of the South. He would take that as a rather left-handed compliment and that would be as I intended it!

As I was in Norfolk on a Sunday, I sang the high mass and Father Prachensky preached in English. That afternoon I myself preached in French at the insistence of a certain family, originally from Roanne, which settled in Norfolk only a year ago. As yet no one in the family can understand a word of English. I promised the devout young girl who made the request for a French sermon that I would preach if she could find twenty people who would listen to me. As she brought along more than thirty Frenchmen to church that evening (and all of them practicing Catholics too!), I was obliged either to break my promise or to give a sermon. This particular Sunday marked the first time in twelve years that Father O'Keefe had so many priests on hand.

I'll not mention anything about the *Merrimac*; I suspect that the newspapers say enough about it. No reason to tell you either that I went over to see Captain [Robert M.] Sands at his camp, which is only about four miles from Norfolk, and that while I was there I saw quite a few of our former students: W[illiam] B[ell] Rohmer, [John] Burns, [Henry?] Muldon, J[ohn] Daily, among others. I missed [John] Innerarity because he was confined—awaiting a court-martial. The poor fellow got drunk and insulted one of the officers. While I was in Norfolk, the Third Alabama Regiment (part of which is made up of the Mobile Cadets) was judged to be the best behaved and the most gentlemanly regiment stationed in this area. The ladies in town decided they would give a beautiful flag as a token of their high esteem for the regiment, and the presentation ceremony took place on the same Sunday that I referred to above. I myself therefore had the honor of observing the worthy Mobilians march down the main streets of Norfolk, and I must say, to their credit, I had reason to be mighty proud of them.

That very same evening I heard that the Yankees had landed a large number of troops at Old Point or Fort Monroe and that it looked like they would try to maneuver their fleet up the York. I'll let you picture for yourself how fast I flew out of Norfolk in the direction of my own Peninsula, heartsick that I had left it in the first place and chagrined that I had missed the battle that was probably taking place there at that very moment. I arrived in Richmond. A dispatch had just come to the Minister of War from General Magruder; some of the troops had already engaged the enemy, and within a few hours the fighting should become general. More reason for self-reproach and anguish. I should have gotten out of Richmond that evening, but it was impossible. I wasn't able to budge until 7:30 the next morning. What an endless night! I could hear the cannons; in my mind's eye I could see Yankee bombs raining down amidst the flames of Yorktown. And then at last it was 7:30. I left with a

Florida boy whom I had met the night before. During the past few weeks he had been sick, and now he too was on his way to rejoin his regiment. The two of us got as far as West Point. No news there from the Peninsula; that was already a good sign. Then after the two-hour boat trip we found ourselves gazing at a peaceful Yorktown—not a single scar of battle could we detect. Just as soon as the boat touched the wharf, I jumped off and dashed out to find my friend Henry Miller. He told me the great noise we had heard came from an insignificant skirmish of absolutely no importance—way on the other side of Bethel.

When I heard this all of my anxieties faded away, with the result that I began to feel myself again, and instead of bewailing my Norfolk trip, I could now congratulate myself for having taken it. My friend Henry invited me to spend the night in Yorktown. He promised to find me a softer bed than that one of happy memory which his hospitality had afforded me on my last visit. I thanked him and very willingly accepted. He brought me over to the home of the only Catholic people in Yorktown. These people, a man, his wife, and a female domestic, are not natives here and they plan to stay just until the end of the war. They operate a small grocery store for the soldiers, and no one could say that they live in any kind of luxury—not by any means. Still, they put me up in what was without exaggeration a cubby-hole in their very modest house, and they put at my disposal a small bed, a tiny chair and an undersized desk. Here I spent the night and, like a prophet, it is here that I return every time that I pass through Yorktown.

When I awoke the next morning I was not feeling very well, and Mrs. M., my hostess, noticed that I had caught a chill. Right away she hurried down to the little shop nearby, where she bought the last shawl that the proprietor had in stock. Then, protesting that it wasn't really costly at all, she insisted that I accept the shawl as a gift. I did, and

I assure you that it has proved to be a priceless possession. It is a coat during the day, a blanket at night, and a wrap during morning prayers. I'm looking forward to showing it off to you, if and when I return to Spring Hill; and if nobody steals it from me in the meanwhile. Mr. and Mrs. M. show me the greatest respect and charity and they always insist that I eat alone, as they feel that they are unworthy to sit down at the same table with me. Once when I was at their place I imprudently asked Mr. M. if one could buy a blanket in Yorktown. "No," he said, "But I'll be able to bring you one from Richmond where I'm going the day after tomorrow."

"But I'll need it between then and now, and I'll . . ."

But he didn't give me a chance to finish because he disappeared into the next room, and when he came out again he was carrying a blanket.

"Here's one. It's not new, but it's very good. I wish you would accept it as a gift from Mrs. M."

I felt quite embarrassed to take it, but at the same time I was very pleased. Oh, I tell you, to have friends, especially in this part of the country, is a wonderful thing! And thanks be to God, I have them all over this area (except perhaps in my own regiment), and I do wish you could meet each and every one of them.

I spent only one day in Yorktown since I had to push on to Lee's Mill where my regiment was stationed. As I wasn't able to procure any means of transportation, either from the quartermaster or from anyone else, I left my baggage with Mr. M. and started walking the eight miles to the camp. On the outskirts of town I met two men in a buggy coming from the opposite direction. One of them addressed me, "Good morning, sir. Where are you going?"

"To Lee's Mill, to rejoin my regiment."

"Well, if you're not in a hurry, I'll take you down when I go back."

"When will that be?"

"In about twenty minutes."

"Why, thank you very much, Sir. I accept with pleasure. But are you sure you know where I want to go?" I had never seen him before in my life and I was afraid that he had mistaken me for someone else.

"Oh, I know your regiment, and I know you too. I've seen you several times."

I then asked him if he could take my bags as well. But of course he could and most willingly at that. Who was this unknown friend that Divine Providence had so conveniently sent to my rescue? He is a planter who lives about two miles from where we are quartered. He had observed me on a few occasions when I walked in the direction of his place reading my office or saying my beads in the quiet of the countryside. This strange sight must have attracted his attention and made a favorable impression on him. He asked me to visit him and I said I would, although frankly I have no intention of doing any such thing. He is married to a young woman whose beauty is the cause of a great deal of loose talk among the officers; and rather than offer them an opportunity to make me the center of their ugly remarks, I decided that I would not visit this man's household. This same reason prevents me from visiting other families in the neighborhood. If you could only realize among what trash I live!

I had no sooner arrived back in camp than I was running off again in pretty nearly every direction. I returned to Williamsburg twice and to Yorktown three times. Michel Prud'homme, whom you knew at Spring Hill and who was a lieutenant in a company of Confederate States Rangers, was the reason for my first trip to Williamsburg. The poor boy had had typhoid fever for three weeks, and just when they thought that he was cured, he suddenly started hemorrhaging. His brother [Louis], who was with him at the time, wrote me asking that I come to administer the Last Sacraments. I left here at seven in the evening and got to Williamsburg around ten. But it was too late. The young lad had died four or five hours even before I received the message. This was probably the first time the city of King William of Orange ever witnessed a Catholic priest, fully vested in cassock, surplice and stole, walking in procession down its historic streets. Wonders never cease. But even more wonderful was the fact that the poor boy was mourned here amongst strangers with no less grief than if he had been buried at home.

During the two or three weeks of his final illness he had been cared for by an Episcopalian family who couldn't have been more solicitous for him had he been their own son or brother. The name of this family is Southall, and more gentle people you couldn't find. On one occasion when I was staying with them, Mr. [Albert] Southall graciously consented to allow me the use of the parlor to say mass. I decided to use the top of the piano as my altar and I determined to say a very early mass, thinking I would be finished before anyone in the household arose, and therefore would avoid making a nuisance of myself. But the family didn't figure as I did. As I began to vest, two little girls all decked out in their Sunday best, entered and quietly seated themselves at the far end of the room. They were followed shortly afterwards by two older girls, and finally by the mother and father who came in and joined the group. I don't know what they did during the Holy Sacrifice, but I didn't hear the slightest movement or whisper until I had finished. Oh, but I mustn't forget: there was only one distraction which almost made me laugh out loud. Just as I made the sign of the Cross to begin the prayers at the foot of the altar, Mr. Southall tiptoed up behind me and with the greatest solemnity whispered: "We've just made some hot coffee, wouldn't you like to take a little right now?"

After mass I packed away the vestments and the other accessories, leaving, however, my breviary on the make-shift altar. It wasn't long before this strange book attracted the curiosity of little Miss Kate, all of nine or ten years old. She went over to the piano where she could observe at closer quarters this mysterious object of her attention, and then after furtively glancing over in my direction (I pretended all of the while to be interested in something else), she reached out and touched first the edge and then the cover of the book. I could see she was dying to give it a thorough examination and so I went over to the piano, picked her up, then stood her in front of me where I was sitting and put the breviary into her hands. She immediately began her investigation, and when she discovered some holy cards she cried out with admiration and delight. I asked her if she would like to have one of them for her very own. Have one! The very idea to keep one of these beautiful pictures was beyond her fondest hopes, and that is why she seemed puzzled at my offer.

"Don't you like them?" she asked.

"Of course, I like them, my dear," I answered picking out the one I thought she liked best and giving it to her, "But it would make me happier for you to have it."

I couldn't begin to describe her delight, and in an instant everyone in the house had to come and admire her pretty picture. Her sister, Miss Virginia, who is two years younger, nudged me and rather sheepishly, yet with confidence, told me that she too would like to see my book. It wasn't long before I parted with the picture that caught her fancy. But no sooner had I given away these cards than I began to feel that I had acted hastily, and that perhaps they would prove offensive to the Episcopalian sensibilities of the parents. Presently, however, my fears were allayed and I realized that my action had not been regarded with disfavor, for Mrs. S. enthusiastically hunted up two nice envelopes for the cards and instructed the girls to take good care of their newly acquired gifts.

I'm also on the best of terms with the older girls. Indeed, one would think from their respectful attention that they were model students of the Madames of the Sacred Heart. And Mrs. S., knowing very well that rations are at a premium in camp, often stuffs my pockets with tidbits. This is such a wonderful family; they are so good to me. I can't help but believe that they are living in good faith and that if they had the opportunity to know us as we really are, they would become Catholics. May the Holy Sacrifice of the Mass which I offered in their home and the little pictures which I gave to the children be the source and the occasion of a great blessing for each and every one of them.

This is not, however, the only family in Williamsburg which moves me to admiration and respect. I've found the same charm in almost all of the people in this city. The afternoon we buried Prud'homme, for example, a young officer of the Fifth Louisiana Regiment introduced me to Colonel [Benjamin S.] Ewell, the Commandant of the Williamsburg Post. The colonel and I left the cemetery together. We had only gone a few paces when this remarkable West Point graduate suddenly turned to me.

"Wouldn't you like to come and have tea with me and spend the night at my home?" he asked.

"Oh, I should be delighted. And you would be doing a service, sir, to these men who have brought me here and who are probably at a loss about finding a bed for me tonight." The matter was agreed upon, and we set off at once to the colonel's house, for it was already dusk.

Before the Secession, Colonel Ewell was President of William and Mary. He still lives in the president's quarters with his eighteen-year old daughter and sister. Young Miss [Elizabeth] Ewell is an Episcopalian; Miss [Rebecca] Ewell, a charming lady in her forties who serves as his housekeeper, is a Presbyterian. I believe that the colonel is also a Presbyterian, although he strikes me as a man too well educated and fair minded to have other than a favorable attitude toward Catholicism. I can assure you, whatever their beliefs, the gracious hospitality of each one of the members of this family made me feel completely at home. In fact, I couldn't have felt more at home with any other family, no matter how Catholic they might be.

After this trip to Williamsburg, I returned on another occasion with the intention of paying a visit to the men of the Dreux Batallion. My intention, however, was provisional; it depended upon whether or not I could find the necessary transportation to take me from the town to the camp. The batallion is quartered on the banks of the James, some six miles from Williamsburg. Thanks to Colonel Ewell, transportation was easily come by. I had but to express my wish and at ten the next morning, I beheld, at the bottom of the stairs awaiting my command, a carriage drawn by two splendid gray horses. It took me an hour to get to Spratley's Farm where I was immediately surrounded by my old friends of the Dreux. I was pleasantly surprised to meet again some of my Pensacola friends like John Augustine and [Thomas] Raby, and especially young [James] Masterson who is now the lieutenant colonel's personal orderly. These lads are just like the boys all over: they manage somehow to get plenty of food even though the other soldiers suffer from hunger. When that young rascal Masterson greeted me, for example, he had jam all over his hands and face.

Although I stayed two days and two nights in this camp, I wasn't able to do very much, as the men were bustling about getting their quarters ready for the winter that had already given us a warning that it wouldn't be long a-coming. But, at any rate, there were some confessions and communions for me. There was nothing extraordinary about my stay, however, except perhaps, my confessional box. As I didn't have a tent to myself, I persuaded my penitents to join me in an evening stroll along the James. When we were about a quarter of a mile from camp we came upon a huge tree trunk that the tide had washed up on shore. It was bathed in a magnificent moonlight. Here, I thought to myself, is my confessional, and so here it was that each man, sitting beside me looking as if he were carrying on the most ordinary conversation, settled his affairs with God. Perhaps I should also say a word about the place where I said mass. I'm sure that if Father [Joseph] Desribes saw it, he would cry: "My, the poor Lord! What will the good Father subject him to next!"—an axiom already abundantly illustrated in my own correspondence. So much for Spratley's Farm.

I returned to the Ewell's in hopes of obtaining transportation back to camp. The colonel once again put his carriage at my disposal, and this was not all. He also invited me to return to spend a week at his home in order that I might have the leisure to visit all of the sick in the hospital. On the way back to Lee's Mill I learned that my regiment had been sent to Bethel Church to harvest the corn and to see if their presence couldn't entice the Yankees out of Fort Monroe. I didn't like this state of affairs one bit. Now either I had to join my regiment at Bethel Church or I had to stay in the camp with the sick. If I chose to rejoin the regiment I would run the risk of exposing myself to the rain and frost, since I had only one blanket and we would certainly have to sleep out under the stars; moreover, I would deprive myself of the consolation of saying daily mass. But if I chose to remain in camp I would run the risk of dying of starvation, because the captain with whom I took my meals was with the regiment and had taken his servant with him. There was absolutely no one at Lee's Mill to take care of me. But that's neither here nor there. As there wasn't the slightest possibility that there would be a skirmish at Bethel, I chose the second alternative as the lesser evil, and I remained in camp.

For a whole week, however, I suffered all the pangs of hunger. There were three days when I had but a few biscuits and some scraps of salt pork that the Negroes gave me. When the week was up I learned that my regiment was going to stay on at Bethel, and therefore I decided that under the circumstances it might be well to keep my promise to Colonel Ewell and return to Williamsburg for a little visit. He welcomed me as I knew he would, and I remained as his guest for five days. There was only one disadvantage: I wasn't able to offer daily mass because there was no one present to assist. On Sunday, however, I particularly wanted to say mass because some of the sick in the hospital had expressed the desire to receive Communion. I mentioned this to the Ewell ladies, and sure enough it was the best possible way to find a place to offer the Holy Sacrifice. Because of her regard for me and her sympathy for Catholics in general, the aunt was delighted to have the opportunity to enable the Catholics to fulfill their religious duties; and the Colonel's daughter, hoping to provide the opportunity for many of her friends to observe a Catholic mass—a spectacle which promised to be a real novelty for them—was no less enthusiastic. The ladies, then, took over all of the preparations, and at nine o'clock on Sunday the eighth, I had the chapel of the lunatic asylum at my disposal.

And so here it was in the largest and most beautiful building in Williamsburg that I offered mass before a dozen or so Catholic convalescents and some twenty Episcopalian ladies. I have no idea what the impressions of the ladies were since they did not undertake to confide them to me. That evening, however, some of them paid a visit to the Ewells with the rather obvious intention of seeing me. With one exception, all were most charming and friendly. This one declared that she was a heretic, and boasted that, although she had been to Rome, she had neither kissed the *scala sancta* nor asked the pope for his blessing. As her manner was rather arrogant and impertinent, I decided to say simply this: "Madame, I find it difficult to see how your failure to kiss the *scala sancta* or to ask for the papal blessing can in any way stand as a condemnation of those who judge it proper to do so." With that she made a profound curtsy and said in French (for she spoke a little French): "*Bonsoir, Monsieur*," and left the room. As soon as she was out of earshot the other ladies made it clear that they thoroughly disapproved of her provocative remarks.

Later on that same evening I was honored by a visit from the Episcopalian minister, [Thomas Ambler] himself. As he greeted me, he put on a mask of sweet innocence which he wore rather unconvincingly during the series of barbed questions and ever-so-polite objections which followed. Once again the ladies were shocked at seeing me treated with such rudeness in their home, where my status as guest should have given me immunity against this sort of outrage. Once again the aunt came to my defense by showing herself to be a much better theologian than the minister. For my part, not wishing to be drawn into a controversy that might lead me to say something offensive to my friends, I confined myself to one remark: "If the Reverend Gentleman would but consult Catholic authors on these matters of Catholic dogma," I said, "his questions might easily resolve themselves."

I cannot venture to say whether he will take my advice. At any rate, as I was leaving Williamsburg, young Miss Ewell asked me if I could give her the "Poorman's Catechism" which I had previously shown her. I was only too glad to do so. And the devout aunt, for she is indeed a very devout woman, took me into her confidence on some matters which greatly consoled me. May God enlighten these good souls and grant them all the graces which they need in their present circumstances.

I am very fond of the people of Williamsburg, and it seems unfortunate that there is not a single Catholic home here around which a priest might build a parish. If there were, I feel sure that it would not be long before one could have a sizeable congregation. But really now I must end this letter, lest I forfeit all chance of its being read. *Adieu* dear Father. I have not been especially well these last few months; but I do manage to get along, despite the cold—which is becoming more noticeable, particularly during the nights—and despite the hunger, which I experience from time to time.

My regards to all of Ours, to Dr. Rohmer and to Mr. Parada. In union with our Holy Sacrifices, I am *totus in Christo tuus*,

H. Gache, S.J.
Chaplain, 10th
Louisiana Regiment

COMMENTARY

In his second extant letter from Virginia, addressed to Dominic Yenni, Father Hippolyte named many individuals, beginning with two fellow chaplains, both Jesuits, whose demeanor offered him the opportunity to manifest his sharpness of wit, which at need showed its sting not only with a flicker of his black eyes and mischievous smile, but also with the point of his devastating pen. Chaplain Darius Hubert (b. Toulon, France, January 19, 1823–d. Macon, Georgia, June 14, 1893) arrived in New Orleans in 1847 while yet a scholastic, and was dispatched to Grand Coteau under the eye of Hippolyte Gache. When the First Louisiana Regiment was organized, its commanding officer Colonel (later Brigadier General) Albert Blanchard requested Father Hubert by name to accompany the Louisiana troops to Virginia. One month later the Jesuit received his appointment. The second chaplain, Joseph Prachensky (b. Eger, Prague, Bohemia, June 22, 1822–d. Fordham, New York, July 8, 1890) had come to Alabama in 1848 at the time of the great exodus of Jesuits from revolutionary Europe. He remained in Mobile until he joined the Third Alabama on the Peninsula in September, because "Col. Lomax and Captain Sands and other officers and men of the Mobile Regiment have sought him—and his superiors have consented." Sometime between that date and November, Prachensky cultivated "a moustache and a little tuft of chin-whiskers" like that sported by one of the Spring Hill carpenters, François Minoret (b. Saar, France c. 1830).[51]

This innocent affectation, added to Prachensky's pretentions to the title "major" and to his decision to wear the uniform of the Confederate officer (a dress which Gache's former protégé Hubert had also adopted) drew a sneering condemnation from Hippolyte. Such a seeming over-reaction could indicate Gache's pettiness, but these outward symbols were seen as an affront to Jesuit *ésprit de corps*, and because there were no dress regulations for Confederate chaplains, Catholic priests in the army normally did not opt for such attire. Father Egidius (Giles) Smulders, C.SS.R. (b. Endhoven, Holland, November 1, 1815–d. St. Louis, Missouri, April 2, 1900), the chaplain to the Eighth Louisiana, recollected that in "all the divisions of the army (Catholic chaplains) always met with the greatest politeness and respect from the officers and men, and generally the colonel or major would give up his tent to us for confessions and Holy Mass. Even the Protestant chaplains treated us with the utmost deference, although we never would associate with them, nor adopt their uniform."[52]

Most probably whenever he was in camp, Gache wore his Jesuit cassock, with rosary beads attached from the cincture, and with a biretta placed squarely on his head. In December he requested that Father Jourdan send him a new cassock since the one he had brought with him to Virginia was showing its age. Such clerical attire was entirely proper "for the perfect country priest" who, in January, purchased a bell so that the village church in the middle of the camp would be yet more authentic. Among the men of the 10th, Gache's appearance should have caused no wonder; but once when a soldier from a Virginia regiment had seen Smulders similarly dressed he noted in his diary a description of the "old priest clad in a black gown hanging down to the ground with a singular hat on his head and with his beads around his neck and with a face representing the Virgin Mary, etc."[53] When traveling, Gache was sure to dress "in a guise so humble and so indicative of another calling" than that of a Confederate officer; however, there is evidence that he wore his cassock on the battlefield.

Besides Hubert and Prachensky Gache mentioned six other Catholic priests in his letter to Yenni. One of them was the pastor of Lynchburg and traveling companion of Hubert, Oscar Aloysius Sears (b. Alexandria, Virginia, 1830–d. Lynchburg, Virginia, November 5, 1867). A convert from Methodism and a one-time Jesuit novice, Sears was a man with whom Gache would have dealings later in the war. Ordained in 1857, Sears remained at Lynchburg until 1865 when he was sent to Martinsburg to rebuild the church which the Federals had used as a combination prison-stable. In 1862 a Catholic priest was needed for the sick and wounded in the many army hospitals at Lynchburg, and therefore Sears was appointed chaplain.

Father David Whelan (b. Baltimore, Maryland, January 25, 1822–d. Cincinnati, Ohio, December 18, 1867) was the brother of the bishop of Wheeling, Richard Vincent Whelan (1809-50) and was well known to the Spring Hill Jesuits, because in 1861 he had been the chaplain at the Visitation Convent in Mobile. Also, at one time he had been the pastor at St. Joseph's Church, Petersburg, Virginia, a position now held by another priest Gache described to his correspondent, Father Thomas Mulvey (b. Kilbride, County Meath, Ireland, 1810–d. Petersburg, Virginia, December 15, 1872).

One of the best known of the Virginia clergy that the Jesuit singled out was Father Michael O'Keefe (b. Waterford, Ireland, May 11, 1828–d. Towson, Maryland, January 28, 1906), the pastor at St. Mary's Norfolk. Shortly before the war O'Keefe completed building his church, modeled after the cathedral of his native Waterford. The structure was so challenging and the design so ambitious that even Father John Cambiaso came from Louisiana to study it during the early stages of its construction. This is especially significant because Cambiaso was not only a deadly marksman, a talented linguist and an efficient administrator; he was also a professional architect who had designed and built the Jesuit church on Baronne Street, New Orleans.

O'Keefe was known and admired for his dedication to the people of Norfolk during the pestilence of 1855 when, with his own hands, he dug graves for the dead. In one respect he was very different from Gache: one of his closest friends was a Presbyterian minister with whom he had entered a compact to the effect that if the 1855 fever caused the death of the one, the survivor would bury the victim. When Prachensky resigned his commission for "duties in the ministry calling me to the Southwestern frontier,"—and then promptly went to the Northeast—Blanchard requested that O'Keefe be appointed "chaplain for the whole brigade." Surprisingly, this request was granted by Secretary of War George Wythe Randolph (1818-67), and O'Keefe received his letter of appointment on April 16, 1862—two months before Blanchard was removed from duty. Like Sears, O'Keefe did not give up his parish when he was appointed chaplain, and when the Federal troops entered Norfolk on May 10, 1862, O'Keefe remained behind. In March 1864, he ran afoul of Gen. Benjamin Franklin Butler.[54]

In this letter Gache mentioned the name of a second priest who had experienced Butler's wrath. This was the Jesuit Robert Kelly (b. Mullangar, County Westmeath, Ireland, August 23, 1828–d. Mullangar, County Westmeath, Ireland, June 15, 1876). When he entered the Society of Jesus with Father John Serra at Lyons in 1854, Kelly was also an ordained priest.

In 1858, with the excitable Serra as his companion, he arrived at Spring Hill. He was to remain there until with the outbreak of the war he was reassigned to Grand Coteau. Eventually Butler, "the beast," had him visaed back to Ireland because of his strong opinions, loudly and frequently expressed, on the real and supposed qualities of "the invading Yankee army" that had occupied St. Laundry Parish after the fall of New Orleans. But he did not stay muzzled long. Once back in his native land he founded the Association of the Sacred Thirst, a total abstinence league whose *Illustrated Monitor* was an attempt to provide a cheap religious journal for the poor. The *Monitor* reflected the spirituality of Vals, as might be expected, and it also presents one more unexplored source for research into the prevailing religious attitudes of Southern Jesuits, contemporaries of Gache.

The final cleric mentioned in this letter was Joseph Desribes (b. Tissoire, Auvergne, France, July 30, 1830–d. Fordham, New York, January 19, 1903), a man marked from the day of his birth for the bizzare, the dramatic, the extraordinary. Convinced that a Bourbon prince had been sequestered in the Desribes chateau during the revolution of 1830, a crowd invaded the premises causing Madame Desribes to go into premature labor for the birth of Joseph, her seventeenth child. At the age of seven the boy was arrested for chopping down a republican tree of liberty, thereby demonstrating for all the world to see that he was not one to take uncompromising stands on sensitive issues. After the war he took Dr. Richard Hooker Wilmer (1816-1900), the Episcopal bishop of Alabama to court in favor of some orphaned children of a dead soldier. Thanks to his lawyer, Henry St. Paul, Desribes won his case, and then joined Prachensky as a chaplain in the asylums and hospitals on Ward's Island, New York.[55]

Gache informed Yenni that he had met three Virginia families during the fall of 1861: the Hintons, the Southalls, and the Ewells. William E. Hinton (b. Petersburg, Virginia, March 13, 1815–d. Petersburg, Virginia, June 22, 1894), was a prominent banker, civic leader, and wealthy descendant of the founder of Petersburg. In September 1856 he married his second wife, Ellen Coxe McGowan (b. Petersburg, Virginia, 1830–d. Petersburg, Virginia, June 21, 1892), the daughter of the wealthy and socially prominent merchant William McGowan and his Irish-born wife, Margaret Phelan. William Hinton had become a Catholic in 1855 after the death of his first wife, Mary Jane Whyte (1822-54), also the daughter of a successful Irish immigrant. When Gache and Mulvey were received at Folly Castle, Hinton's three surviving children were part of the household. The two eldest, Mary Ellen (1845-1933) and Martha Jane (1853-1936), were his daughters by his first wife. Mary Ellen subsequently married Waddy Thompson, M.D. (1841-1916) of New Orleans, the brother of

Hugh Smith Thompson (1834-1904), twice governor of South Carolina, and Martha Jane married Alden Spooner Dunn (1849-1903) and settled in Scotland Neck, North Carolina. Margaret (1858-1918) was his only child by Ellen McGowan, and like her half-sister Martha Jane, Margaret married a scion of one of Virginia's most distinguished families: Randolph Tucker, U.S.N., C.S.N. (1849-1928).[56]

Father Mulvey had not always been as welcome at Folly Castle as he was when he visited the Hintons with Gache in November 1861. On Easter Sunday, 1860, he delivered "the most vulgar, indecent, intemperate and abusive tirade that ever disgraced a Christian pulpit in this city or elsewhere." Such was the opinion expressed in a letter to the bishop of Richmond, John McGill (b. Philadelphia, Pennsylvania, November 4, 1809–d. Richmond, Virginia, January 14, 1872), by one of Petersburg's most distinguished Catholics, Anthony M. Keiley (1833-1905), later mayor of Richmond (1875-85), and minister, first to Italy and then to Austria under President Grover Cleveland. "Mr. Hinton," continued Keiley, "who is as warm a friend as Father Mulvey or Catholicism has in Petersburg, left the church in utter disgust and he informed me this morning that his wife wept for an hour on reaching home, concluding hereafter never to attend late mass. Mr. Hinton has just called on me to say that no child of his shall ever be forced to listen to such indecency from the pulpit or elsewhere, and I heard more than one intelligent Protestant, who was attracted by the beautiful Easter service to attend on Sunday, declare that they would publically mob any minister of theirs who should pour such filth into the ears of their wives or daughters. I must certainly advise my sisters and younger brothers to leave the church invariably before sermons if this obscenity continues." Precisely what Mulvey said in his earthy eloquence on the most sublime feast in the Christian calendar has not been preserved, but McGill must have blanched when he read further in Keiley's letter that "a prominent member of the congregation publicly states, as one did in my presence today, that he should *insult* the priest the first time he spoke to him and *had cause to make the threat* . . ." The bishop was warned that "unless the 'amending hand' is applied the worst consequences to religion and constitutional accord must ensue" at Petersburg.

There is no record that Mulvey ever felt the pressure of the "amending hand" extended from Richmond, but a second letter from Keiley a week later assured McGill that ruffled feelings had been soothed. The pastor had not been challenged to a duel; Mrs. Hinton had dried her tears, and the Hinton and Keiley children continued worshiping at St. Joseph's. One fact to which Keiley's letter attested was the cordiality between the Protestants and Catholics of the Petersburg visited by Gache in 1861. A year earlier Keiley had informed McGill that "no Protestant can enter the Catholic church without the certainty of insult, and to save the feelings of their friends, Catholics invariably discourage their Protestant acquaintances from attending services." The implication is that Protestants had felt that they were now welcome at Catholic services. Moreover, Catholics apparently discussed the impropriety of their pastor with their Protestant neighbors on a level which transcended sectarian differences. Gache observed later in this correspondence that, despite cases of bigotry and ignorance he encountered, Virginians on the whole were accepting of Catholics. The fact that Mulvey, the rough and ready, florid and kind Irishman, remained, like his Norfolk compatriot, dear to so many in the Protestant community for so long a period of time is not insignificant.[57]

Although not as prosperous as the Hintons, the Southalls of Williamsburg represented one of Virginia's most prominent families. While yet a teenager, Albert Gallatin Southall (b. Charles City County, Virginia, 1808–d. Williamsburg, Virginia, August 26, 1862) became the ward of John Tyler (1790-1862), Governor of Virginia (1825-27) and President of the United States (1841-45). In 1834 Albert married Virginia Frances Travis (b. New Kent County, Virginia, December 4, 1814–d. Williamsburg, Virginia, August 31, 1879), who counted members of the Virginia House of Delegates and a number of patriots among her distinguished forebears. At the time when Gache was the recipient of the Southall's hospitality, four of the six children were living with their parents. The Louisiana chaplain refers to two of these: "Miss Kate" and "Miss Virginia." They were Catherine Hardyman (b. Washington, D.C., January 18, 1849–d. Baltimore, Maryland, September 2, 1902) and Virginia Atkinson (b. Washington, D.C., September 27, 1852–d. December 21, 1899). Gache also refers to the two older girls, Mary Fisk (b. Williamsburg, Virginia, July 9, 1838–d. Richmond, Virginia, April 1894) and Elizabeth Bouche (b. Williamsburg, Virginia, March 20, 1846–d. Fitzgerald, Georgia, March 19, 1922). The older son, Tyler, (b. Williamsburg, Virginia, November 9, 1834–d. Macon, Georgia, March 27, 1872) had been detained, during the course of the war, in Washington from where his brother Travis (b. Williamsburg, Virginia, July 23, 1836) had earlier made a daring escape to enroll in the Third Virginia Cavalry. But no sooner had the young fighter for the cause arrived home than he was arrested as a spy and sent off to a North Carolina prison. "There exists in Williamsburg bitter feeling against the father of young Southall," wrote John Tyler to President Davis, "and I have little doubt that the father is struck at by these parties through the son." John Tyler and Albert Southall had long since disagreed on many political questions, but there was no question about the latter's loyalty to his native state, and Virginia's elder statesman was indignant by the trumped-up charges against Travis and by the meanness shown his family. These charges and injustice of her son's imprisonment compelled Virginia Southall to write Jefferson Davis. "All I ask, Mr. President, is that (Travis) may be heard, his case examined into. If he prove guilty, though his mother I can say let him be punished; if innocent let him be discharged at once and join his company." This letter, accompanied by uncontestable evidence and sworn depositions from a number of Williamsburg ladies, who later would charm Gache, "tell their own tale," Tyler explained to Davis, "and show conclusively that the young man's heart beats in the right place." Travis was pardoned and joined his company where he was serving when Gache visited his parents. A present-day reader of this correspondence cannot but be impressed that this woman, who gave her son's bed to a dying Louisiana soldier and who allowed the family piano to serve as a makeshift altar for a Catholic Mass, was indeed a worthy descendant of a long line of proud, independent and brave Virginians.[58]

The description Gache has given in this letter, and in those that follow, of the Commandant of the Williamsburg Post, Col. Benjamin Stoddert Ewell (b. Georgetown, D.C., June 10, 1810–d. Williamsburg, Virginia, June 19, 1894), is a reiteration of those virtues acclaimed by the biographers of this well known Virginia educator. Like his equally famous brother, General Richard Stoddert Ewell (1817-72), "Buck" Ewell, as Gache came to call him in later years, is a recognized figure in American history. In these letters, however, Gache brings into the light two women who were close to the President of William and Mary during much of his life, but whose personalities have been obscured by time. Rebecca Lowndes Ewell (b. Georgetown, D.C., December 3, 1815–d. Williamsburg, Virginia, August, 1867), kept house for her brother and his only child, Elizabeth Stoddert Ewell (b. Williamsburg, Virginia, August 8, 1842–d. Williamsburg, Virginia, June 9, 1911). Elizabeth (or "Miss Lizzy" as she was called to distinguish her from her aunt after whom she was named), cherished the catechism Gache had given her in 1861, corresponded with him for forty years, and always considered herself the Jesuit's godchild. Gache was by no means the first Catholic the Ewells had encountered. As a youth the Colonel had attended Georgetown College and Rebecca had been a teacher in a Catholic school in the 1830s. Moreover, she and her brothers and sisters were reared at "Stony Lonesome," near Nokesville in Prince William County, at Georgetown and in Blandensburg, Maryland, by a free Black servant who remained all of her life a fervant Catholic. Rebecca's father, Doctor Thomas Ewell, "insisted that Fanny Brown, the faithful Mammy of his children, should always have beer on Fridays as she was too strict a Roman Catholic to touch meat on days of abstinence." "Mammy" Brown died shortly before Gache was received by the Ewells, having been nursed tenderly during her last prolonged illness by Rebecca and Miss Lizzy. Rebecca's Catholic background, as well as her singular virtue, explains why Gache judged her a better theologian than the Reverend Thomas M. Ambler (b. Fauquier County, Virginia, 1829–d. Williamsburg, Virginia, February 13, 1907), the rector of Bruton Parish, a clergyman that he came later on, despite himself, to respect more than he did at his first encounter. It was said that Ambler, who had received his military appointment the day before Gache's first visit to Williamsburg and who served as chaplain at the Chimborazo General Hospital, Richmond, after the fall of Williamsburg, was "of a genial and happy temperament, defusing mirth and even merriment around," and that he loved God and his fellowman. Gache detected less redeeming qualities in his personality, dispositions of nature which placed into bold relief the goodness and gentility of the ladies Ewell.[59]

Research has not revealed the names of the Yorktown grocer and his wife introduced to Gache by Henry Miller, but seeing that they were not natives of the region and that they had planned to move on with the army, this fact is not surprising. Records indicate that many small grocery stores similar to the one described by Gache were operated by Irish immigrants throughout the South; and, given the deference Mr. and Mrs. M. showed the priest, it is probable they were an Irish couple which vanished from Yorktown long before 1870. The census of 1860 for the city of Norfolk lists ten French-born inhabitants, but by 1870 that number had decreased to six. So, the family from Roanne and others which constituted the French colony that Gache had discovered there had also emigrated to other centers after the war.

As Gache indicated in his September 11 letter, the 10th, now part of the Seventh Brigade, had moved camp a number of times since coming to the Peninsula. But by the first of October they had settled down near Lee's Mill on the Warwick.[60] Directly across this rivulet was the farm of Thomas Curtis, aged forty, and his twenty-five year old wife, Maria. Although many records of Warwick County were destroyed during the war, the Census of 1860, which is not always reliable, indicated that this couple had been married during the course of that year. The location of the Curtis farm and a description of this couple, make it highly probable that the "planter" whom Gache had met on the Yorktown road was Thomas Curtis (b. Warwick County, Virginia, 1820–d. Warwick County, Virginia, March, 1880). Moreover, a contemporary map indicates the wooded path where Father Hippolyte was able to give full play to that contemplation which was keynote to his life and which afforded escape from the ennui that had settled down so imperceptibly on the camp.[61]

Fortunately, most of the Spring Hill alumni that Gache mentioned in this letter can be identified, beginning with Captain Robert Martin Sands (b. Cantonment Brook, Tampa Bay, Florida, October 12, 1825–d. Mobile, Alabama, November 7, 1903), a former instructor at the Jesuit college who formed the Spring Hill Cadets in December 1859. After the election of officers a few days before Christmas, this expanded unit became known as the Mobile Cadets; then Company A in the Third Alabama Regiment under Col. Tennent Lomax (1820-62). Captain, later Colonel, Sands was married to Josephine (1825-1915), the daughter of Charles Le Baron II, and was a graduate of the college in 1843. Henry Hotze (1834-87), who himself married into the Sands family, joined the Cadets when they were first formed because they "proudly and justly claimed to be the elite of the youth of Mobile." Hotze observed that at "dress parade no regiment could form a more exact line, and at the order 'parade rest' the row of white gloved hands was a geometric marvel to behold." Apparently, as Gache reported, the ladies of Norfolk were no less impressed by geometric marvels than those of Mobile, but the days of dress parades and flag presentation ceremonies for the Cadets were drawing to a close. At Appomattox there were but forty of the original 1,651 men of the Alabama Third left to witness the surrender; yet not all of the elite youth of Mobile had been left behind in Virginia graves. Two days before Lee's surrender, one of the cadets with whom Gache had visited near Norfolk in 1861, walked a bride down the aisle of St. Vincent's Church, Mobile, where the Stars and Bars were yet unfurled. This was John Bell Rohmer (b. Black Creek, East Feliciana Parish, Louisiana, October 16, 1841–d. Bay St. Louis, Mississippi, August 21, 1922), who had enrolled in the Cadets on April 23, 1861, and was discharged from the regiment because of disability on March 1, 1864, but who continued to serve at Byrnes Hospital, Mobile, until the city's surrender when he took the oath and was paroled. Rohmer was one of the few Spring Hill students to whom Gache referred in these letters that survived him. After the war Rohmer became a medical doctor, and for forty years at Bay St. Louis, Mississippi, he was "a friend to the poor; attending them at all times, regardless of pay." Like his father (Gache's good friend, the college physician), the younger Rohmer was "an inventor," as his obituary categorically stated. "In fact, he was a genius."[62]

Four more Spring Hillians from Mobile that Gache referred to in this letter had much in common, sharing the same ethnic, social, and cultural background that had produced the Lyons brothers. These were John Burns (b. Mobile, Alabama, July 7, 1839–d. Mobile, Alabama, September 1, 1875); Henry Muldon (b. New York City, New York, April 6, 1844–d. New York City, New York, October 2, 1871); John Daily (b. Mobile, Alabama, March 12, 1841–d. Spotsylvania Court House, Virginia, May 8,

1864), and James Hugh Masterson (b. Tuscaloosa, Alabama, July 3, 1849). The fathers of each of these soldiers and the mothers of all but one were Irish born. John Burns enrolled at the college on December 2, 1857 to follow the academic career laid out by his older brother, Robert (1824-61), and enlisted in Captain Sands' Company for a twelve-month period in the spring of 1861, going with the battalion to Virginia. But because of his brother's death he was discharged from the army in December. His own health broken by camp life he remained an invalid until his death.[63]

Although Gache did not specify which of the two Muldon brothers he had met in the Third Alabama camp, it was probably Henry, whom he had known as a student, but it could have been Henry's older brother, James Michael (b. Mobile, Alabama, June 17, 1835–d. Mobile, Alabama, June 11, 1886), who had been at the college with Robert Burns in 1842. James also enlisted in the Mobile Cadets in April, 1861, but resigned in November to accept a commission in the Pelham Cadets, Light Artillery. He spent the remainder of the war in Columbia, Georgia. Henry achieved the reputation of being an outstanding soldier, and even though he had been recommended on a number of occasions for a lieutenancy, he never rose above the rank of corporal. He participated in every battle fought by the 3rd, and from the day he enlisted until the day of his capture, in February 1865, he never requested a furlough.[64]

Burns' father was an engineer; Muldon's a merchant, but John Daily's father was a bayman, who was able to send three sons to the college, thanks in part to the "supply calls" the Jesuits would take on weekends and during the summer months. John enrolled at the college in 1853, and on September 1, 1861, the twenty-year-old Mobilian enlisted at Yorktown, as the seventeen-year-old Henry Muldon had done before him, but the vice-president's Diary recorded that John Daily was back at the college in December, to pay "a visit after a glorious campaign in Virginia." Father Cornette added shortly afterwards that a number of restless boarding students had run off to join the army in Virginia. Wounded in 1862, and later captured, John Daily was finally killed in action.[65]

Despite the similarity in background, the military career of James Masterson was considerably different from the other former students from Mobile whom Gache had met on the Peninsula. For one thing, James enlisted at Richmond on June 1, 1861, for a twelve-month period in Company F (Orleans Cadets) of Rightor's First Louisiana Battalion. Moreover, when Gache had encountered him with "jam all over his hands and face" Private Masterson had just turned twelve years old! His North Carolinian mother and his father died in 1850, leaving him in the care of a guardian uncle who followed them to the grave four years later. Another uncle enrolled him at Spring Hill in 1858—he was nine at the time—but there is no record how long he remained at the college. Shortly before Gache had met him, this "young rascal," who was now Rightor's orderly, had fallen victim to the fever which decimated the battalion and he had been nursed in the Seminary Hospital, Williamsburg. Research has revealed nothing about him after 1861, and the rolls of Rightor's Battalion are incomplete. His father had left him modest property in Alabama, which it seems he never claimed.[66]

The chaplain wrote that he could have mentioned many other former Spring Hill students he had seen while visiting the Third Alabama at the camp near Norfolk, but he passed over all of these to single out one individual he did not see. This was John E. de Villiers Innerarity (b. Pensacola, Florida, 1841–d. near Richmond, Virginia, July 1, 1862), who was later judged guilty at the court-martial to which Gache referred in this letter. But seeing that he was one of the 207 casualties the regiment sustained at Malvern Hill, he did not live long enough to pay off the fine. John's parents were cousins and therefore he was the grandson of both James (1777-1847) and John Innerarity (1783-1845), the Scottish brothers from Brechen, Forfarshire, who had, in 1817, taken over from John Forbes (1769-1823) what had been the powerful Panton, Leslie and Company of Pensacola and Mobile. The older John had married Marie-Victoire, granddaughter of the Chevalier François Coulon de Villiers (1712-94), the founder of the Coulon de Villiers family in Louisiana, whose brother had forced George Washington to surrender Fort Necessity to the French, July 4, 1754. At the time when Gache wrote this letter John E. de Villiers' only brother, Albert (1847-1922), was a boarding student at the college; later he would run off to join the army.[67]

Thanks to Colonel Ewell, Gache was able to visit Spratley's farm where Rightor's Battalion was bivouacked, and besides James Masterson he named two more Spring Hillians he had encountered there. John Augustine (b. New Orleans, Louisiana, February 14, 1838–d. New Orleans, Louisiana, February 5, 1888) had been with him at Pensacola, and undoubtedly was one of the "Frenchmen" about whom the chaplain bragged in his letter to Father Cornette, but Thomas C. Raby (b. Napoleonville, Assumption Parish, Louisiana, 1843–d. Terrebonne Parish, Louisiana, October 19, 1888) enlisted at Yorktown on August 28 for a one year's stint. Augustine, who could cite eminent Louisianans among his ancestors and who became the father of a fallen hero of the Spanish-American War, had been with Col. Charles Dreux when he was mortally wounded, and then on April 8, 1862, he himself was wounded during the skirmish at Lee's Mill. When Rightor's Batallion was decommissioned, Augustine returned to Louisiana where he was instrumental in organizing Fenner's Battery at Jackson, Mississippi, and after the war he followed in his father's footsteps by becoming first a district judge and then the United States Commissioner in New Orleans. Thomas Raby, like James Masterson, had been confined to the Williamsburg Seminary Hospital, and in December, by a special order from Colonel Ewell, he was permanently assigned to the hospital as a guard. It is tempting to speculate why Ewell went out of his way to liberate an eighteen-year-old Louisiana boy from the arduousness of camp life. It is a coincidental fact that at this time Gache was developing the friendship with the Ewells that would last the rest of his life.[68]

The chaplain had been introduced to Colonel Ewell, a former Georgetown student, at the funeral of Michel Prud'homme (b. Opelousas, Louisiana, August 13, 1838–d. Williamsburg, Virginia, November 5, 1861), the young lieutenant of the 10th that had been nursed by the Southall family. Michel and his brother Louis (b. Opelousas, Louisiana, August 12, 1835–d. Opelousas, Louisiana, November 26, 1862) were the only children of Louis and Caroline (Barton) Prud'homme. The two boys had transferred from St. Charles, Grand Coteau, to Spring Hill in 1853, and both enlisted in the 10th the same day, Michel being commissioned 1st lieutenant and Louis 2d lieutenant in the Confederate States Rangers, Company K. On November 26, Louis was elected 1st lieutenant and Seton was formally appointed to take his place, but on the following day Louis left the Peninsula with Michel's remains for Opelousas, where in January he resigned from the army.[69] Michel Prud'homme's funeral may well have been, as Gache asserted, the first time the city of William of Orange witnessed a Catholic priest, vested in cassock, surplice and stole, walk solemnly through its streets. But in 1861 Hippolyte Gache had no way of reckoning that he was not far from where the ill-fated Jesuit mission of 1570 had once stood, a center, however brief, for papist ceremonies more than three hundred years before a Confederate Jesuit came to Williamsburg to assist at a Louisiana boy's funeral.[70]

Camp Lee's Mill
December 5, 1861

Rev. Father Jourdan
Spring Hill College

Dear Father, Pax Christi

I have just received a letter from Father Prachensky giving me the news you recently sent him. In this same letter he tells me that you have charged him with the responsibility of inquiring whether I have need of anything, and if so how it should be sent. I am very grateful, Father, for your thoughtfulness, but really there isn't a single thing I need. When I left Spring Hill, I took all my winter clothing and even your own frock coat, which the Clothes' Room Brother gave to me. This should see me through the winter. I think I will have enough blankets too, seeing that I have acquired another one since I arrived at Lee's Mill. Nevertheless, if you insist on exercising your charity towards me, I would certainly not object to your sending me a new cassock, as mine is already two years old; nor would I mind receiving my old cassock coat, if you can find it. You might also send on a few bottles of white mass wine and a few bottles of brandy, if you have any good brandy; if not, whiskey will do. Brandy and whiskey, which are excellent means of warding off the ever present danger of diarrhea, are very much in demand and are very expensive here in camp. A bottle of the most ordinary kind of brandy costs 2 or 3 piastres and whiskey is $1.50. You might also include one of those little alarm clocks that you have no need of where you are. Then wrap everything up in an old, but not too old, blanket. This blanket will certainly be better for me than the straw which I am now obliged to use. No need, of course, to tell you that everything ought to be well packed, and that the bottles should be carefully separated from one another. But once more let me say that

I have absolutely no need for any of these things, and if you can't send them without paying more than they are worth, far better not to send them at all.

You can also give me some information. I would like to know what would be the best and the safest way of sending you $200, of which $100 is to reimburse Father Gautrelet for the money he gave me when I left, and the other $100 is for Father Curioz for the same purpose. I am anxious to pay this debt for the following reasons: First, I have the money now and I'd like to cancel the debt. Second, the sum is made up of notes which have been issued by the various banks in all of the states. Since these bills are legal tender in this part of Virginia, I cannot say how long I'll be able to hold on to them. Third, I know that although procurators in the Society cheerfully give, they even more cheerfully receive; and, as you know, no one is more sensitive than myself to the preferences of others . . .

A few days ago I wrote a monstrously long letter to Father Yenni. It must already have reached Spring Hill by now. I could write another of the same length and still not succeed in describing all of what has been happening; but aside from the fact that my fingers are too frozen to write very much now, I want to be sure to take advantage of tomorrow morning's mail collection. Until another time then, Father, for those little details which seem to please you so much, and which I am always so pleased to give you!

At the present time the men here are busy building log houses for the winter. Some of these cabins are finished and are already occupied. It is terribly cold living in the tents; I don't dare keep water in my pitcher for fear that the ice will break it. On the feast of St. Francis Xavier [December 3] we had a little snow. All of this makes camp life, which was never very pleasant, even more arduous to endure. You would have to see for yourself what these poor soldiers have to suffer in order to understand what I mean. Last month all the able-bodied men had to spend two weeks harvesting corn near Bethel, where they had to sleep on the ground without so much as a tent over their heads and with but one blanket to protect them from the elements. We have had many sick among the officers and the men, but fortunately we've had few deaths. So far we've only lost four men on the Peninsula, and two of these were accidentally killed. I won't say anything to you about the war; you know more about that subject than I do.

Adieu, Father. My respects and best wishes to all of Ours, and to our dear doctor and to Mr. Parada. Please pray and ask others to pray for him who is your Reverence's servant in Christ.

L.H. Gache, S.J.
Chap. 10th La. Reg.

P.S. We have a man in Richmond who takes care of packages; consequently, if you send me anything, the safest way would be to address it to:

Rev. L.H.G.
c/o Col. Marigny
10th La. Volunteers
Richmond

COMMENTARY

Although Gache indicated in these letters that he wrote on a number of occasions to his rector, the imposing Anthony Jourdan, the preceding letter is the only piece of correspondence which has survived. The reason for this fact seems clear. Jourdan, whether issuing orders from the saddle at Antwerp or from the superior's chair in Mobile, was a man of high resolve and serious temperament. No doubt his sense of integrity compelled him to destroy any letter in which his subject in Virginia manifested the slightest hint of personal or confidential matters. But the light humor of this letter and the deprecatory tone, which gives it a nice edge of irony, were not designed to sustain the attention of the man whose own frock coat had found its way into Gache's baggage. Jourdan, who had so imperiously sacked Father Hippolyte from Baton Rouge in 1852, undoubtedly turned over this silly letter with its outrageous requests to the attention of a subordinate, and then went about trying to keep the college together during the increasingly difficult days of the first year of the war. The letter was written the day after Gache had been paid $50, his salary for the month of November. Gache was therefore in a position to reimburse the treasurers at Spring Hill and New Orleans, "who cheerfully give and more cheerfully receive." His friend Francis Gautrelet was now responsible for the college books and Aloysius Curioz (b. Valleiry, Savoy, April 27, 1816–d. Grand Coteau, Louisiana, December 17, 1903), was the mission superior in New Orleans who had advanced Chaplain Gache $100 and ordered him to report to Bishop Blanc for a military assignment. Curioz had led the sensational escape from Marseille with de Carrière and twenty-two others during the revolutionary days of 1848. Two months after Gache wrote this letter Curioz came to Spring Hill as the third Jesuit president and Jourdan assumed once again the position of mission superior.[71]

Gache's complaint about the scarcity of sacramental wine was in fact no more acute at Lee's Mill than it was in many other parts of the Confederacy, including Mobile. The Provost Marshall in Richmond, Brig. Gen. John Henry Winder (1800-65), personally rationed out a specified amount of altar wine to each priest whose written request had received Bishop McGill's endorsement. At Spring Hill Doctor Rohmer cultivated scuppernongs that grew wild on the hills, and before the end of the war the fermented juice from these indigenous grapes were used at mass.[72]

Camp Lee's Mill
near Yorktown
January 17, 1862

Rev. Ph. de Carrière, S. J.
Spring Hill College

Reverend and dear Father, Pax Christi

Sometime ago I received your note telling me of the death of your dear mother. I need not tell you that my heart went out to you in your bereavement, and I immediately arranged to offer for her soul the masses that our friendship would give you every right to expect.

I thank Father Jourdan for the message added to your letter, and particularly do I thank him for promising to send the things I requested. I am surprised, however, at not having received another letter from Spring Hill assuring me that the package has already been sent, and containing the receipt from the express company. I fear that such a letter has been sent, but that it has met the same fate as so many others—namely, that it has been lost. There are many things that do not run smoothly in our new Republic, but nothing that runs less smoothly than the mail service. It is really *monstrueux, fabuleux*—as some of our sergeants are wont to remark. Please God your precious package has not met a fate similar to that of the letter, for we lose proportionately just as many packages as letters.

It was because of this distrust of the mail that in Richmond the other day when I met a captain (he was of the Eighth Alabama, where as you know, I have many friends), I took advantage of the opportunity to give him a letter for Father Jourdan. This letter requested that Father Jourdan entrust to the captain [Patrick Loughry], as the surest way of my receiving them, a half-dozen bottles of mass wine. I hope that the good Father will not grow weary of my entreaties, especially since this is probably my last request and since I will send him very shortly a draft which will amply reimburse him. There is still some wine in Richmond—Madeira, Port, Sherry and the like—but the merchants themselves, although they charge you anywhere from $1.50 to $5.00 a bottle, frankly admit they cannot vouch for the contents. You can understand how distressing all of this is and why I prefer to exhaust every possibility of obtaining wine elsewhere.

As I already mentioned I was in Richmond recently. I went there shortly after the first in order to go to confession and to do some shopping. During my week's stay I had the good fortune to encounter Father [Joseph] Bixio, S.J., the brother of the famous Italian general of the same name. When the war broke out Father Bixio had been pastor of a parish that lay on both sides of the Virginia-Maryland border. During the battle at Manassas he happened to be in the Virginia part of his parish, and ever since then he hasn't been able to return to the Maryland side. But this hasn't bothered him a bit; he has simply volunteered as a Confederate chaplain. He seems to be quite successful in the various places where he serves, and he has the good fortune to be in a part of the country where he has known many people for as long as ten years.

As for me, I always manage somehow. We're all living now in our winter quarters—log houses which are comfortable and rather pleasant-looking structures. I am so fortunate as to have one all to myself. My Irish boys built it for me. I should now be quite snug in it, if only I had not made the terrible mistake of having it built in a low spot where all the water tends to collect. After a recent thaw the cabin looked as if it had been built on pilings! I could have avoided this misfortune, but now the only thing to do is to have the house moved one hundred yards closer to the camp. Once it is moved, I'm also going to have a little church in the same style built alongside of it. Up till now the colonel has not wanted me to build a church, but

I'm hoping that my Irishmen will construct one even without his cooperation. If they do, I'll be a perfect little country priest.

Already the camp has taken on the appearance of a small village. Each morning at 7:30 I ring the bell for the eight o'clock mass, which I say in my room. I went ahead and got a bell, by the way, because no one associates a roll of the drum with a call to mass. Normally there are four or five that make up the congregation every morning. After my mass and thanksgiving I generally have breakfast with Lieutenant Colonel, formerly Captain, Waggaman, who is my only friend among the officers. I then visit the sick in the hospital and in the cabins. Next I read or write until dinner, which is served around three o'clock. After dinner I say my office, read, and so forth, until it is time to retire. This country is too damp and foggy for an afternoon jaunt. On Sundays I say mass at ten o'clock, but as my room is so tiny, there are only a few who manage to squeeze in. Such then is my daily routine, partly missionary and partly parochial.

Regularly every month I make a trip into Williamsburg or to some place not far from there. Last month I went to a place about eight miles from Williamsburg, a place called Bigler's Mill. It proved to be a most agreeable and valuable discovery. Bigler, the former owner of the estate, was a Yankee who fled the country as soon as war broke out, and his house, confiscated by the Confederate States, was transformed into a hospital. One of our soldiers among the sick there had sent for me to give him the Last Sacraments. I left camp immediately, and despite the twenty-five mile journey, I was soon at Bigler's. Upon arriving I went directly to my sick man, who turned out to be not so sick as I had been led to believe. When I finished visiting with him, another of the soldiers who is also a patient there, said to me: "Father, there is someone in the next house who wants to see you."

I assumed that it must be another soldier, because most of the servants' quarters on Mr. Bigler's property were at that time occupied by the sick. But I was mistaken. When I arrived at the house I found there three or four Irish families—about nine people altogether—among whom there were two women. As I entered, one of these women respectfully took hold of my hand, although she was weeping and could not manage to speak. She seemed, poor thing, almost as if she were out of her mind. I then learned that some of these people hadn't seen a priest in three or four years, and that they would have to go to Norfolk to find one. The woman whom I judged to be deranged was not indeed completely sane, but the weeping was the result of her joy at seeing a priest. All of this took place on a Wednesday, and they begged me to come back to say mass for them the following Sunday. I told them that I couldn't because I had to say mass that day at my camp, but that I would return the next day, that is Thursday, if they wished. They most willingly agreed. The next morning the master of the cabin where I had met these people came himself to Williamsburg to fetch me in something like a tilbury. It was this man's wife who had wept so when she saw me.

When I arrived at Bigler's Mill I found everyone in a holiday spirit. My Irishmen had put on their Sunday clothes and had gotten excused from work. Six of them came to confession and received Communion. I said mass in the bedroom of my worthy host, who was one of the communicants. He couldn't have been happier for such an honor. "Father, after having had the blessing of a mass said in my room, I'll sleep sound tonight."

The overseer of the whole property, even though he was a Protestant and even though he was still convalescing from a broken leg, knelt throughout the mass, and nearby the altar, at that. After mass he waited to meet me, and later he attended a splendid dinner that they had prepared in my honor. He was so pleased with everything that he insisted that I return soon, and that in the future I stay at his house. This I certainly will not fail to do, as I cannot afford to offend him. He and his wife live all alone in a huge mansion maintained by an army of domestics. I plan on visiting him next week.

But Williamsburg is really the place of my predilection; it is almost another Pensacola for me, even though there is not a single Catholic family there. It is partly on account of a few good and pious ladies there who show me such consideration and esteem and who welcome the opportunity to do little favors for me. The last time I was there two of these ladies presented me with a little woolen mattress that they had made—a gift which is literally priceless in camp during the winter. There is also the fact that the Protestant ministers themselves are all courtesy in my regard and lavish their kindness upon me. For instance, the last time I was there the Episcopalian minister [Thomas Ambler] repeatedly besought me to stay with him whenever I might pass through town. He also asked me to say some prayers for one of his flock, a person who had previously shown an interest in me. We are almost always arguing with one another—and I don't spare him a bit—but that doesn't spoil our friendship. I intend to dine at his house next week. The Baptist minister [William Martin?] visits me every time I stay at the Ewells. He tries to get me to come and visit him, offering me the use of his library and, if it had not been converted into a hospital, his church. He truly treats me as a brother, but I'm not going to give him any encouragement. I take advantage of every occasion to tell him and the others of his ilk that I don't see them under any other aspect than as gentlemen, but that certainly I don't consider them as ministers of the Gospel.

I find that in this part of the country, where there isn't a single Catholic, the Protestants are more religious and more sincere. In more than one family I've seen nothing which is not edifying. May it please God to illumine the souls of these good people! The other day a lady told me that for two years she has been *longing* to meet a Catholic priest so that she might obtain the spiritual direction which the ministers had not given her. And then, just like a novice, she gave me an account of her conscience. I am sure that you would be edified if I could reveal to you some of the questions she asked me.

Adieu, cher Père, try to write me a little bit more often; and ask Father Yenni if he has received as yet my last twelve-page letter. I fear that it might have gone astray.

Yours truly in Our Lord.
H. Gache, S. J.

P. S. My best wishes to all of Ours. I am getting along very well here in spite of the obligatory fasts to which I am sometimes sentenced, and in spite of all the petty inconveniences of camp life. One remarkable thing: up till now I haven't had the merest symptom of a cold—I, who for more than twenty years have had more than three or four colds each winter. It is unbelievable. To my mind this is an excellent argument against heated rooms. Here, although I have a fireplace where I can make a tolerably good fire, there is no danger of my being exposed to the inconvenience of a warm room. But do you know what I do to preserve my precious health? I'll tell you in a low voice. Now don't be scandalized, and whatever you do, don't tell anyone else. I've been taking w-h-i-s-k-e-y. Of course, I don't like it and I never will. But certain trustworthy people assure me that it is a *sine-qua-non* for the life I lead. Hence reason dictates, despite the taste, that I finish off a bottle every ten days. At any rate, it will never make me fat!

COMMENTARY

"The Jesuits were perfect soldiers in their demeanor," wrote an anonymous Englishman who fought with the Confederate troops during the early part of the war. This artillery lieutenant had little use for chaplains in general, but he confessed an unqualified admiration for members of the Society of Jesus. His sketch of the Jesuit chaplain's qualities was not executed without a certain romanticism, for in his mind the Jesuit was "ever at the head of a column in the advance, ever last in retreat; and in the battlefield a black cassock, in a bending posture, would always betray the disciple of Loyola, ministering to the wounded or dying. No hospital could be found wherein was not a pale-faced, meek, and untiring man of this order. Soldierly in their education and bearing, (Jesuits) are ready for anything—to preach, prescribe for the sick, or offer a wise suggestion on military or social affairs." Now, at this time there were only three Jesuit chaplains in Virginia: Gache, Hubert, and Prachensky. It is possible that the English officer could have had a composite of these in mind when he depicted the archetypal Jesuit serving the Confederacy. But his further commentary rules out the possibility that these three priests alone were the models for his impression. "It is to the foresight and judgment of one (Jesuit)," he continued, "that Beauregard and Johnston escaped death or capture at Manassas, for had they not met one of these missionaries during the heat of the conflict, and heeded his modest advice, one or another of these calamities must have inevitably ensued."[78]

Seeing that there was no Jesuit chaplain in Virginia when Johnston and Beauregard defeated the Federals at Manassas in July, 1861, the question is: who was the mysterious Jesuit to whom Johnston and Beauregard were indebted and whose disciplined bearing so impressed the English lieutenant? Unquestionably, it was the Jesuit whom Gache reported having met in Richmond in January, 1862—Joseph Bixio (b. Genoa, Kingdom of Sardinia, May 23, 1819–d. Santa Clara, California, March 3, 1889), the incarnation of the tartuffish Jesuit, every bit as ingenious and resourceful as he was double-dealing and cunning. He had entered the Society with Aloysius Curioz in Turin. When the Jesuits were expelled from the Kingdom of Sardinia during the 1848 uprisings, Bixio came to northern Virginia where he remained until 1855. Then he joined his Piedmontese Jesuit confreres who had resettled in California. Having a nose for trouble, he returned to Virginia as war clouds gathered, and assisted at a parish in whose territorial confines was Manassas. As Gache advised de Carrière in this letter, Joseph was the brother of the famous General Nino Bixio

(b. Genoa, Kingdom of Sardinia, October 2, 1821–d. at sea off the coast of Java, December 16, 1873), Garibaldi's right-hand man in the struggle for Italian unification, an excommunicate described by Alexandre Dumas as "an indefatigable conspirator, with a passionate love for his country which bordered on madness." One of Nino's early biographers recalled that the general's older brother Joseph was "a mischievous, troublesome hooligan," a young boy who was nevertheless alert, street-wise and clever, and who, when "drawn to studies and the religious life, he decided on the most military order in the church, and so entered the Jesuits."[74]

During the war the chaplain to the Fourteenth Regiment, James B. Sheeran, C.SS.P. (b. Temple Mehill, County Longford, Ireland, June 21, 1819–d. Morristown, New Jersey, April 3, 1881), kept a journal, and in these pages the former street-wise and clever Genoese emerges as a sly cicerone of unfailing chicanery and competence who spent an inordinate amount of time slipping back and forth across the Federal lines. Gache had met Bixio in Richmond in January 1862. In the Spring, a Union chaplain wrote that Bixio had been in Federal camps "where he had gained the hearts of both officers and soldiers," and by the summer he had turned up again in Richmond.[75] In his memoirs George Clark (1841-1918), captain of the Eleventh Alabama, described meeting a priest at the Battle of Gaines Mill, June 27, 1862. This priest was undoubtedly Bixio, for he was the only Italian priest in the vicinity. The Alabama officer, later Attorney General of Texas (1874-76) and unsuccessful candidate for the governorship of that State (1893), recalled that, having been wounded in battle, "I was sitting on an old log awaiting my turn [for treatment] when a Catholic priest came up and told me he would dress my arm if I would permit him, as he had a great deal of experience in the Italian army in the war between France and Austria. He ripped the sleeve of my coat, and took it off of me and most carefully washed and dressed the wound, telling me I would not need any attention during the night. To my surprise after thanking him for the kindness, he felt around his pocket and pulling out a bottle of brandy, he told me the doctor would allow me to take a drink after the first twenty-four hours after being wounded."[76]

In September 1846 Sheeran had been captured and was a prisoner behind the Federal lines when he came across Bixio again. He noted in his journal that the ubiquitous Jesuit was "now playing Yankee chaplain in company with several Yankee officers," and drawing Federal rations at Winchester, Virginia. At this date Bixio was posing as Father Leo Rizzo da Saracena, O.F.M. (1833-97), the Italian-born chaplain of the Ninth Connecticut Volunteers and later President of St. Bonaventure College, New York (1877-80).

Father Leo, stricken with typhoid fever, had been hospitalized and was hovering between life and death when Bixio "slipped into the sick priest's tent and stole his chaplaincy credential and uniform." In his new disguise the Jesuit personally conned General Philip Sheridan into having cartloads of Union supplies assigned to his charge. The captured Sheeran did not betray the bogus Connecticut chaplain's true identity, but when Sheridan learned that the supplies were diverted across the lines to Staunton and that he had become the butt of Staunton jokes, he realized to what extent the vanished Jesuit had "deceived me and acted meanly." Exasperated he turned his full wrath on Sheeran whom he had thrown into a wretched prison to expiate for Bixio's hoax.[77]

Meanwhile, Gen. Benjamin Butler received a distorted version of the swindle, and thinking Father Leo was the guilty chaplain, bellowed: "Find him, and shoot the Dago at sight." Even though the Franciscan had served the Union long and loyally, and had been seriously wounded in battle on one occasion, "he was almost shot for espionage or treason when as an American citizen he was still only a babe in arms." The friar was fortunately able to prove that he was unconcious and writhing with fever at the time Sheridan and Bixio were sharing promises. But while he was pleading for his life his fellow countryman was back in Staunton doling out the Yankee haul, and it was here that Bixio received "a polite message" from an unidentified general other than Sheridan, and most certainly Butler, "to the effect that, if ever caught, he should be hanged to the first tree."[78] But caught he never was, and after the war he arrived in Georgetown "with a trunkful of Confederate script—hundreds of thousands of dollars, expecting to found a college with his treasure." Just how he came upon this script and how long he had it before he showed up at Holy Trinity Church in the spring of 1865 has not been recorded. He left Virginia after the war, worked awhile in Australia, and finally returned to California where the Jesuits were feuding with the Archbishop of San Francisco, Joseph Sadoc Alemany (1814-88). In no time Bixio charmed the prelate, became his trusted confidant, and founded a number of parishes for him in Santa Clara and San Mateo counties before dying at the Italian Jesuit *collège-en-exile* at Santa Clara.[79]

In 1853 a land speculator and entrepreneur, James Bigler (b. Binghampton, New York, February 6, 1818–d. Newburg, New York, July 16, 1910), bought the deed to "Ripon Hall," a 2400 acre tract northwest of Williamsburg along the James. Almost two centuries earlier, in 1687, this estate had been purchased and beautified by Sir Edward Jenings (1659-1727), the predecessor of Alexander Spotswood to the governorship of Virginia (1706-10). After erecting the mansion destined to become famous in history and in fiction, Jenings died and the property passed into the hands of Col. Landon Carter (1709-78), the famous diarist of "Seneca Hill" in Richmond County.[80] Bigler subdivided the estate and a small community bearing his name sprang up around the lumber mill he had built below Carter Creek. The census of 1860 shows that there were a few Irish-born families employed at this site, all of whom had left before 1870, by which date the mill itself had been abandoned.[81] Extant records do not conclusively identify the Baptist minister that Gache mentions in this letter. The 1860 census names William A. Crandal as a Baptist clergyman at Williamsburg, but most probably before 1862 he had been replaced by the saintly and scholarly Reverend William Martin, M.D. (b. Loudoun County, Virginia, August 1812–d. Williamsburg, Virginia, December 15, 1866).[82] Undoubtedly the unnamed Williamsburg lady who so edified the former master of novices by giving him an account of her conscience was Rebecca Ewell. In a letter to Rebecca's sister, another Elizabeth Stoddard Ewell (b. Georgetown, D. C., December 11, 1813–d. Washington, D. C., January 1901), Gache recalled that her late sister's "soul was so noble, so upright; her conscience so delicate; she would not have failed to embrace the truth, had she seen it. Sometimes in our private conversions [sic], I thought I was listening to a nun." But Rebecca was a potential nun who "unfortunately had read some Protestant books which had too much injured her mind." Elizabeth had become a Catholic many years before and had tried the cloistered life at the time when Rebecca was considering conversion. "Pain and unhappiness enough had been produced by Elizabeth's change," their mother wrote Rebecca in December 1842, "if you change too I do not know what the consequences will be, as of course you would go into the convent too." But the fare at the Georgetown Visitation Convent was beyond endurance for Elizabeth, and so she settled for being the organist at Holy Trinity Church near Georgetown College. When she died, her niece, "Miss Lizzy," wrote to Gache offering him some of her effects. " I will receive some, the beads, for instance," the dead woman's longtime spiritual director replied, "but I advise you to keep her crucifix yourself. This image of our dear blessed Lord dying for us on the cross is a source of blessings in the houses where it is kept."[83]

J.M.J.

Camp Lee's Mill
April 5, 1862 (Sat.)

To Rev. Father Cornette, S. J.
Spring Hill College

Reverend and very dear Father, Pax Christi

Father Gautrelet must have received sometime ago the letter in which I informed him that package number one has finally arrived, after considerable delays and hindrances, at Yorktown. I learned just today of the happy arrival of package number two at Lee's Mill.

Early last Sunday afternoon, I saw two gallant horsemen approaching my modest abode. As they drew closer I was delighted to discover that they were none other than Captain [Patrick] Loughry and Father [James] Sheeran. Captain Loughry's Eighth Alabama had been encamped at a place called Harwood's Mill, and Father Sheeran's Fourteenth Louisiana at Ship's Point on the James, not far from Newport News. Major General Magruder, judging his forces to be insufficient for the defense of these places, ordered these regiments and a few others to withdraw to our side of the line. The Eighth Alabama and the Fourteenth Louisiana accordingly found themselves temporarily camped about four miles from Lee's Mill, at a place called Wind's Mill. The proximity of our campsites made it possible for the captain and the chaplain to pay me a little neighborly visit. Another reason why they rode over from their camp was to invite me to pick up my package. One would have suspected that Captain Loughry felt more keenly responsible for this item than for all of the other treasures in his possession.

While I was at Wind's Mill I saw someone whom you yourself had seen not long ago, a person whom you seemed to have captivated. I refer to the brother-in-law of Mr.

[James] Tierney. This good soul thinks that you are the finest man in the world and that the race has not yet produced your equal. All of this because you had showed him something that no one else has ever shown him—your physics laboratory. I didn't attempt to disabuse the young man, for such an effort would have been to no purpose, and might even have given him the impression that it was my judgment that was amiss. After all, if it comes to a choice, I should prefer that people overestimate your acumen than that they underestimate mine. There are occasions when one's love of truth must yield to higher values. I also saw Cornelius Lyons of Mobile at this camp. He is in good health and he is, as he always was, a fine fellow. Along with ninety-five men in Captain Loughry's company he received his Easter Communion the week previously from Father Sheeran.

When I returned to my camp that same evening, I learned that the regiment had received orders to move ahead to serve as an advanced picket eight miles below Young's Mill. To my great consolation these orders had been served and executed during my absence. The men were to remain at this new outpost only four or five days where I know there would be no engagements because if the enemy decided to challenge them, our troops would have to retreat behind our lines, and the 10th in particular would have to return to this camp, which is the best fortified on the whole line. So, I decided not to follow the men to their new position. Besides, during the last fortnight I've had a frightful cold which has left me quite ill. I didn't feel I had the strength for such a march and it would have been very imprudent on my part to spend the nights as one must on these marches—that is, out in the open exposed to the cold, and even, often to the rain.

But in escaping the Scylla of exposure, I fell victim, so to speak, to the Charybdis of hunger. Whenever the regiment is away from camp those who remain are hard put to find something to eat. This time I availed myself of the services of a good Irish woman, the wife of one of our soldiers, and I arranged to have her see to my meals. Ordinarily she works as a washerwoman, and this permits her to follow her husband with the regiment. The dear soul —her faith and piety empowered her to work miracles with the meager viands at her disposal. Of course, when I say "miracles" I don't mean to imply that I was dining on pheasant-under-glass. On the contrary, another month of such cuisine would have been enough to put me out of commission altogether.

You are nonplussed perchance at my habitual references to the gastronomic crosses I must bear. You fancy perhaps that I have become a glutton? A glutton— alas, not that! A glutton, as far as I know I have never been, and there is small chance of becoming one now. I would venture to say even that I have made progress in sobriety, perhaps indeed in mortification, though I daresay that Father de Carrière would disagree. The good Father seems to have been scandalized and to have conceived certain serious misgivings in my regard upon his learning of my taking an occasional shot of w-h-i-s—ah, but no: we dare not mention the shocking word! However, you know well, dear Father, that though man does not live by bread alone, he does not live without bread; however abstemious and mortified he may be, he inevitably finds, when this sustenance is denied him, that he can ill endure its absence. Ever since the beginning of my military career, I have never had enough bread. Whether you find this credible or not, it is neither more nor less than the simple truth. Such is not the misfortune of everyone; it is rather the result of my particular position. But in the long run, the reason does not alter the fact. The cassock which I could scarcely button at my departure from Spring Hill now goes around me twice. Yet in the face of all of these things, Father de Carrière takes umbrage at my little indulgences. Oh, hardhearted, pitiless man! I wouldn't have him as my director if he were the last man on earth!

But this whole business reminds me of a little anecdote which I must tell you. Sometime ago I was coming back from Richmond on the James River steamer. The day was a Friday. Since I had eaten a very light breakfast at the convent of the Daughters of Charity where I had said my mass, I was not displeased when dinner was announced. Nor was I the last to take his place at the table. But just as I was about to go into operation, I became aware of a very grave problem. At one end of the table was a golden brown turkey, at the other end a tender suckling pig, and in the center a succulent veal-quarter. No point in dwelling on the leg of mutton and the roast beef; suffice it to merely acknowledge their presence. Now, as I have already told you, it was a Friday. So this is the problem that presented itself: Was I to observe the law of abstinence and be satisfied with a piece of bread, a few sardines and a plate of potatoes (for this seemed to be the only alternative to the dishes mentioned above), or ought I to make use of my military privilege and take a bit of turkey, a small serving of veal, and perhaps even a tiny morsel of the suckling pig? I would have you take note of the following circumstances, either attenuating or aggravating as you may choose to interpret them. On boarding the steamer, I had purchased my ticket; strictly speaking I had not purchased my dinner, as meals are served free of charge on the river boats; yet it was my ticket that gave me the right to take my place at the table. Therefore the price of the ticket was the same whether I ate or did not eat, and, if I ate, whether I availed myself of the whole menu or only a part of it. What ought I to have done? What would you have done in my place? I have a rather strong suspicion as to what you would have done, and I shall not tell you what I did since you probably are too worldly-minded to appreciate my choice. I shall merely say that while I was sitting at the table I was well aware of the fact that I would have no supper that evening, and I know that not once during the next two days would I have a full meal. As it turned out, I just managed to get by on some scraps given me by the few men who remained in camp while the regiment was on the march and who could ill afford to part with the little they had. Now judge and tell me whether I could with a perfectly clear conscience, have taken advantage of my dispensation. If you say no, not even under these circumstances, I would suggest either that you review your theology, or better, that you come and see what life here on the Peninsula is like. That would bring you down to earth!

Don't think, however, dear Father, that all of these privations and hardships make life disagreeable or make me regret my assignment. Not at all. By God's grace my life up till now has been utterly free from tedium, and I am more content with my lot today than I have ever been before. I have never been more certain that this is where God wants me to be and that I am doing His will. From January to the middle of March I was not very active. During this time the weather was invariably bad. Why? Obviously, because we had to make so many marches and counter-marches. Since the beginning of Lent, though, things have improved. Now each morning I have a good number at mass. Every evening right after the seven o'clock roll-call, I conduct a service consisting of rosary, catechetical instruction, and night prayers, which is attended by thirty or forty persons. That's about all that can fit into my little log house. The number of confessions and Communions has picked up too; every day I have at least a few. I would like to have as many as three hundred Easter Communions, and I'm hoping that there will even be more, either from my own regiment or from some of the others.

April 10 (Thurs.)

This letter was interrupted last Saturday [April 5] by our good friends the Yankees. They made their appearance on that day in the field opposite our camp on the other side of the creek. As soon as we were aware of their presence we hastened to salute them with a salvo from our cannon. They returned the greeting in kind. Then during the course of the day they fired on us some twenty times, but no one was injured or even really frightened, though many of their shells exploded in the midst of our troops. During a period of one hour, four of these shells passed right over my quarters. The Yankees' aim was always too high. Our own artillery reciprocated with more effect: one shot blew up one of their caissons (I saw this myself from the height of one of our ramparts where I happened to be), and another managed to knock an officer clean off his horse. On the next day, Sunday, we were still exchanging occasional volleys, but to no one's advantage; and ever since that time the cannons have remained silent. But the skirmishes which began Saturday night along the creek have continued up till now. The Dreux Batallion, which is encamped right alongside us, has been more involved than we in these brushes with the enemy. Five of their soldiers have already been wounded, although none very seriously; nevertheless, they're now *hors de combat*. One of them is John Augustine. His injury, a leg wound, is the least serious of the lot. One was killed. He was the nephew of the bishop of Natchez [William Henry Elder] and, as a matter of fact, one of my best friends. Just five days before he died he had gone to confession and had received Holy Communion. The Tenth Georgia, another regiment encamped nearby, has also had some killed and four or five wounded in these skirmishes. I'm finally beginning to have a lot of work on my hands. The big fish, frightened by the sound of Yankee cannons, leave their deep holes and come up to where I can catch them.

April 5, 1862

It looks as if we're going to have not just one major battle, but a series of major battles. The enemy are attacking simultaneously at as many as five or six points all along our lines. And there are so many of them! Some of the prisoners we captured put their number at 100,000. But we're rather well fortified and we're receiving fresh reinforcements every day. During the past three days it has been raining and it's probably as a result of this that we've had no serious engagement up until now; however, as soon as it does clear up we're going to have a hot time of it here on the Peninsula. May God help us! I might very well be taken prisoner, and if there is anything I fear it is that. *Adieu.* Pray for me, one and all.

Your friend and brother,
H. Gache, S.J.

P.S. All my best to dear Doctor Rohmer. How is he? I'm afraid that things are not going too well for him. Give my regards also to Mr. Parada. I'll write you again as soon as I am able. I forgot to thank you for all of the packages, but this doesn't mean that I'm not grateful for receiving them. The first time I get to Richmond, if I manage to get there at all, I'll send you the payment for them. Again, *adieu.*

COMMENTARY

Exasperated by McClellan's procrastination on the Peninsula, President Lincoln was urging the general to action when Gache began this letter, two days after Shiloh had fallen to the Union offensive in the west. The skirmish which interrupted his writing was followed by intensified military operations that culminated in the Battle of Yorktown, on the third and fourth of May; the Battle of Williamsburg on the fifth, and the evacuation of Norfolk on the ninth. The young soldier killed at Lee's Mill was James Willcox Jenkins (b. Baltimore, Maryland, January 2, 1836), the son of Juliana (1809-46), Bishop William Henry Elder's sister, and through his father, a descendant of a family conspicuous in the history of early Maryland.[84] Research has not yielded conclusive evidence relating to "Mr. Tierney's brother-in-law" who had been so impressed by Father Cornette's physics laboratory. James Tierney, Sr. (b. Ireland, 1825–d. Mobile, Alabama, September 26, 1899), the proprietor of the Gulf States Bakery, came to Spring Hill the year after Gache returned to the college from Baton Rouge, 1853.[85]

The Jesuit was unquestionably pleased with the way Lent was observed in camp. Even though the troops had been dispensed from church law to fast and abstain from meat—a privilege about which he was annoyingly coy—the chaplain was encouraged by the success of his Lenten program.[86] That he anticipated more than 300 Easter Communions from his own regiment no doubt contributed to the assurance that "I have never been more certain that this is where God wants me to be and that I am doing His will." The fact that his "little log house" was able to accommodate up to forty men for catechetical instruction and devotions is a telling indication of how extensive was the space his "Irish boys" had provided for him. But it is not inconceivable that Gache's earlier complaints about having so little to do in camp contributed to Bishop McGill's letter to William Henry Elder (1819-1904), James Willcox's episcopal uncle, suggesting that there were already too many Catholic chaplains in the army.[87] Bishop Elder's diocese included the whole state of Mississippi.

J.M.J.

Richmond
June 11, 1862

Rev. Fr. de Carrière S.J.
Spring Hill, Alabama

Reverend and dear Father,

I had resolved not to write to you for fear that I would call down upon my head an avalanche of reflections and counsels on the dangers of drink, confirmed by sundry examples from the lives of Malloy and other lushes. But a particular circumstance in which I find myself, and which might prove to be of some interest to you, has led me to put aside my fears. The circumstance is that I am now in the hospital. Yes, after walking around on the brink for such a long time, I finally fell into the well myself—along with many others.

I don't think very highly of these "masterful retreats" of General Johnston; although in the future when they speak of the famous retreat from Williamsburg, I'll be able to say, and not without pride: "I was there." At the present, however, I want to say something about the hospital. After a week of fatigue, general malaise and a touch of dysentery, I decided to go to the hospital on the day before Pentecost. My first night there was a miserable one, thanks to the medicine they gave me; nevertheless, I felt I really ought to say mass the next morning, not only because it was Pentecost Sunday, but also because, if I didn't, the poor sisters would have to walk all the way to the cathedral which is a good mile from their convent. But no sooner had I finished the Epistle than I was overcome by such severe weakness and nausea that I had to leave the altar and return to my room. I was never quite that sick again. There is no more dysentery now, but I'm still as weak as a cat, and I've been having headaches which the doctors cannot explain any more than I can. But even more mysterious than the headaches is the fact that I have no appetite at all—a strange state of affairs for one who has been hungry for six months! The sisters, however, are very good to me; they lavish their care on me and spoil me with specially prepared dishes, which, alas, I am not able to relish. But the result is that not only do I find this illness bearable, but I'm afraid that I'll end up taking real pleasure in being sick. May God preserve us from such nurses at Spring Hill! If we had them there, everyone would be sick all the time and no one would ever get well. It was they who came to fetch me at the bishop's house when they learned that I had been struggling there with my illness, utterly destitute of all help, for three days. In the bishop's residence there is no one to care for the sick, as the servants there are too busy being masters. As matters turned out, however, the sisters had no other room for me except their own parlor, of which they deprived themselves for my sake. I couldn't even begin to tell you how indebted I am to these saintly Daughters of Charity, nor could I begin to enumerate all that they have done for me since my arrival in Richmond. Only last week, for example, after I had vainly spent days searching the stores for a pair of shoes, I finally managed to get what I was looking for through the efforts of the good sisters.

Young George Spotswood of the Second Florida was admitted here to the hospital last week. The poor boy, he'd have been a goner anywhere else. Divine Providence, however, willed that Doctor [Alexander] Semmes, who had visited us at Spring Hill, was with old Doctor [William] Spotswood in Richmond when they brought young George in from the Peninsula, and it was he, Doctor Semmes, who spoke so highly of the sisters that Doctor Spotswood agreed to entrust George to their care. He had no reason to regret his decision either. What a lovable old man Doctor Spotts is, and what a pity it is that he has received no religious education at all. At any rate, he is not so upset anymore about George's becoming a Catholic, and he no longer heckles him about practicing his religion.

Also with me here are two wounded boys from the Third Alabama. One is named [Edward] Livingston. His family lives on the Shell Road near Mobile. The other lad's name is [Lemuel] Lincoln. He is a cousin of Mr. [Charles] Dorrance and he knows Father Gautrelet. He was wounded in the jaw, but the wound is not serious. He is a good Catholic and I have heard his confession and have given him Holy Communion. Livingston is an Episcopalian. He had heard Doctor [John] Innerarity speak of me, and so when I told him who I was he recognized the name and began to weep like a child. He has around his neck just about all of the rosaries and medals that the sisters possess. He was wounded in the leg, and seriously too. They're afraid that they're going to have to amputate, and late amputations like this are rarely successful. But I'm going to have to stop now; my eyes are getting bleary. Another time, then, for the news about the war. The newspapers probably keep you well informed about the war anyway. *Adieu, mon bon Père.* My regards and best wishes to all of Ours and to Dr. Rohmer and Mr. Parada also, if he is still at Spring Hill.

Yours sincerely in Our Lord,
H. Gache, Chap. 10th Reg.,
La. Vols.

P.S. Please tell Father Gautrelet that I was given as an indemnity $20 at the Express Office for the objects that were missing in the box he sent me. I have no way, however, to send this money down to him.

COMMENTARY

The two months which intervened between this letter and the last were, in contrast to the eight months Gache had marked time in Virginia, filled with derring-do—marches, countermarches, battles, bivouacs on the Chickahominy—all of which won glory for the 10th, and for its chaplain a bed in the St. Francis de Sales Hospital, Richmond. The regiment, "marching to its place with the accuracy of a parade drill" at the Battle of Yorktown, had been singled out for special commendation by General Magruder.[88] But Southern spirit and military discipline were no match for the numerical superiority of McClellan's army, and so the Peninsula was abandoned. Then, as May gave way to June, events in the Shenandoah Valley, where Lt. Gen. Thomas Jonathan "Stonewall" Jackson (1824-63) was amassing an army to thwart McClellan's plan to march on to Richmond, revitalized Confederate hopes. On May 31, one week after the chaplain had been hospitalized, Gen. Joseph Johnston, about whom he would have kinder things to say as the war progressed, was seriously wounded at Seven Pines, enabling Gen. Robert E. Lee to assume command of the Army of Northern Virginia. On the very day that Gache wrote this letter bemoaning Confederate set-backs, Brigadier, soon to be Major General, James Ewell Brown Stuart began his four day spirited ride around McClellan, thereby setting the stage for the defense of the capital, and eventually permitting Lee to go on the offensive against the Army of the Potomac. Meanwhile, the news from the west was ominous: New Orleans surrendered on the first of May, and Corinth fell on the twentieth.

In this letter Gache advised de Carrière that a fellow patient at St. Francis de Sales was his former student, George Willis Spotswood (b. Pensacola, Florida, 1844–d. Mobile, Alabama, December 28, 1908), the oldest son of Doctor William Augustine Washington Spotswood (b. Orange County, Virginia, October 2, 1786–d. Mobile, Alabama, September 8, 1891) and Mary Reese Eastin (1822-91). "Doctor Spotts," who had visited both patients, was the great-grand nephew of George Washington and a distant relation of General Lee. His wife was the niece of John Gayle (1792-1859), governor of Alabama (1831-35), and cousin by marriage to General Josiah Gorgas, C.S.A. (1818-83), who became president of the University of Alabama in 1878. Doctor Spotswood began his medical career in the United States Navy in 1829. He later participated in the Seminole and Mexican wars, and distinguished himself at Norfolk in the cholera epidemics of 1830 and later at the siege of Vera Cruz. In January 1861 he resigned from the Federal Navy, and was immediately appointed chief of the Bureau of Surgery of the Confederate Navy, and ordered to

Richmond where he served until the end of the war. George had come to Spring Hill in 1855 from Pensacola, where his father was the medical officer at the Warrington Naval Yard. On April 7, 1860 he became a Catholic and the following year left the college to enlist in Company A, the Pensacola Rifle Rangers, of the second Florida Regiment. ". . . he is very anxious to go to the ranks as a volunteer," Dr. Spotswood wrote in September 1861, "but as he is very young his mother wishes him to defer it." Never making a sufficient recovery from the fevers which had brought him to St. Francis de Sales, the young soldier was given a medical discharge from the army on August 6, 1862, but remained in Richmond working for the Navy Department until 1864 when he returned to Alabama to enlist in Company F of the Alabama Fifty-third Regiment.[89]

The surgeon who had persuaded "Doctor Spotts" to entrust George to the Daughters of Charity was Alexander Jenkins Semmes (b. Georgetown, D.C., December 17, 1812–d. New Orleans, Louisiana, September 20, 1898), brother of Thomas Jenkins Semmes (1824-99), the Attorney General of Louisiana (1859-61) and representative from that state to the Confederate Congress. Dr. Semmes was also the first cousin of Rear Admiral Rafael Semmes, C.S.N. (1809-77) and a relative of James Willcox Jenkins, Bishop Elder's nephew who was killed at Lee's Mill. Like the Virginia Spotswoods, the Maryland Semmes were closely associated with Spring Hill College before and after the war. Doctor Alexander was appointed surgeon to the Eighth Louisiana when it formed in 1861, but later he was assigned to the hospitals in northern Virginia, where in 1864, he was commissioned medical inspector for the department. In the Fall of that year he was united, in an Episcopal marriage ceremony, to Sarah Lowndes Berrien (1837-72), the daughter of John McPherson Berrien (1781-1856), the United States senator from Georgia who founded the Know-Nothing Party in that state, a former member of Andrew Jackson's cabinet and the United States Attorney General in 1829. Eventually the couple separated and Dr. Semmes was reconciled to his own church. Returning to New Orleans to practice medicine, he soon gained worldwide acclaim for medical research, but then suddenly gave up his brilliant career to become a Roman Catholic priest in Georgia. Almost immediately after his ordination in 1873, he was appointed seminary rector in Savannah, and here he served until his retirement to New Orleans in 1895.[90]

The third doctor Gache mentioned in this letter was John Forbes Innerarity (b. Mobile, Alabama, 1813–d. Mobile, Alabama, November 2, 1868), the son of James (also known as Santiago) Innerarity, mentioned above, and Heloise Isabel Troullet (1792-1847). After the death in 1795 of her father, Pedro Troullet (1752-95), Heloise's mother, Marie Isabella Narbonne, presumably married John Forbes—one more detail which renders the convoluted genealogy of this distinguished Gulf family yet more complex. Doctor John was the brother of William Panton Innerarity, also mentioned above, and uncle of John E. de Villiers Innerarity. Married to Fanny Wemys Scarborough Johnstone (1818-70), John Innerarity was well known to the Jesuits at Spring Hill.[91]

Besides George Spotswood, Gache singled out two other patients: Edward Livingston (b. Mobile, Alabama, 1838–d. New Orleans, Louisiana, November 23, 1898) and Lemuel Lincoln (b. Little Rock, Arkansas, 1840–d. New Orleans, Louisiana, March 25, 1900). Both soldiers were in Captain Sands' Company of the Third Alabama. Livingston's military career was short lived, seeing that he was wounded at Seven Pines, a mere nine days after he had enlisted on May 23 for a two-year stint. Despite the priest's dire predictions, Livingston kept his leg, although he remained confined to the hospital until April 1863, when he was discharged from the army and sent back to Mobile where more problems awaited him. Unsuccessful in reclaiming the clerk's position he had left when he joined the army, he spent eight discouraging months trying to find employment. Finally, on January 8, 1864, he addressed an appeal to Christopher Gustavus Memminger (1803-88), Secretary of the Treasury in Richmond, expressing the desire "for serving my country in a civil capacity as I have done in a military one." But apparently Memminger was not able to honor his request.[92]

Livingston's friend Lincoln had enlisted in the Fifth Louisiana on May 20, 1861, but was discharged for health reasons shortly after the regiment arrived on the Peninsula. Later he and Livingston enrolled on the same day in Capt. Sands' Company, and both were wounded on the first of June and sent to St. Francis de Sales. When Lemuel Lincoln left the hospital he carried with him his second set of discharge papers from the army, but shortly afterwards he enlisted in the Third Virginia defense command, an outfit formed for the defense of Richmond. When President Davis fled the capital during the last days of the war, he was ironically escorted by a Lincoln as far as North Carolina where the escort detail to which Lemuel had been assigned was disbanded. The war over, "Major" Lincoln, sometimes president of the Benevolent Association of the Army of North Virginia, turned to journalism in New Orleans where he became prominent in the struggle to overthrow the Louisiana carpetbag government. By his marriage to Adrienne Hulluin (1870), Lincoln allied himself to an important Assumption Parish family. In this letter Gache reported that Lincoln was also related to Charles W. Dorrance (b. Warren, Rhode Island, 1810–d. Mobile, Alabama, February 10, 1873), a prosperous Mobile merchant whose second marriage made him part of the Sands family. In 1866 Dorrance and James M. Muldon, Sr. were two of several leading citizens who signed the "Petition of Leading Merchants and citizens of Mobile praying the President of the United States to pardon Rafael Semmes and admit him to the benefits of the Amnesty Proclamation of the 25th of May 1865," and that "His Honor will remove the military prohibition which prevents him from performance of his military duties as Judge of the Probate Court of Mobile County and City."[98]

Richmond
July 8, 1862

[André Cornette]

Reverend and dear Father, P.C.

A few days ago I managed to get a letter off to Father Gautrelet; however, you shouldn't be too upset if in the midst of all these terrible events taking place around Richmond I fail to send you the news with the same regularity as in the past. I say this because a remark in Father de Carrière's letter of four or five days ago has made me wonder whether I have answered your last letter.

You know—or at least you've heard tell, for not being a Frenchman yourself you wouldn't have direct experience of it—you know, I say, that we French are reputed to have a great love of war. By the grace of God, I am as French as any man alive, albeit I have never liked the idea of fighting others, and even less have I relished the thought of their fighting me. Just the same, I do love to see an army in battle array. I thrill to the thunder of artillery cannon and to the crack of infantry rifles; my blood tingles when I watch cavalry manoeuvers–not practice manoeuvers on parade grounds, but authentic manoeuvers on the very field of battle. But alas, the events of Monday, Tuesday, Wednesday and Thursday have surfeited my appetite for war. I have now seen enough carnage to last me for life.

Monday [June 30] the battle began about 6:00 p.m. and lasted until about 9:00—too late for me to be able to witness much of it; moreover my regiment took no part in the fighting at all. But what a spectacle the next morning presented along the four miles of road where we had pursued the enemy. The place where the battle had begun was covered with the dead, Confederate dead for the most part—since we had attacked and it is ordinarily the offensive side which in the beginning suffers the greater losses. Some bodies were lying along the edge of the woods, but there were many strewn out over the open fields. About a half mile further on we began to see the wounded lying alongside the dead, and from here on it was all Federal troops. Thanks to the speed of noble Fanny (Miss Fanny is the name of my horse) and to the occasional halts the brigade had to make, I was able to stop and see some of these poor lads and to give them at least a few words of encouragement. Many of them were pitifully mutilated, lying in the dust under a fierce sun. Some of them didn't even have the strength to turn their faces to the shade. Here they had lain, anywhere from fifteen to twenty-six hours without so much as even a sip of water for their burning thirst. How deeply moved they were when they saw that those whom they had considered the perpetrators of all this misery were approaching them and offering help. For I must remark that our soldiers who are depicted by the newspapers of the North as cruel, barbaric monsters, acted with great kindness toward the wounded. The Irish lads of my own 10th were especially outstanding in this respect. Each time the brigade came to a halt, dozens of men broke ranks and ran to cut down branches to provide shade for the wounded. Sometimes they would fix those branches into the ground beside the poor unfortunate Yankees; sometimes they would even gather up four muskets and bayonet them into the ground as a framework to support the branches. They would then give the men water, biscuits, and other bits of food that they happened to have. I have said that the Federals generally reacted with surprised gratitude to this kindness from their enemies; there was one, however, who just about died of panic when he saw the Confederates approaching him. The poor boy, frightfully mutilated and weakened by a great loss of blood, imagined that our troops were coming to put him out of the picture for good. In spite of all their solicitude and friendly words, three or four of our boys were not able to reassure him of their good intentions. I then came to him, told him I was a priest, and asked him if by chance he was a Catholic. "Oh, yes, Father, I am," he answered, pitifully attempting the sign of the cross, "I'm a Catholic and I'm a Democrat too."—meaning that he wasn't an Abolitionist and had done nothing to merit Southern wrath. Right then and there I spoke to him about the affairs of his soul and heard his confession. He died, I believe, that night. But among all of the wounded I found only six Yankees who were Catholics. I heard the confessions of four of them; the other two were not gravely wounded and said that they preferred to go to confession at the hospital after having a better opportunity to examine their consciences.

The non-Catholics showed me very great respect and were sincerely appreciative for the spiritual advice I gave them, willingly repeating the short prayers and aspirations that I suggested. Among others there was one old colonel who had received a blast of shot in his chest. When I saw him he was very weak. I told him to recommend himself to God and to ask pardon for his sins. To which he replied: "I have already done that, but I'll do it again. And I do thank you for your advice. I also pray that God will bless you for the kind words you have said to me and for the sympathy you have shown me. I really have no right to this at all."

Another, when I inquired whether he was a Catholic, answered: "No I am not, but my wife and children are Catholics. I like their church very much. It is the only one I attend."

"Have you ever been baptized?"

"No, my mother and father were Baptists; they didn't have me baptized when I was a child and I didn't have myself baptized when I grew up."

"Well would you like to be baptized now? You realize that without baptism you cannot be saved."

"Yes, I would like to be baptized."

"And in the Catholic church, I suppose?"

"Yes."

I assured myself as best I could that he had the faith and necessary depositions, baptized him, and left him in a state of joy and gratitude to God and appreciation for what I had done. He kept saying over and over: "Blessed be the Lord. Now I will die in peace."

Tuesday evening [July 1] I witnessed another manifestation of the work of grace. The time was about six o'clock. I had been in the saddle all day visiting the places where the battles of Tuesday and Wednesday had been fought, places which were now veritable cemeteries. Or more precisely, I had been visiting the make-shift hospitals which had been set up in these places where the battles had been fought. I had had no opportunity to eat or drink since seven that morning. I was exhausted and on my way back to Richmond when I noticed over to my right a small house surrounded by tents. It was obviously another camp hospital. But I was so weary; besides, I had to get back to the infirmary at Richmond by ten o'clock that same evening so as not to cause more inconvenience to the good sisters. And Richmond was another fifteen miles along the road; so oblivious to everything except my own fatigue and the necessity of returning to Richmond I continued on my way. Then suddenly the thought occurred to me: "Who can tell? Perhaps there is some Catholic back there in one of the tents gravely wounded and sorely in need of my care." So, I pulled back the bridle, turned around, clapped the spurs to my horse, and galloped back toward the little cabin. Ah, the ways of Providence! I had no sooner dismounted when I was greeted by a surgeon whom I knew by sight. "Father you've arrived in the nick of time. There's a Catholic here among the wounded who's been calling for a priest." The poor soldier had reason to call for a priest, too, as he had been away from the sacraments for a long time and had scarcely any time left in this world.

I had hoped that my regiment could have gone through the campaign without being involved in any of the actual fighting. But this was not to be. The 10th took part in the battle on Tuesday, and like all the other regiments in the twilight action of that disastrous day, we sustained heavy losses. Twelve of our men were killed, thirty-five were wounded, and thirty-three are still missing. My dear friend Colonel Waggaman is listed among the missing. Please God he has not been wounded; although he must surely have been, as he was at the head of his regiment when it made a charge against a battery of thirty-two cannons. I miss him very much; his loss is and will be irreparable. The night before the battle the poor fellow took me aside and said: "Father, I'd like to make another short confession" and so the two of us withdrew from the rest of the troops for a few moments and I obliged his request. The following morning before I finally settled down to get some sleep (we had marched during most of the night and weren't able even to snatch a few winks until 3:00 a.m.), I noticed that the colonel spent a long time at his prayers. This much is for sure: if he has to face death in some Yankee prison, he'll not be unprepared.

We have three priests here who have been taken prisoner. Two of them are Jesuits, Father [Joseph] O'Hagan of Georgetown College and Father [Peter] Tissot who was a student of mine at Mélan and who some of the Fathers at Spring Hill may know. All three assure us that there is no doubt at all about the North's determination to conquer the South, and that even if McClellan's army is defeated, they'll raise another that will sweep right through the Confederate States. I'd like to feel that these priests are quite mistaken about this, and that President Lincoln will find that issuing a call to arms is one thing and actually raising an army is quite another.

Our Louisiana officers are trying their best to persuade the government that all of Louisiana's troops now in

Virginia ought to be sent back home. There is some reason to hope that their efforts will not be unsuccessful. If so, we'll be seeing one another shortly. But there now, I've told you something I ought not to have mentioned at all. My health is quite good as long as I stay in the infirmary, but it is invariably wretched after two or three days on the march. These starvation marches will be the death of me yet. The rest of life is bearable. But, oh how I long for the day when there will by no more marches!

At the present time we have the Yankees in an angle formed by the confluence of the Chickahominy and the James. I hope we don't let them slip by. What I fear is that their gunboats, which patrol both rivers, will keep us from making a quick concerted attack on their position; and the longer we hold off, the more chance there is that they'll receive reinforcements; in which case they'll be able to make a powerful counterattack against us. As far as our soldiers are concerned, we have an admirable, indeed an incomparable army. You have no idea until you see them in the heat of battle just how brave and patriotic these boys are. But on the other hand, our officers, even those of highest rank, are, for the most part, quite mediocre. I have no doubts but that half of our losses are due to their lack of judgment, their ineptitude, or their sheer negligence. I'll wait until I get home to tell you about the retreat from Williamsburg; it's an event about which I have many interesting anecdotes.

Adieu, mon cher Père, my twin brother in religion, the companion of my spiritual childhood and youth; pray for me (if you know how to pray), and give my very best wishes to all of Ours. And don't forget to remember me to Dr. Rohmer and to Mr. Parada.

Yours, wishing you everything you strive for in the Lord,

H. Gache, S.J.
Chap. 10th Reg., La. Vols.

COMMENTARY

The day Hippolyte Gache wrote this letter to Father Cornette "in the midst of these terrible events taking place," a concerned President Abraham Lincoln arrived from Washington at Harrison's Landing on the James to confer with General McClellan and to review the wounded Army of the Potomac which had completed its retreat to the Peninsula after the inconclusive Seven Days Campaign. Richmond had been saved for the Confederacy but the exhausted Army of Northern Virginia was not able to follow up on the victory.

After an ironic and not atypical comeuppance to Cornette for having the misfortune to have been born a Savoyard, the French chaplain explained that his 10th had not been engaged in the confused Battle of White Oak Swamp which had taken place on Monday, June 30. But he did administer to the wounded and dying, singling out for special mention a mortally wounded "old colonel." The only man that fits this description was Seneca Galusha Simmons (b. Vermont, December 1808–d. Glendale, Virginia, July 1, 1862), the commanding officer of the Fifth Pennsylvania Regiment who had assumed command of the Third Division on May 27, after the capture of Gen. John Fulton Reynolds, later killed at Gettysburg. Fort Simmons, Maryland, was named for this professional soldier and recipient of Gache's kindness on the battlefield near Glendale.[94]

The day following the Battle of White Oak Swamp, Tuesday, July 1, the final important engagement of the Seven Days Campaign was fought at Malvern Hill. This battle was as futile as it was costly for Lee's Army and the losses sustained by the Tenth Louisiana and the Third Alabama were particularly staggering. The latter reported 207 casualties out of 345 men and officers, a fact which was undoubtedly not known to Gache at the time he wrote this letter giving an incomplete tally of his own regiment's losses. Waggaman's charge up the slope of the hill and his seeming contempt for the enemy's artillery emplacements was later seen to epitomize the courage, suffering, and endurance of the 318 men of the 10th who followed their commanding officer. The aggregate loss of this charge represented more than 27% of the regiment: 13 killed; 36 wounded and 38 captured, among whom, as Gache reported, was the valiant Waggaman himself. Sent first to Fort Columbus, New York, and then to Fort Warren, Massachusetts, the colonel was exchanged on April 5, 1863, and returned to Louisiana. Early in 1864 he was put in command of the Louisiana brigades in Virginia, a position he held at Appomattox, where he had thrown away his ancestral sword rather than surrender it.[95]

Gache reported to Cornette that he had encountered three Union chaplains who had been captured during the course of the Seven Days Campaign. One of these, like his correspondent, was a Savoyard Jesuit, Peter Tissot (b. Megève, Kingdom of Sardinia, October 15, 1823–d. New York, July 19, 1875), a former student Gache had known at Mélan that followed his mentor to the Avignon novitiate in 1842. The same political conditions which had forced Father Hippolyte to leave France for Louisiana in 1846 set Tissot to New York, and on May 25, 1861, he was commissioned chaplain to the Thirty-seventh New York Infantry Regiment in which he served until his resignation on June 22, 1863. Tissot was a prolific writer and some of the war letters to his brother in France were judged edifying enough to be published in Pauline Jaricot's *Annales de la Propagation de la foi* and in the journal *Etudes.* This serious, pious and decidedly humorless man also kept a diary that was posthumously edited and published. It is in this diary that Tissot gave the circumstances of his capture on June 30 as well as some interesting reflections on the Catholics of Richmond, whom he was surprised to find, "if we except the Germans and a few Irish, strongly for the South." He learned to be careful about speaking politics with his host Bishop John McGill, who was "very kind, but very strong in his Southern convictions." On one occasion, after an altercation with a Richmond priest on the subject of the war, Tissot asked McGill for faculties to hear confessions. The bishop gladly granted his request—for Northern soldiers. "This did not satisfy me," the testy Tissot wrote. "I explained how I might be in some place where there might be Catholics living. Why could I not hear their confessions?" No doubt Gache had confided to the missionary-minded Jesuit his own experience with the French at Norfolk and the Irish at Bigler's Mill. " 'Well, you may,' he said, 'provided you do not talk against the South.' He (then gave) me the honor to make his confession to me. Before leaving . . . I offered him some money, which he refused to take."[96]

In late September 1861, when another New York infantry regiment, the 73rd, was formed and made part of the Fourth Excelsior Brigade, one of the first items of business was the election of a chaplain. The clergyman who won, and who was appointed to this post on October 9, reported the circumstances of his victory to a friend: ". . . over four hundred voted for a Catholic priest; one hundred fifty-four, for any kind of a Protestant minister; eleven for a Mormon elder; and the rest said they could go to hell without the assistance of the clergy." This chaplain was Tissot's fellow prisoner in Richmond, the Jesuit Joseph B. O'Hagan (b. Clogher, Tyronne, Ireland, August 15, 1826–d. at sea off the coast of Costa Rica, December 15, 1878). O'Hagan was somewhat less than impressed by the regiment that had honored him with such a vote of confidence. He noted that the

73rd was made up for the most part by first and second generation Irish Catholics, "but all the Catholicity they had was the faith infused into their souls by baptism. . . . Such a collection of men, I think, was never before united in one body since the flood. Most of them were the scum of New York society, reeking with vice and spreading a moral malaria around them." Long before his capture at Fair Oaks, O'Hagan and his flock had come to a better understanding; both the men and the chaplain had changed. "What an apostolic priest I was," he confessed, recalling his introduction to the 73rd, "ready to cry like a homesick girl, because I (had) not found every rough soldier a cultivated gentleman and a perfect Christian." Even though the men of the Louisiana Tenth never seemed to reach the same spiritual heights achieved by the troops of the New York Seventy-third, Gache admitted a similar reevaluation of his own regiment; without, however, reevaluating his own prejudices. O'Hagan's priorities were also similar to those of Gache: "I had a neat chapel built and I prepared a large number of young men for their first confession and Communion. They became attentive to their religious duties and I had as much to do in the ten regiments of the division as I could well look to. My work, though hard, became a labor of love." Resigning from the army in September 1863, at the request of his religious superior, O'Hagan reenlisted the following September, and in 1872, he was appointed president of Holy Cross College, Worcester, Massachusetts, a position he maintained until his death six years later. Tissot also became a college president after the war, serving in that capacity at Fordham in New York, but his delicate health which brought on an untimely death, forced an early retirement from college administration.[97]

In his diary Tissot identified the unnamed prisoner in Gache's letter, the third Union chaplain who shared McGill's hospitality with Gache, Bixio, Smulders, O'Hagan and Tissot. This was the colorful Thomas Scully (b. Ireland, March 24, 1833–d. Malden, Massachusetts, September 11, 1902), an Italian-educated priest from the Boston diocese who was chaplain to the Ninth Massachusetts Regiment from April 15, 1861 until October 31, 1862, and who, like his fellow prisoners, was destined to play a leading role in Catholic education after the war. During the acrimonious debates over an 1889 bill designed to outlaw parochial schools in Massachusetts, Scully was spontaneously and humorously defended by Thomas Wentworth Higginson (1823-1911), wartime commander of the First U.S. South Carolina Volunteers, later the Thirty-third Colored Infantry. To the consternation of adversaries to the Catholic position, this Protestant Yankee eulogized the scrappy Scully before the State Committee on Education, describing him as a liberal, a "healthy hornet" who, with the possible exception of the pope, feared no one—not even the redoubtable

Alonzo Ames Miner (1814-95). Miner was a Universalist divine, trustee of Harvard University and former president of Tufts College (1862-75) who spoke loudly and often against the danger of Catholic schools. This controversy made Scully a well-known figure in Massachusetts; but, at the time of his death, Protestants vied with Catholics to pour forth encomiums on the fallen combatant. In July 1863, however, he was not considered threatening enough to be even recognized by his captors who let him and his fellow priest prisoners of war "simply go without any condition or promise of any kind," barely two weeks after their capture.[98]

J.M.J.

Richmond
August 20, 1862

Rev. Father de Carrière

My dear Philip, P.C.

Here I am back from the campaign of Cedar Run or, if you will, Cedar Mountain, unscathed, but so worn out and exhausted that I have come to Richmond for a few days' rest. It is not exactly a pleasant one, this military life, especially under General Jackson. On [Monday] August 4, I left Richmond to join my regiment, and I caught up with them the next day at Gordonsville. They had brought my horse and baggage ahead with them. No sooner had I arrived than the regiment received orders to move ahead some eight miles farther in the direction of Orange Court House. I had no choice but to go with them. After a few miles march, made all the more difficult by a very slow pace, we halted in the late afternoon at the foot of a hill, where we made our camp on the slope, and awaited the dawn. Although I hadn't slept on the ground for the past two months, I managed fairly well. At any rate, I wasn't pestered by lice and bedbugs and that's more than I can say for some other beds I've slept in. Have you ever reflected that a bed stands or falls on the quality of its pillow? Now I am fortunate in having ready to hand a most excellent pillow. Mine is not a pillow of moss, nor is it of linen made, nor of cotton, nor yet is it with feathers stuffed. Pillows of such kind, you see, do not lend themselves to commodious transport. No, dear Father, difficult as it may be for you to believe this, my pillow is the saddle of my horse. With a saddle under one's head, one scarcely feels the pebbles that lie beneath him, be they the size of walnuts. It might be well here to add that nothing abounds more richly in this part of Virginia than rocks—small rocks, large rocks, all kinds of rocks. But back to the slope where we awaited the dawn.

Having received orders the next morning to continue the march, we finally got under way about ten o'clock. A snail's pace brought us to Orange Court House around one o'clock that afternoon. Five miles in three hours—that's not what I would call forced marching. Nevertheless, when we reached our destination we were more weary than had we covered the same distance in an hour's time. We had been obliged to endure an oppressively hot sun for three long hours. When we arrived at Orange Court House, we were given orders to halt right in the middle of the road, but within twenty minutes officers and soldiers alike had scattered off in all directions looking for shade. Orange Court House is a pleasant little town, agreeably situated in a valley and on the slopes of two small hills. As far as I could ascertain there was only one Catholic living there, and him I was not able to see. We had expected to leave town about four or five o'clock, but instead we camped, as we had the previous night, on a nearby slope.

The next morning, Saturday [August 9] distant drums and bugles began to sound at dawn. All of us knew what this meant. I got up and like everyone else went through the motions of grooming myself. No need, really, to dress, as we sleep fully clothed when on the march. I had just taken out my canteen and had poured out onto the corner of my towel the one or two drops that were to serve me for my extensive morning toilette, when I glanced over to the spot where I had tied my horse the previous night. Alas, she was nowhere in sight! Had she broken loose of her own free will in search of unchartered pastures, ungratefully abandoning her master—her master who had loved her as ardently as any horse has the right to expect—or had she been stolen? At that moment the reasons for her absence seemed less important than the fact that she was gone.

Immediately I began to search for her among the horses of all the regiments in the vicinity. Two men in different places told me that they had seen a pair of stray horses wandering about. This news raised my hopes, but a further search left me again disconsolate. Finally someone suggested that she might be in the company of a dozen or so assorted quadrupeds grazing in a nearby meadow. I went to see for myself. It was not yet daybreak, and although I had no trouble distinguishing the horses from their friends of other species, I did have some difficulty seeing the markings on those horses which were grazing. Their mere silhouettes, however, sufficed to assure me that my horse was not among them. Then I happened to notice two horses lying down in the grass some distance away. Could one of these be my Fanny? Twenty steps toward the first were enough to send me on my way to the other, the very last of the lot. Imagine my sentiments when this beast coyly whinnied her greetings! Immediately I saw that someone had removed the nice white rope I had put around her neck the night before; so I grabbed her by the mane and led her back to camp. By the time we arrived, everyone had finished his breakfast—all of the horses and all of the men. We were too late; and though it was all Miss Fanny's fault, it was I who had to suffer most.

It wasn't long after this that we broke camp and were on the march once again, this time at a faster pace. Around ten we crossed the Rapidan, rested briefly and then moved on. Toward noon we could hear a cannon firing not far away. The sound echoing through the valleys seemed to echo also in the hearts of our men, filling them with an emotion that found expression in lusty rebel yells. We pushed on eagerly; we didn't want to be late for this performance. Soon we could hear not only the roar of the cannon but even the crack of rifles; we knew for certain that our troops were routing the retreating Yankees. We pressed on even harder. What a pleasure it was to pursue an insolent enemy who had come to slaughter us and who was now fleeing in panic before us! I think this was the greatest thrill of my life, seeing our shells exploding in the midst of those confused and terrified troops!

Serious fighting began about two o'clock with an exchange of cannon fire, and by four the engagement had become a major battle. But it was not until a little before six o'clock that we took our place on the line, relieving a brigade that had been doing splendid fighting. The enemy was now retreating too rapidly for our infantry to keep up with them. All we could do was send some cavalry ahead to round up those who had the misfortune of not being able to run as fast as their companions-in-arms. While my battalion was slowly advancing in battle formation, I made a thorough tour of the area where the principal action of the day had taken place, and where the dead and wounded were still lying where they had fallen. The scene which now confronted me was no less horrible than what I had witnessed on the banks of the Chickahominy in the last days of June and the first days of July. There were at least as many dead and wounded as there had been there, and the sight of these unfortunate was no less heartrending. Faced with this carnage, I quite forgot the joy I had experienced when first I heard the sound of cannon and fusillade. All at once I was overwhelmed by a profound sadness: so many men only a few hours before so full of life now lying wounded, mutilated and grotesquely contorted: some dead; some in their last agony; some struggling desperately for life; some still fully conscious and therefore able to suffer more keenly, were calling out for doctors, for wound dressers; for something to drink, for help. One took me for a surgeon and begged: "For God's sake, cut off my leg! Now. Above the knee." He said he could feel the gangrene setting in. And he was right: the lower part of his leg was already purple. I told him I wasn't a doctor, that I was a priest, and that whereas I could do something for his soul, there was nothing I could do for his leg. The poor fellow was a Protestant Yankee; what I was saying meant nothing to him. "But don't you see, if they don't cut it off," he pleaded, "I'll be dead in a matter of hours." "That is quite possible," I replied. "Therefore, all the more reason, my boy, to think about your soul." After a few more words I left him, and went on to see if there were others that I might help.

I didn't find a single Catholic among the wounded, either of the North or of the South. Night was now falling and I was resigning myself to the fact that I had to leave the field without having been of any real help to anyone. The only good result of my activity was that it had caught the attention of a young Virginian, and perhaps even gained his admiration. In the past, this young man, who is a courier for one of the generals, had always greeted me respectfully and courteously whenever we met. He now found me assisting a Yankee who had been horribly wounded in the chest and in the arm. This poor lad had fallen head downwards into a small ditch, and there he had lain unable to move. I had just pulled him up to level ground and was trying to make him as comfortable as possible when the Virginia gentleman approached me and asked: "Do you think these dogs deserve any pity?"

"I do indeed," I answered. "When an enemy is vanquished and can no longer do you any harm, he is no longer an enemy; he is simply an unfortunate human being who has a right to Christian charity. Besides, I'm a Catholic priest and my work here doesn't allow me to make any distinction between Yankees and boys from the South. I see all men as redeemed by the Blood of Jesus Christ. Believing this I can hardly do otherwise than show sympathy to all and animosity to none. Don't you see what I mean?"

"Maybe, but that's not the way they acted toward us."

"On that point, then, they're wrong; and that's their affair. But it doesn't follow that we should act without justice and magnanimity merely because they lack these virtues in dealing with us. On the contrary, if they treat us badly, all the more reason why we should treat them well. This isn't worldly wisdom, but it is Christianity, and that, after all, is what I'm trying to practice."

"Oh, that's true. Of course, that's true. I'm not a Catholic myself, but I have a lot of friends who are. And I admire them too. What impresses me about Catholics and the reason why I respect them is because of the unshakeable tenacity with which they hold to their beliefs. Once they adopt a principle as an article of their faith, that's all there is to it. The case is closed. As far as they are concerned, the principle stands for all times and all places."

"Quite so," I replied. "And don't you understand why that is? It's because they have certitude that they have the truth even though other religions are always changing their principles. You've noticed this, haven't you?"

"Uh, maybe."

And on that note we parted. Now every time he sees me he gives me a warm greeting and reminds me of the circumstances of our first meeting. I should tell you, by the way, that a true Virginian as a rule is very religious, and he always shows a great deal of respect for any "minister of the Gospel." Before I left this scene of carnage, I witnessed another sight which I will not soon forget, a sight which at the same time disgusted and infuriated me. While I was circulating among the dead and wounded, I noticed that some of our soldiers were doing the same thing. These wretched men (and their number was greater than you might suppose) were not concerned with bringing help to the wounded, but in emptying their pockets and stealing their clothes. They had remained behind on some pretext or other while the brigade advanced, and they were now busy at their shameless and disgusting work. There were some who went so far as to strip a dead man of every last piece of his clothing to leave his body lying naked in the dust. I came upon two of these ghouls kneeling on either side of a corpse they had just despoiled fighting about who should keep the poor man's canteen. I felt such revulsion that I simply had to say something. But what could words mean to men who had been insensible to the grim scene itself?

It was close to seven o'clock when I rejoined my regiment. They had advanced only a mile or so from the place where I had left them. We marched along slowly for about another half-mile, and then just as we had reached the top of a hill, we were given the order to stop. Now one of the most interesting operations of the battle was about to take place. Facing us, less than a mile away, was another hill crowned with a rather thick forest of pine and oak. Hidden under the hospitable foliage of those woody perennials was a whole brigade of newly arrived Yankee troops. The Federals we were pursuing thought we didn't know that there were reinforcements at this point; consequently they assumed that we would continue along the road through the forest and eventually be trapped between them and the new troops who could close in behind us. But we were not so naive as they supposed. General Jackson was perfectly aware of the situation. Thanks to his scouts, he knew that the enemy had taken cover in the forest and he knew that backing up these troops was a considerable force which had just arrived. So what did he do? He ordered us to continue the march down the slope as if we were unaware of the trap. Then when we arrived at the bottom of the valley, he ordered us to halt and allowed us to rest without breaking ranks. Meanwhile, he brought three pieces of artillery up from the rear and placed these in a hidden position near the summit. No sooner were these cannons in place than they were put into action. For almost thirty minutes bombs and shells were bursting in all parts of the woods. I won't go so far as to say that our shells fell as thick as hailstones, but during the entire time of the bombardment few of their troops could enjoy a single moment of safety. It was thrilling to watch the shells streaking through the air, then bursting against the trees with a blast as loud as that with which they had been fired; or to see them fall between trees into the air. The affair was a success in every respect except that the gathering darkness and the thickness of the trees prevented us from enjoying the sight of Yankees fleeing in panic from the very place where they had hoped to entrap us.

About eight o'clock we resumed the march, passing through the woods from which we had dislodged the enemy. Soon we were on the far side of these woods, in a clearing of high grass with only a few trees here and there. Ahead of us, about 500 yards away, was another wooded area where the Yankees had taken over. I was under the impression that our artillery had followed us and was soon going to do to the second wood what it had done with notable success to the first. Shortly afterwards a few volleys about a mile away on the left confirmed this suspicion. (We were on the extreme right flank). The order which came at the same time to advance fifty paces into the field in battle formation and to lie down in the grass removed all doubt. As I had not made my evening prayer, I thought that now would be a good opportunity to do so. I took my horse by the bridle and led her back near the edge of the wood to a little meadow where she could graze and where I could pray in peace. Hardly had I begun my act of faith, hope and charity when—zoooom—a shell exploded against a tree, scarce twenty-five feet away. "Well now, what was that?" I mused. "Could it be that our troops don't know we are here, or can their aim be so poor that they are missing the enemy and hitting us?" Hardly had this question formed itself in my mind when I was further distracted by a second blast, so powerful that my horse lost all interest in her food. The poor beast was not accustomed to music with her meals. Wishing to reassure her, and fearing that she might be concerned about my safety, I decided we had best remove ourselves from the line of fire. After all, I reasoned, the source of these projectiles matters little; it is their destination that counts. A few moments later I found myself in the presence of the regimental commanding officer. "What is the meaning of this, Major?" I asked, "Is it our friends or our enemies who are shelling us?" "It isn't our friends," said he, "And for your safety let me recommend that you lie down and keep quiet." I readily complied with his suggestion and lay down on the grass next to him, still holding the bridle of my horse, who, incidentally, seemed to find courage in the reassuring presence of the major's horse.

What had deceived me when I first noticed the firing was the fact that the two wooded areas became very close together at our extreme left flank, and this fact, together with the darkness of the on-coming night prevented me from telling which side the shots had come from. After the Yankees had sufficiently amused themselves by shelling the woods where they supposed us to be and where in fact no one was, they had the unhappy inspiration to begin shelling the field where in fact we were. As long as the projectiles were falling fifty or more yards away the affair still possessed a certain charm. When they began falling into our ranks and even to pass between the major and me, who were scarcely two yards apart, and then to pass between our two horses, who were even closer together; when shells began to explode just above our heads and strike some of our men in a manner that was rude and inconducive to good health—well, that was a different story altogether! Besides, at every instant we expected to see a whole brigade of carbine-shooting Yankees rushing at us from out of the woods, less than a hundred yards away. Had they, in fact, so appeared, they could with a single volley have killed half of us and put the rest of us in critical condition. Let me assure you that this was not a particularly enjoyable thirty minutes lying in that field while bombs and shells were exploding on all sides, and I am convinced that many who haven't prayed since God knows when recommended themselves more than once to the Blessed Virgin. I had no fear of death for myself, but I was concerned about the others, particularly those who were not at all prepared to die. More than once I said a *memorare* for them, begging our dear Mother to divert the shells from their direction.

This barrage finally stopped about a quarter to nine, enabling us to retire to the wooded area that I spoke about previously. Here we stretched ourselves out and were soon snoring loudly, our slumber utterly unimpeded by any overindulgence in banquet fare. Naturally we had lookouts posted between our bivouac and the Yankee encampment. Several times during the night these frightened guards came running back with what always turned out to be false alarms: they saw Yankees coming from all directions, marching in formation, yet crouching as low as possible in order to take us by surprise. But in spite of those panicky interruptions, the night passed quickly, and as soon as it was light enough we could see the enemy calmly setting up batteries on a height just in front of the wooded area where they had fired on us. Soon they would be ready to continue the bombardment which night had interrupted.

I couldn't understand why we weren't doing anything to stop them from setting up these positions, and at any moment I was expecting to hear a volley from one of our *tormenta bellicosa* that would send them running like sheep, or I expected to see some of our cavalry or infantry storm their positions. What I didn't realize was at that very moment they outnumbered us four to one, and they were most anxious for us to provoke an attack, thinking that this would give them the opportunity to make up for the losses of the previous day. But if I was ignorant of their strength, our general in command was certainly very much aware of it, and while we were impatiently awaiting the command to charge, he gave the order to retreat. Seeing that we hesitated to begin battle, the enemy began firing at us; so, in order to confuse them we advanced a bit then retreated; advanced again, retreated again, and continued doing this for several times. Then, as soon as the baggage was a safe distance away, we retreated slowly and in perfect order. It was a fine retreat; I don't think a single piece of materiel was lost. During the two day engagement we had only three killed and four wounded from our regiment; yet the number of our casualties was the highest of the whole brigade. Even though I was with the men all of the time, there were only two of these to whom I could be of any service. Indeed, there were but three that I spoke to at all; the others were either already dead or had been rushed back to the rear in ambulances by the time I learned of their injuries.

At seven o'clock we were back again at Orange Court, and here I learned that General Jackson intended to follow a new plan in dealing with the Yankees, one which called for no immediate engagements with the enemy. Here I also took stock of my own physical condition and tried to determine what plans I should make for the future. These past twelve days on the march—at night sleeping on the bare earth, soaked to the bone by the icy dew which covers everything; during the day exposed to the fierce heat, and moving about in an ever present cloud of dust; eating next to nothing (for three whole days my stomach had to content itself with hardtack and spring water, a diet that did more harm than three months of wholesome food would have done good)—these twelve days on the march, I say, utterly wore me out. Add to these physical hardships the total lack of all spiritual consolations. During the whole campaign not once was I able to offer mass—not even on

Sunday, not even on the feast of the Assumption [August 15]. Taking all of these circumstances into consideration, I decided to spend a few days in Richmond at the sisters' convent to consider whether I would be capable of rejoining my regiment; and, if so, whether I ought to do so. As difficult as my first year of military service had been, it now seems that my second would be even more so, and I'm beginning to have grave doubts as to whether I will be able to stick it out. I'm very sorry that the blockade prevents me from communicating with Father Jourdan. His decision would relieve me of all worry as to what I should do, and it would leave me secure in the quiet peace of obedience.

Father Hubert, even though we are both in the same brigade, was not at the Battle of Cedar Creek, as his regiment had been detained at Richmond, for some reason or other, two or three days before the battle began. And anyway, despite all his military enthusiasm, he was by no means eager to be there. Nor would I have advised him to go, even had this been possible. I met him shortly after I took leave from my regiment, and he's looking very well indeed. He is much better situated than I: his regiment is composed solely of gentlemen, among whom there is a considerable number of good Catholics who take excellent care of him. It is quite otherwise with me.

Adieu, mon bon Père. Father Cornette requested that I send long and frequent letters. I'm afraid from the length of this missive you'll find that I took his suggestion a bit too literally. Next letter I'll try to keep within bounds. Every best wish to Ours and my affectionate greetings to Doctor Rohmer and to Mr. Parada.

Your brother and friend in Our Lord,
H. Gache, S.J.

COMMENTARY

After Malvern Hill General McClennan withdrew to the Peninsula where he remained planning a new offensive against Richmond. To facilitate the execution of his plan, Maj. Gen. John Pope (1822-92), now in command of a newly formed and potentially larger army in the northwest, that is, in the Shenandoah Valley, laid out a complementary strategy in mid-July designed to draw the Confederate forces from the southeast. Anticipating Pope's threat, Lee had already dispatched Gen. "Stonewall" Jackson's decimated division from the Army of Northern Virginia to the northeast. After July 19 Jackson dug himself in at the important railroad junction town of Gordonsville to await reinforcements, part of which was a newly organized Second Louisiana Brigade under the command of Col. Leroy Stafford (1822-64). This brigade, made up of five regiments, one of which was the 10th, and two special batallions, was sent by rail to Gordonsville on the thirty-first where it was assigned to Jackson's division. Two days later Pope began his offensive by marching south from the Culpeper area toward Orange Court House. Meanwhile, Stafford's Brigade had been detached from Jackson's division, which was already comprised of brigades commanded by Thomas, Branche, Archer, Pender, and Field. It was during these days crowded with anticipation that the 10th set up a new encampment some four miles from Gordonsville, and here it was on Monday, August 4, that Gache joined the regiment. Then on Thursday, the seventh —Monier incorrectly stated that it was the sixth—the Light Division broke camp and began the snail's pace march toward Orange. Finally, after a day of confusion, frustration and blistering heat, Colonel Stafford's Louisiana Brigade fell in behind Pender's at dawn on Saturday the ninth, and continued the march toward the rendezvous with the Federals beneath Slaughter's Mountain that claimed 2,381 Union and 1,307 Confederate casualties.[99]

Gache informed de Carrière that when he arrived at the battlefield, about 6:00 p.m., he did not remain with the brigade that was being kept in reserve on the left flank, but that he went ahead visiting the terrain where most of the action had taken place between four and five o'clock, that is where the famous Stonewall Brigade had broken when the Federals encircled their flank. It was here also where the first brigades of the Light Division had passed and where the chaplain met and conversed with an aide-de-camp to one of the generals. Who was this Virginian? The most likely candidate is Capt. Murray Forbes Taylor (b. Falmouth, Virginia, December 24, 1843–d. Spotsylvania County, Virginia, November 20, 1909), an aide-de-camp to Maj. Gen. Ambrose Powell Hill (1825-65), whom Gache never identified by name, even when he referred to him later in this letter. Hill was ignorant of how the Light Division was to fit into General Jackson's overall plan and, therefore, he kept his aides busy racing from one congested Brigade to another. Such a courier would have been highly visible to the troops of Stafford's Brigade, particularly on the eighth of August. Moreover, since Taylor had been on the spot near the 10th during the Seven Days Campaign, it is highly probable that the chaplain and the courier had noticed one another. Finally, this eighteen-year-old Virginian was the only one of Hill's aides not wounded at Cedar Mountain, and therefore the only one who could have saluted Gache so warmly whenever the two met after the battle, reminding the priest "of the circumstances of our first meeting." Taylor enlisted in the Thirteenth Virginia Infantry on April 17, 1861 from the Virginia Military Institute and was assigned to the task of drilling raw recruits. He so impressed the commanding officer of the 13th, the then Col. A.P. Hill, by "his good moral and mental qualities," and Gen. Joseph E. Johnston, who concurred with Hill's judgment, that despite his age, Taylor was commissioned 1st lieutenant on June 14, 1862 and assigned to Hill as an aide-de-camp. It was Capt. Murray Taylor who brought the news from Chancellorsville to Lee that Jackson and Hill had been wounded in battle and that Stuart had been ordered by the latter to assume command. After Hill's death, Taylor served Longstreet and was present at Appomattox with Lee. The war had impoverished the captain who moved first to Alabama and then to California where, in 1892, he was employed by recently widowed Phoebe Apperson Hearst (1842-1919) as overseer to her 48,000 acre Rancho Piedra Blanca in San Luis Obispo County. Under the Virginian's management this former Mexican land grant became the nucleus of the fabulous San Simeon Ranch. Taylor was handsomely rewarded for his services to the Hearst family and when he retired in 1908, Phoebe Apperson presented him with the deed to "Fall Hill," the Taylor ancestral estate in Spotsylvania County. So it was that the young lieutenant at Cedar Mountain returned to his native Virginia.[100]

Murray Taylor was wounded once during the war, at Petersburg, while he was with Col. William Johnson Pegram (1841-65), the commanding officer of Pegram's (Virginia) Artillery—"the boy artillerist"—who fought his way up from a private to a colonel and who was killed at Five Forks, seven days before Appomattox. At Cedar Mountain it was Pegram who provided the intense artillery fire that so delighted Gache, giving him the opportunity, despite the growing darkness of the evening, to see "Yankees fleeing in panic from the very place where they had hoped to entrap us." By that hour the chaplain had joined his regiment which was engaged in the mopping up exercise after Branche's victorious pursuit of Rolland's Brigade on the left side of the Orange-Culpeper road. Passing through the bloody wheat field, then through some wooded area, and finally down to a grassy meadow, the regiment experienced an artillery barrage from the Second and Fifth Maine Batteries of Ricketts' Brigade. The unnamed commanding officer with whom Gache huddled on this occasion was William H. Spencer (b. Kentucky, 1823–d. Manassas, Virginia, August 30, 1862), the erstwhile editor of the Opelousas *Courier*, who had been elected major on January 16, 1862, and assumed command of the 10th after Waggaman's capture at Malvern Hill. Spencer had come up to New Orleans from St. Laundry Parish with the Prud'homme brothers in the spring of 1861 and was elected captain of the Confederate State Rangers, Company C of the 10th, after July 22.[101]

In a letter to his nephew, more than twenty-five years after Cedar Mountain, Gache gave one more detail of the events of that memorable day. He recalled that he had been in the saddle when the Maine batteries began their barrage and that one shell fell so close that his poor horse "went right down on her belly for a few seconds without harming me at all." Gache never mentioned when he had managed to commandeer this beast which seemed to cause him so much trouble and to which he had a genuine attachment. He certainly had her during the Seven Days Campaign, as he himself has indicated. Also the records show that he requested forage for the month of June. "Inadmissible" was the response from the Quartermaster General's Office which reminded him that "Chaplains of the Mounted Regts. only, are allowed forage." But apparently Bixio was not the only *débrouillard* in Virginia.[102]

J.M.J.

Lynchburg
November 18,1862

Reverend Father Cornette
Spring Hill

Reverend and dear Father, P.C.

In a letter I wrote to Father Gautrelet about two weeks ago, I promised to inform you of my whereabouts as soon as I was settled. Today I am finally able to keep my promise. I'm now in Lynchburg, but for how long nobody knows. I am truly sorry that I had to take leave of the tribe of Dan, because, even though Virginia is not the Promised Land and even though I was not living amidst the Chosen People; nevertheless, I did see wondrous events in Danville, and I was able to do more good there than I can ever hope to do here. By the time I left I had an active little congregation of about eighty persons. They were all very conscientious about attending Sunday Mass, and in spite of my halting speech and my accent, they listened to my catechetical instructions with flattering attention. Some of them even appeared to have been pleased with what they heard. The Protestants (and there were always a few of them present) were delighted to hear Christian doctrine presented with such clarity, precision, and economy—qualities which they have never observed in their own ministers. "I've listened to sermons preached hundreds of times on baptism," one was heard to remark, "but I declare, I didn't know what it really meant until I heard that priest there explain it."

Because there isn't a single priest in the vicinity, my presence was all the more necessary; for never have I seen a place where Protestantism reigned with such absolute sway. The only notions which the local people have of Catholicism are derived from ridiculous and slanderous fables which thrive in a Protestant milieu. You know what I mean: hackneyed yarns about confessions, indulgences, worshipping the saints and the like. And, of course, all of this nonsense is accepted as Gospel truth. These people honestly and sincerely believe Catholics are low scoundrels of the most unscrupulous type, capable of committing any crime (even idolatry) that has ever been attributed to us by the Reformers. I met only one person there who was an exception to this rule—Mrs. [Elizabeth] Stuart, the mother of the general who has done such wicked things to the poor Yankees.

Two days after my arrival in Danville, this good lady came to the convent to see the sisters (I think it was her first visit) and to ask them if they could lend her a life of St. Ignatius Loyola. I should explain that she had spent her early years in St. Louis, Missouri, and it was here that she met Mère [Philippine] Duchesne, a Religious of the Sacred Heart. On one occasion the Reverend Mother had given the young girl a biography of St. Ignatius to read, and Mrs. Stuart had found the book captivating. She now explained to the sisters at Danville that she wanted to re-read this fascinating life of the founder of our Society. Mother Superior explained that although there was no life of St. Ignatius in the convent, there was something even better—a son of St. Ignatius, and that perhaps he could procure the biography. Then: "Do you mean to say that there is a Jesuit here?"

"Yes Madame, our present chaplain is a Jesuit," Mother Superior replied.

"Oh, I would be delighted to see him. Here is my card. Would you kindly present it to him for me, and beg him to pay me a visit at his earliest convenience."

Mother Superior promised that she would convey the message, and about a fortnight later I found myself engaged in a conversation with a marvelous old lady who was every bit as charming as I had anticipated. She told me that she had always had the highest esteem and the utmost respect for Catholic priests. Then she informed me that when she was a girl she had been forewarned, as so many Protestants are, against us, but that later on, having had the opportunity to associate with Catholics and to read some of our books, she came to the conclusion that somehow, either through malice or through ignorance, we had been falsely represented. This discovery had led her to seek further information, and at last she made up her mind that Catholics were as good as anyone else, and probably were no further from the truth than were the Protestants. "Right now," she went on to assure me, "I believe most of the doctrines that Catholics hold and the Protestants reject. For example, I believe in miracles, in the Communion of Saints, and I also believe in confession."

"Well now, Mrs. Stuart," I said, "you're more of a Catholic than any other Protestant I've ever met. Let's hope that one of these days you'll come all the way over and have done with it."

She laughed at this, but said nothing further. However, during our conversation she told me that she liked our churches very much as she found their silence and their atmosphere conducive to prayer. For this reason, she explained, whenever she was in a city where there was a Catholic church, she made it a point to drop in for a visit to say her prayers there. What a pity it is that she had no contact with a Catholic lady with similar tastes and background. One, for example, like Mrs. [Mary] Dorrance. Undoubtedly her becoming a Catholic would be no small matter. Perhaps I myself could have been instrumental in this conversion, as well as in the conversions of three or four others in the region, if only I had stayed at Danville. . . . But Divine Providence had other plans for me, and there is no point in thinking about it any further.

The work here at Lynchburg will never put me in an early grave. The local pastor [Oscar Sears], a very pleasant young Virginian, has been appointed hospital military chaplain (the additional eighty piastres alloted to the "Reverend Captains" will considerably augment his meager salary), and he and I have divided the thirty Lynchburg hospitals between us. This means that each of us has from 1,500 to 2,000 patients to look after. If all of these sick and wounded were Catholics, or even if they were interested in becoming Catholics, we would have more than enough work to fill our idle hours. But alas! It's hardly an exaggeration to say that about one out of every twenty is a Catholic. And of this number only about one-fifth are sick enough to be confined to bed. This should give you some indication that the Catholic hospital chaplains at Lynchburg are in no danger of being crushed by the burden of overwork.

You might be tempted to ask: "Well, don't you do anything for the Protestants?" Very little; except perhaps in the hospitals run by the sisters. What, after all, could I do? The men who are not sick enough to be confined to their beds are never any place in sight. The bedridden are easy enough to approach, and if they are not suffering too much, they are glad to have a visitor, but we're not any further advanced on that account. Generally the poor men have been warned against Catholics; so what good would it do to argue with such people? And how, in the midst of their sufferings and ignorance, can I draw their attention to the type of serious instruction that they need? You'll say: "But you only have to give the essential points." That may be true; but I have found very few who are well enough disposed to give me their attention at all, and even with these few I've been able to do next to nothing. After I had instructed them and had given them sufficient preparation for baptism (for I was always sure that they were going to die), a minister would come along and undo all my work. The next time I would see them, I would find them completely changed and unwilling to discuss the matter further. They would say: "I don't believe it would do me any good," or, "I'll be baptized when I go home."

In the hospitals of the Daughters of Charity the situation is somewhat different. The presence of the nuns working long hours in the midst of the sick, and the care and attention that they lavish on them is a constant sermon which, if it does not enlighten the understanding of men, touches at any rate and wins their hearts, and disposes them in a wondrous way to be receptive to the priest's instruction and to receive the faith. Normally it is enough for the sick to see these saintly women at work for a period of three or four days; then they are willing to believe in the "sisters' church." For these men the proof of the Catholic church is the life of the sisters. I have asked some men in the hospitals conducted by the nuns if they would like to be baptized Catholics. "Oh, no," they'd reply, "I don't like that church a bit! I've never seen a Catholic, but I've heard a lot about them. The sisters' church is the church for me!"

"But the 'sisters' church' is the Catholic church," I'd say.

"Oh, I don't think so. At least nobody has ever said that."

"All right then," I'd add. "Let's ask one of the sisters," and I'd call one of the nuns over to the bed. "Sister," I'd ask, "is it true that you belong to the Catholic church?"

"Yes sir, it's true," she'd reply. "And that's the source of the greatest happiness I have in this life."

"Well, I declare," the patient would say. "I'd never have suspected it. I've heard so many things . . . I thought Catholics were the worst people on earth."

"I hope you don't think so now."

"Well, sister . . . I'll tell you. If you say you're a Catholic, I'll certainly have a better opinion of Catholics from now on." And the next thing you'd know they'd be asking on their death beds to be baptized in the Catholic church.

Here's another story about the sisters that you might find interesting. It was told to me by an eyewitness. One night during the Battle of Richmond a company of Texans was on picket watch near the Chickahominy. Five of them were brewing coffee on a rustic hearth which they had improvised 'neath a noble oak, with the intention of using this stimulating liquid to repulse the advances of Morpheus. Whilst the Brazilian brew was slowly absorbing calories propelled from the blazing pine chips beneath (forgive me if my description is a heresy in physics; my doctorate is not in that science, as you know)—whilst all of this was, I say, taking place, the talk turned to the subject of religion. As all five were Protestants, it wasn't long before someone added a dash of anti-Catholic seasoning. Others might have said more along this same line, but they were cut short by one member of the group who cried! "Stop friends, stop! I don't know what Catholics are, what they believe, nor what they do; but since I was attended, in my sickness, by the Daughters of Charity at Richmond, I swore never to allow anyone to speak against their church in my presence. Please do not oblige me to go further to fulfill my oath." The remaining young theologians, who expected to hear anything but a warning like that, stopped short and changed the subject.

In their capacity as nurses in the military hospitals, the Daughters of Charity, scarce though they may be, do a great deal of good for the church. They are in daily contact with a multitude of persons: doctors, army officers, government agents, and particularly with the ordinary soldiers. Most of these men either know the church not at all or know it through the sermons and scurrilous pamphlets of Protestant ministers. But because of their esteem, their repect and their admiration for the sisters, those who were once wary of us become less wary or, sometimes, even favorably disposed. Let us hope that this good impression made by the sisters will not be easily forgotten, and that it will be a source of salvation for many. When I consider how little I have been able to accomplish, it's consoling to think of all that these sisters have done. And, as these good women could never remain in Lynchburg unless I stayed with them as their chaplain, or unless they could find another priest to take my place, I feel that I can appropriate to myself, as *sine qua non*, some of the good works they do.

As far as living conditions are concerned, they are much better here than they were at Danville. The building in which we are presently lodged is a two-storied, four-towered castle. Each floor consists of four very large rooms of equal size divided by a hallway running north and south. The doctors occupy three of these rooms on the ground floor (the fourth being reserved as the sisters' parlor) whereas we have the upper floor to ourselves: the sisters live on one side of the hall and Our Lord and I live on the other. I have my own entrance into the chapel, the connecting door from my room. I might add that I've put my bed against the wall near this door, not only in order to say that I sleep on the doorsill of the Lord, but also in order to remain as near as possible to the altar. I realize that you are not religious enough to understand such a sentiment. Hence, I have not recounted it for your benefit, but rather for the edification of Father de Carrière, who, as is generally agreed, is more otherworldly than yourself. This bit of information will serve, I hope, as fitting response to a remark he made some time ago. But lest I seem to disparage your own piety, let me remark that I have noticed a new spiritual refinement in you since you began preaching to the Visitation nuns. Delicately pious sentiments now flow so freely from your pen—to my great surprise, but to my even greater consolation. And then there was that pretty little holy card with our own two names written on the back. You have no idea what that meant to me! But shall I try to tell you? Do forgive me for speaking so frankly, but I have never thought of you as an apt pupil for the school of convent piety. It gives me great pleasure now to discover how grievously I have underestimated you. But now in all seriousness, be sure, please, the next time you go to the convent to thank the nuns for their good prayers, and assure them that I think of them often, especially at mass. Meanwhile, back to my chateau.

The greater part of the compound now serves as a hospital; our building, formally the home of the president of the college, was originally built in the grand style of an Italian villa by a wealthy man who then put the property up for sale. It was subsequently purchased by a company of speculators who added two more structures (which from the outside look exactly like the original private home) and turned the whole shebang into a college. Today this notable architectural composition, with its twelve crenelated towers, its balconies and colonnades, its Gothic doors and windows, seems to take itself quite seriously. But when all is said and done, it is just a great pile of bricks, a pastiche of chicken coops, replete with nooks and crannies and quaint little closets, in the whole vast expanse of which you would have trouble finding two or three practical, ordinary rooms. It would be hard to imagine a more disagreeable or more inconvenient place to live. The very existence of this assemblage argues convincingly that the New World has not yet come of age.

I could, dear Father, continue to write more in this vein and to illuminate yet many a page with the same fine brush, but let me not run the risk of wearying you. Besides, I would never want to encourage you to believe that the format of my letters is always eight pages, neither more nor less. So let us be done with it. Now that you have become so lovable let me send you a brotherly embrace along with the wish that you have a happy, and particularly tranquil New Year. Finally, let me assure you that I am your "*Frère de lait*" and will remain so until such time as your growth in beauty matches your growth in virtue.

L.H. Gache, S.J.
Chaplain C.S.A.

P.S. My very best regard to all our fathers and brothers, and please remember me to good Doctor Rohmer and to Mr. Parada, if he is still with you. When you see Bishop Quinlan please, if you remember to do so, give him my most respectful greetings.

COMMENTARY

The five Daughters of Charity eulogized by Gache in this letter came from Richmond to the military hospital at Manassas in January 1862, but in mid-March, when this installation was then destroyed, three of the sisters were reassigned to Gordonsville where, as North Carolina-born Sister Angela Heath (1830-1912) noted in her journal, "the sick were very poorly provided for, although the mortality was not as great as at Manassas." But then Gordonsville was judged too close to the Federal lines, and so the nuns were once more ordered to move, this time to far off Danville where, joined by two more companions from Richmond, they arrived on May 2. At this prison camp center "most of our patients were Catholics, at least in name," observed Sister Angela, possibly with some exaggeration, and their spiritual needs were met by the ubiquitous chaplain of the Eighth Louisiana, who in late summer was "transferred" to Warrenton, North Carolina. Egidius Smulders' departure left the sisters without a chaplain, a fact which most probably explains why Gache was assigned to Danville, after being detached from the 10th which, now reassigned to Johnston's division under the command of Brig. Gen. William B. Taliaferro (1822-98), had sustained great losses in the follow-up battles after Cedar Mountain at the end of the month.[103] Gache did not note the exact date when he arrived at Danville, but most probably it was before these series of engagements, subsequently called Second Manassas, since he was credited with room and rations at his new post from September 1; although he was not officially detached from the 10th and assigned to Danville until November 29, at which date he was already in Lynchburg.[104] Nor did he make mention in this letter of the living conditions at his first hospital assignment. No doubt they were an improvement on camp life, but Sister Angela also reported seeing "wondrous events in Danville" of a different nature from those recorded by the new chaplain. The makeshift convent, she wrote, "would have been a kind of luxury had it not been the abode of innumerable rats, of whom we stood in greatest awe, for they seemed to be the proprietors of the mansion. During the night, shoes, stockings, etc., were carried off, and indeed, safe we did not feel for our fingers and toes, which we often found, on waking, locked in the teeth of our bold visitors."[105]

In this letter Gache recounted a conversation he had with Gen. J. E. B. Stuart's mother, Elizabeth Letcher (Pannill) Stuart (b. Pittsylvania County, Virginia, January 4, 1801–d. near Lebanon, Russell County, Virginia, August 31, 1884). At the time of Elizabeth's death, her daughter-in-law, Ellen Spotter (Brown) Stuart, recorded in the family Bible that this woman, who had such a powerful influence on moulding the personality of her celebrated son, was herself "one of the most intellectual and cultured women in Virginia." Gache's account of their chat in the improvised Danville convent is an attestation to the fact that this epitaph was not exaggerated. But, unlike other famous members of the Pannill and Letcher families, Elizabeth Pannill has surprisingly passed all but unknown into history. In 1817 she married Archibald Stuart (1795-1855), a compulsive gambler who, within two years of the marriage, had wagered and lost "Seneca Hill," his handsome estate in Campbell County, and had exposed his wife and rapidly growing family to financial ruin. Something had to be done quickly, and so in 1819 the improvident Archibald threw himself on the good graces and hospitality of his father, Alexander Stuart (1770-1832), a former United States district judge in the Illinois territory, who, some twelve years previously, had settled at Florissant, St. Louis County, Missouri. The same year Judge Stuart received Archibald, Elizabeth and their young children, Mère Philippine Duchesne (b. Grenoble, France, August 29, 1769–d. St. Louis, Missouri, November 18, 1852) and four Sacred Heart nuns opened a convent and school for Indian girls at Florissant, on property given them by Bishop DuBourg. In 1832 Judge Stuart moved to nearby St. Louis to take his place on the circuit bench; the Archibald Stuarts returned to Virginia, and twelve Jesuits with six slaves arrived from Maryland to settle on the DuBourg farm at Florissant, the modest beginning of St. Louis University. It was therefore somewhere between late 1819 and early 1823 that Elizabeth Stuart first met Philippine Duchesne, certainly one of the most intellectual and cultured women in Missouri, and received from her a biography of the founder of the Society of Jesuits, St. Ignatius Loyola. Ellen Stuart further recorded with telling emphasis in the family Bible that her mother-in-law "though charitable to all denominations, was a *High Church Episcopalian.*" Gache's letter shows that at the time when the long controversy between the evangelical and high-church movement in Virginia had become most bitter, Elizabeth Stuart clearly preferred the beauty of worship and the centrality of ritual acts. Presumably she maintained this position, through the schism of 1873-74, right up to the day of her death.[106]

If Gache failed to describe his Danville quarters, he more than made up for this omission by a flamboyant sketch of his Lynchburg lodgings. Despite fires and trends, which have slightly modified its original design, the structure in which Gache lived from 1862 to 1865 still stands at 1300 10th Street, Lynchburg. It was built between 1845 and 1850 as a residence for Charles K. Craille, and immediately was given the name of "Craille's Folly" because, like Father Hippolyte, the citizens of Lynchburg regarded it as pretentious. On February 12, 1856, Nathaniel H. Campbell, Craille's son-in-law, sold it and the adjoining property for the outrageous sum of $8,000 to the trustees of the Old Lynchburg College, a Methodist institution which did not survive the war.[107] In this letter he cited only one new name, that of Mary A. Dorrance (b. Georgia, 1813–d. Mobile, Alabama, March 23, 1865), the first wife of Charles W. Dorrance. A woman of independent wealth, cultivated tastes and civic interests, she was a long time resident of Mobile and a close friend to the Jesuits at Spring Hill and to the nuns of the Visitation Convent.[108]

Lynchburg
March 8, 1863

[Philip de Carrière]

Reverend and dear Father,

Your last letter, the one in which you informed me of the death of Brother [Emmanuel] Brenans, did somehow reach me. It arrived quite by chance; thanks to the erroneous, scandalous, and even heretical manner in which you addressed it, it had already gone astray and was well on the road to gehenna when an acquaintance of mine luckily discovered it and put it back on the straight and narrow path. Why, dear Father, oh, why is it that on the envelopes of those letters which I have the honor and pleasure to receive from you, you insist on indulging a taste for phantasmagoria! Why don't you use the address that I unfailingly send you, at least every time I change my residence? Now just what did you mean by "in care of the Catholic bishop?" Is it that you recognize the existence of bishops other than Catholic bishops? Even if there are others in other parts of the world, Bishop McGill is the bishop of Richmond and there are no pretenders to the title. And what do you mean by "the Catholic chaplain?" Are there any other chaplains than Catholic chaplains? Is it your intention to acknowledge an ecclesiastic character on the souls of the so-called Protestant ministers? If you do, you are simply a heretic, and I'll leave it up to Father Serra to pronounce the sentence you deserve. If you do not mean to recognize such a character, just what distinction do you wish to convey by employing the adjective "Catholic?" Don't you realize that there are many bigoted clerks who work in the post office, and that the word "Catholic" on a letter is reason enough why it should never reach its destination? Furthermore, you wrote "Catholic chaplain in hospital (Lynchburg)." Now far be it from me to find fault with the grammatical ambiguity of this formula (you may work that to death with Father [James] Graves if you feel so inclined); however, do permit me to point out that there are thirty hospitals in Lynchburg, not a single one of which is Catholic. In light of all of this, then, in precisely what mail box would you have had the post office officials put your letter! There now, dear friend—that's the first complaint I have to register with you. The second is yet more grave.

In each of your letters there has been an insinuation, a sort of whining insinuation, that I do not write to you as often as you deserve. Speaking frankly, dear Father (for I am nothing if not frank), I will admit that for a moment I suspected a bit of jealousy on your part; a desire, shall we say, to be the sole recipient of my military correspondence. But on second thought, I knew this could not be the case. How, after all, could my insignificant self be the object or the cause of jealous passions! Were I capable of blushing, blush indeed I would to admit that such a thought had crossed my mind. Then suddenly the light dawned, clearly revealing, to my dismay, the true reason for such insinuations and laments. There are, you know, people whose misfortune it is to be too clever by half; and it is on this particular occasion I seem to have had an excess of illumination. But just how did the light come to dawn on this dark mystery? Well, one day while I was thinking of you, a thing which I do from time to time, I happened to recall various accusations which the fathers at recreation were wont to have laid at your charge—remarks about your buying cheap and selling dear; about your propensity for having grits brought to your own mill. This led me in turn to reflect upon certain methods which you are accustomed to use to defend yourself in argument, and finally upon the half-concealed reproaches which you have made against me. While ruminating on all of these things, I could not help but pose the question: What *is* it that is so reprehensible about that man? That there is *something* is evident, seeing that everyone finds him such a hard pill to swallow. I am aware of it myself, and although I cannot exactly put my finger on it, I am quite sure that not only is there something wrong, but also that it is one and the same thing which underlines all of the accusations. While I was thus pondering over the problem, a sudden light flashed into my mind and revealed with heartbreaking clarity the awful secret. This illumination, this revelation can be summed up in a single word, a word that perfectly defines the mysterious cause of all these reproaches, a word that explains the mysterious element. So long indeed had I sought this term in vain that when I finally found it, I was tempted to cry out "Eureka, Eureka" like Archimedes of yore. Alas and alack, dear Reverend Father, how has it come to pass that you have become so quintessentially Yankee? There I've said it! I've uttered the *mot fatal*!

It has been eighteen months now since I wrote to you that long eight or ten page letter from the Williamsburg country. This letter impressed you enough to extort from you a reply of three whole pages, a fact in itself sufficient to reveal you in your own true colors. Yet there was more: you were the very paragon of amiability; you assured me that this epistolary pittance could not presume to consider itself as a serious reply to my own voluminous offering. So far so good. But how did you follow this up? With two months of silence! That's what I call Yankee through and through.

Knowing that you felt guilty about being in my debt, I decided not to embarrass you with another letter which would only increase your obligation. I decided accordingly to write a really prodigious letter to Father Yenni, well realizing, of course, that I would receive no reply—and so far the good father has done nothing to disappoint my expectations—then finally, I wrote to you a second time, a long eight or ten page letter. In your reply, which was prompt but scarcely three pages long, you excused its brevity on the pretext that there was no news to report. Oh, treacherous, kindless, Yankee villain! I had the simplicity to believe that you were still my debtor, seeing that you had acknowledged that such you were; so, not to increase your indebtedness, I addressed my next letter to Father Cornette. He, to my great surprise (for who is not surprised when that man does something good?), answered my letter immediately, sending all of the news that anyone could ask for. However, I was still awaiting the long overdue payments from you, and awaiting them, of course, in vain. So long did I wait that you indeed must meanwhile have forgotten their very existence. But then I did write; then I wrote a second time; then a third time, and on each occasion your letter was one-third the length of mine. Never once did you anticipate my letter with one of your own. So, resolving to advance no further credit, lest I drive you into bankruptcy, I ceased to write at all, and I assumed that you would understand the cause of my silence and would therefore not attempt to renew our correspondence. I was not entirely mistaken in this assumption, neither was I entirely correct, for not long ago you deigned to begin this correspondence anew, not, however, with the intention of liquidating your arrears, nor even with the intention of acknowledging them. Rather, it was to reproach me for not having written, and to inform me that I had forfeited all right to reproach you. Unadulterated Yankee! Double-dyed Yankee! Yes, I have forfeited all rights to reproach you, if three or four letters of three or four pages are equivalent to three or four letters of eight or ten pages (and I am prescinding them entirely, of course, from the value of the paper and the ink). Yes, I have forfeited all rights to reproach you, if, when once having recognized a debt, you cease to owe it; if once having made a promise, you are disposed from its fulfillment. I have then forfeited all of my rights, providing all of this is true. Dear Father, the Yankees are just no good. I cannot abide them, neither those of the North nor those of the South. Make haste to become once more a true and loyal Southerner. Write to me frequently and unstintedly. I always find your letters very enjoyable—yes, even those whose arrival is a veritable triumph over the nonsense you have written on the envelope.

You will say that it is rather I who have wasted good ink and paper in writing to you in this vein. As I look back upon what I have written, I am inclined to agree. I'm sorry about it; but it is done. When one sets out on a journey with no clear notion of his destination, one does seem to run the risk of getting lost. What assures and consoles me a bit is the observation made by one of our modern theologians that nonsense is an excellent laxative in time of recreation, not only for those against whom it is directed, but also for those who perpetrate it—provided, of course, that there be nothing in it that would distress the rest of the brethren. I hope that you will accept this theological opinion as some excuse in my behalf.

Up till now I've been giving you anecdotes about the war; this time I have something a bit different for you. Have you heard yet about those females rioting in Richmond last week? Probably not, as the government, with good reason, forbade the newspapers to print anything about it. At any rate, around ten o'clock last Thursday morning about one thousand women of all ages, but not of all classes, came trooping into the square that faces the capitol building and the Governor's Mansion. They had come armed with hatchets and revolvers and screamed at the top of their voices for food and clothes. The governor appeared, made them a fine speech, promised that their demands would be met, and then begged them to disperse and return peacefully to their homes. They were deaf to his pleas. Then President Davis himself addressed them; still to no avail. When these representatives of the fair sex saw the authorities were attempting to placate them rather than threaten them, they realized that they had inspired fear (at least that's my explanation of what happened); so apparently under the direction of about two hundred or so men, who moved stealthily amongst them, inciting them to acts of valor, the mob broke up into two bands, one of which headed for Broad Street and the other began the attack on Main. This pillaging, of course, was what they had intended to do from the very outset; it was coldly and deliberately premeditated. Grievances about the shortage of food and clothing, and about the inflation of prices were no more than a pretext, as was clearly demonstrated by the fact that the women did not bother to break into food stores, and by the fact that they refused any food offered them, saying: "Yes, but, what's the good of eating today if we die of hunger tomorrow! We want something we can have today, tomorrow and the next day!" What particularly attracted them were the goldsmiths, the jewelers and the fancy shops. They passed by necessary and useful items in their greed for the more expensive. At last a group of young men, members of the beneficent society called the Young Men's Christian Association, made an appearance and promised that on the following day they would distribute 10,000 piastres which they then had in their treasury. Whether it was because this offer satisfied the women, or whether they had already gotten what they wanted, or whether it was because they were afraid of the police who had begun making arrests—for one reason or another, they broke up shortly before three and went home.

Protestant spitefulness didn't miss the opportunity to heap all of the blame for this riot on the foreign-born—that is, on the Irish and Germans, all of whom, normally, are Catholics. But as is usually the case, *mantita est iniquitas sibi.* ["(False witnesses have risen up . . . and so) such breathe out violence." *Psalm 27:12.*] All of the plans for the riot had been drawn up at two meetings, one held in a Baptist church, the other in a Methodist church, and I find it hard to believe that such pious sectarians would be willing to lend their churches to Catholics for plotting shenanigans. Moreover, the disorders took place on Holy Thursday at an hour when the Catholics were in their churches for the Divine Office. And finally, the only people who lined up the following day to receive the money promised by the YMCA were native-born Protestants. If the Northern newspapers had known of this fracas you can imagine what capital they would have made of it. Something similar had taken place a few days ago at Petersburg, and there was a threat of a possible repetition today of the Petersburg affair here in Lynchburg. But it is now already five o'clock in the afternoon and nothing has happened. Ah, but how long will it be before we have peace!

About a fortnight ago I received a letter from Father Gautrelet. He informed me that you were beginning to worry about my remaining silent for such a long time. I cannot tell you how flattered I am by this solicitude, but grateful as I am, I hasten to assure you that there is no cause for worry. I am in excellent health, even though I have not repaired all of the damage done by a year of life in camp. But should I fall sick, you can be sure that I will not lack for doctors or nurses. What a marvelous invention the Daughters of Charity are—in spite of the fact that they were invented in France! I can't understand why the Spaniards don't want them in Spain; they seem worthy enough of the privilege of being admitted on the other side of the Pyrénées. But let us return to the subject of Hippolyte Gache, a subject, incidentally, which is never very far from my thoughts.

There are two reasons why I have waited a bit longer than usual before writing to you. First, I have been waiting for Father Gautrelet's receipt of the bill of exchange which I sent him in my last letter. Second, my work here seems to be demanding more of my time. I made a resolution to write out an English sermon every week before preaching it on Sunday, and up till now I've kept that resolution. Even though such a chore is not hard work, it certainly does demand considerable time, especially since I am not at all that "man of one book" that Saint Augustine so distrusted. Moreover, there is always someone to be prepared for a good death and someone else to instruct for baptism or for First Communion. As far as those instructions are concerned, it seems that I always have to begin *ab initio*, that is, right with the sign of the cross. And, of course, this takes a lot of time.

In general I am quite content with the patients in this hospital—I mean those of them who are really sick. About thirty-five men have died since Christmas, and of this number I have baptized, I should guess, twenty-five. Four or five died without making any express profession of Catholicism, but being good, simple, country boys, it seemed better to leave them in their obvious good faith since I knew that all of them had been baptized anyway. Also, they were very receptive to the pious thoughts I suggested to them and they readily repeated all of the prayers which I recited for them—even including the Hail Mary. For me their deaths were more than consoling; they were even deeply edifying. One soldier, only twenty-four years old, who was leaving behind him a twenty-two year old wife and two babies, said: "It is a great consolation to me to think that when my people learn that I am dead, they will learn at the same time that I died happy and with a firm confidence that I was going to see my God." "I am satisfied to die," a young Alabaman told me. "After all, why should I be sorry to depart from all this misery. Isn't it better for me to go and see my God and Father? For five years I have tried to serve Him according to my best, in the camp as well as at home. I hope He will forgive me my sins and receive me into His Glory."

I encountered only three men who did not want me to do anything at all to prepare them for death. All three were Freemasons. One of them would have willingly accepted baptism, which he acknowledged to be necessary for salvation, but he knew Freemasonry was proscribed by the Catholic church, and I insisted that he renounce it. He was a Mason though, before all else. To a young French soldier he confided: "If I were given one hour's leave before I died and if I could choose between spending that time visiting my family or my lodge, I'd choose the lodge one hundred times over." Incidentally, this young French boy, who looks just like Mr. [Jules] Maitrugues, is in a Zouave Battalion. Ever since I prepared and gave him his First Communion, he has been a veritable young apostle among the sick. Every day, however, I see how difficult it is to convert members of the secret societies. For instance, the day before yesterday there was a soldier who left the hospital, one that I thought I had really won over. He had been baptized in the church, but had never been reared a Catholic. As he was intelligent, well-educated, serious and honestly eager to learn the truth, I devoted considerable time to him. He appeared to be delighted with what I told him and he was already well enough instructed to make his confession when, purely by chance, someone told him that the church condemned Freemasonry. Immediately when he heard this he came to find out if it was true, and when I told him yes, it was, his reaction couldn't have been different had he been struck by lightening. "I never was in so bad a fix," he finally said. "I want to be a Catholic because I see it is my duty, but I cannot leave Masonry." Because he was so candid and sincere I decided to explain the whole situation to him. He saw my reasons, but he assured me that having arrived at the twenty-third degree in that society he had never once heard anything objectionable to Catholicism. Without telling me openly what his ultimate choice was to be, he turned away sad, like the rich young man in the Gospel, and never came to see me again.

The time before last when I was in Richmond, a young woman came to see me about eight o'clock one evening. She asked me to come right away and visit her father, an old Creole from Santo Domingo or Martinique who at that time was very ill. The young woman, her husband and I set off immediately. As soon as we arrived at the house, I was brought before the sick man. Seeing me there and suspecting why I had come, he pretended that he was too sleepy to speak. His wife, not being fooled for one instant, said: "Go ahead. Talk to him; he'll hear you and he'll understand." After having made a few polite remarks to which he responded with grunts, I offered him my services as a priest. He said nothing. So, I asked: "Now, you don't want to die without the sacraments of the church do you?" The poor fellow, who for several days had been just this side of death and who, during all of this time, could scarcely speak a word, glared at me; then in a clear, strong voice he shouted: "Go to hell, you and your church!" He then sank into his last agony, and the first thing the next morning I learned that he had died. He was a Freemason; so, on the following day he was buried with all the accustomed pomp of his lodge. His poor family had a twofold bereavement: they mourned his physical, and with much more grief, his spiritual death.

I would prolong this letter, but look—I have no more paper. *Adieu* then, dear Father. My fondest to all of Ours and remember me to Doctor Rohmer and to Mr. Parada. Give my respects to Bishop Quinlan when you see him. Believe me, although I may have pulled your leg a bit in the beginning of this letter, that I am always your devoted friend and your brother,

In our Lord,
L. H. Gache, S.J.

P.S. Doctor John Duffel is here with me. I met him in town one day; he was there looking around for a hospital to which he could offer his services. I brought him out here with me and introduced him to our chief medical officer, who, upon my recommendation, assigned him a group of patients to look after. He is doing very well; everyone is pleased with him and I think they have good reason to be. He is very conscientious, more successful with the sick than any other of our doctors, and the chief medical officer thinks that his talent, his knowledge and his tact are really remarkable in a man so young. I've invited him to have his meals with me and to move his bed into my room, and, of course, he was very grateful. Needless to say, one of the most important matters we're concerned with these days is having him make his Easter duty. Please ask Father Gautrelet to have forty masses said for two persons, deceased. I took the stipend with the intention of sending the masses on to you. The first opportunity I have I'll send you the money which, however, is only twenty piastres in this part of the country.

COMMENTARY

Bunglers perhaps, but certainly not bigots rattled about the Richmond Dead Letter Office, a fact about which Hippolyte Gache was most assuredly aware when he wrote this letter. It was the Dickensian professor, Alexander Dimitry (1805-83), first English-edition editor of the New Orleans *Abeille* and first superintendent of Louisiana's department of public education, who ponderously shifted through all of the improperly addressed military correspondence. This "renowned LL.D. of Georgetown, eminent for his classical attainments and grand, Olympian presence," and so well known to the Louisiana Jesuits, would scarcely have been perplexed by the casual, crypto-heretical address affixed by Philip de Carrière on his recent letter to Lynchburg's ultra-orthodox Jesuit chaplain.[109] But Gache's turgid, bombastic style in this letter and in the next can be better appreciated when read with Michael Kenny's recollections of Philip de Carrière in mind. "He may have made mistakes of judgment," Kenny recalled, "and have been wanting in worldly prudence, at times, but he was absolutely unselfish, sincere and true." Then, years after this French nobleman's death, Kenny remembered: "Someone in the community would occasionally tease him by a pretended defense of some bold opinion, only to draw upon his guilty head a shower of indignant and emphatic protests." Knowing de Carrièr's predictable reaction to such teasing no doubt pushed on Gache's pen to absurd limits of sheer nonsense. Then, in this the first of two letters, he made use of a ploy of rhetoric, highly esteemed by his Chambéry teachers, that was designed to render his outraged correspondent benevolent. He reminded Philip of the evils of Freemasonry. In doing so, Gache was of course sincere. Still, Kenny's recollection about the excitable old missionary he had known when he was a young scholastic is pertinent: "The very name of Freemasonry was enough to arouse the sleeping lion within the heart of Father Philip." Rising lions supinely placed always seemed to appeal to the sporting blood in Hippolyte Gache.[110]

In his description of the Richmond bread riots the Jesuit reported how easily latent anti-Catholicism could be aroused in the city that had suffered so long from the privations of war. The loyalty of Catholics, particularly the foreign born was always suspect, another fact which may put into better perspective Gache's facetious accusations regarding his correspondent's "Yankee" characteristics. The day after these riots, the Richmond *Examiner* described the perpetrators of the violence as "prostitutes, professional thieves, Irish and Yankee hags, gallows birds from all lands but our own."[111]

Few places in his correspondence did Hippolyte Gache show himself more chauvinistically French than in this letter when he commented on the Daughters of Charity not being accepted "on the other side of the Pyrénées." This religious family was founded in France in 1633 by St. Vincent de Paul (1580-1660) and St. Louise de Marillac (1591-1660), and from their modest beginning these sisters became conspicuous for their devotion to the most poverty-stricken and for their distinctive habit and bonnet, the ordinary dress of peasant women during Monsieur Vincent's day, depicted by the painter Louis Le Nain (1593-1648) in his painting "The Peasants' Supper." In 1790 the first convent of the Daughters of Charity was established in Spain, and when Gache wrote this letter there were more than one hundred convents in that country. During the next seven years this number doubled. But when the sisters crossed the Pyrénées they doffed their cornets, exchanging them for Spanish veils. In 1856 the Superior General of the Vincentian Order, Jean-Baptiste-Etienne, C.M.

(1801-74) tried to insist that the Spanish sisters adapt their millinary apparel to comply with the post-revolutionary Paris style. The Spanish sisters resisted. Described on the southside of the Pyrénées as a "religious Napoleon," Etienne sent a task force of ten corneted French sisters to Madrid where they were patronized by the unpopular Queen Isabel II, and set up in a special convent on the *calle Hortaleza*, appropriately named Santa Isabela. Predictably, they won little respect from the poor; yet this is the group to which Gache referred in his letter. But if Etienne met a religious Waterloo of sorts in Madrid, he gained a victory in Emmitsburg, Maryland, where in 1810 St. Elizabeth Ann Seton (1774-1821), with the help of the ever present Bishop Louis DuBourg, had founded a convent of the "Sisters of Charity." In 1850 these sisters, for whom Gache was a chaplain during the remainder of the war, affiliated with the French community, adopted the Rule of St. Vincent de Paul, and put on the gray-blue habit, the white bonnet and the very distinctive, Gallic cornet. Thus the Daughters of Charity had their beginning in the United States.[112]

In Lynchburg each Daughter of Charity was paid $18.50 per month for nursing at General Hospital #3, which incorporated the college building, Division #1, and Ferguson's (Tobacco) Factory, Division #2.[113] Reports of the sick and wounded for these hospitals, and for General Hospitals #1 and #2, are not extant before June 1863, and even then it is not possible to obtain an official tally of the number of patients or the number of deaths at each of the various hospitals, although the hospital rolls for the college are complete after June 1863.[114] Another source gives the number of Confederate soldiers who died in the combined Lynchburg hospitals as 1,251 in 1862; 677 in 1863; 593 in 1864, and 51 in 1865; moreover, during this same period a total number of 187 Federal soldiers died.[115] One of the doctors who attended to these patients was singled out by Gache, John Duffel (b. New River, Ascension Parish, Louisiana, April 6, 1838–d. ? 1887), the son of Doctor Edward and Desiré Landry Duffel of Mulberry Grove Plantation in Ascension Parish. The prefect noted in the Register Book, when John enrolled at Spring Hill College in 1852, that his first language was French. He received his A.B. from the college in 1857 and his M.D. from the University of Louisiana in 1861. On October 19, 1861 he enrolled as a private, the assistant to Dr. Semmes, in Company K, "Phoenix Company" of the Louisiana Eighth. On October 6 he had written a letter to an unknown source complaining that he had never been paid "since the date of my commission," July 4; then on November 21, 1861, he resigned his commission, "much to the satisfaction of the Regt." as some unidentified hand wrote in his permanent record, before making a half-hearted attempt to scratch out this unkind judgment. In April 1863 Duffel who had relatives in Virginia, was under contract to the Surgeon General to work at the Lynchburg Hospital #3 for $100 per month. It is difficult to say how long he remained at the post, but on November 7 he was captured at Rappahannock Bridge. After the war he was the coroner of Ascension Parish, but despite his prominence in society, research has not revealed the place of his death.[116]

The identity of the French Zouave, who became "a veritable young apostle among the sick" after receiving religious instructions from the chaplain, has not been determined, but the three Jesuits he named for the first time in this letter have been easily identified. The Zouave reminded Gache of Jules Maitrugues (b. Pontarlier, Doubs, France, January 28, 1836–d. New Orleans, Louisiana, September 18, 1878) who was at that time a scholastic at Grand Coteau and who afterwards wrote a short history of St. Charles College. Brother Emmanuel Brenans (b. Domon, Jura, Switzerland, March 2, 1797–d. Spring Hill, Alabama, February 15, 1863) had been the factotum at the college since the day of his arrival there in 1847, and Father James Graves (b. Lebanon, Kentucky, December 1824–d. Louisville, Kentucky, August 21, 1897) was a professional rhetorician, noted for "his masterful elucidation of that subject in the classroom." In Mobile after the war, he became as well known as he was controversial for polemical sermons delivered against Episcopalians.[117]

J.M.J.

Lynchburg General Hospital
May 19, 1863

(Address boxes to:
Sister Rose
College Hospital
Lynchburg, Virginia)

Rev. Father Carrière[1]
Spring Hill College
Alabama

Reverend and dear Father, P. C.

In April when I wrote you my last letter, I had hoped that having pointed out your errors, I would receive a humble acknowledgment of guilt and a sincere promise of immediate amendment. The response to my letter, however, has convinced me that I had set my hopes for you a bit too high, and that instead of being a skin deep Yankee, as I had tried to believe was the case, I find that you are, alas, a Yankee right to the very substance of your soul. Not only do you not acknowledge your crimes, you seek to justify them in a tone that one might mistake for that of innocence sorely put upon, were it not, that is, for a certain shameface effrontery which ill conceals the guilty conscience. Moreover, the means which you have employed, far from diminishing your guilt, have only augmented it. Take, for example, the question of my address.

[1]I hereby send you the "r" I omitted from your name on the envelope of my last letter. I withheld this "r" for a very good reason: I wanted to give to you a name that would be proper rather than common [(*la carrière*, n. quarry)]. Besides, relying on a principle learned in childhood and thereafter never questioned, I have always thought that in French there were no ironclad spelling rules for proper names. You, however, have put in a claim for this "r," a letter which is so dear, as I now recall, to all of the inhabitants in the valley of the Garonne; besides, I could never let myself forget the axiom of St. Augustine, "Restitution or Damnation." Therefore, here it is; it would never do to go to hell for one, single, solitary, purloined "r."

I was displeased first of all with your use of the terms "Catholic bishop" and Catholic chaplain," since this seemed to imply a recognition of non-Catholic bishops and chaplains. Adroitly parrying my thrust, you wrote: "I call a thing by its right name. If you choose to take exception to this terminology it is either because you do not consider yourself as a Catholic chaplain, or because you consider the title a dishonorable one." In the first place, I resent your subsuming me under the category of things. In the second place, the question is not whether the title is accurate, but whether under the circumstances, it may be fittingly used. It is to this question that you should have addressed yourself. And furthermore, apart from the implication I have already mentioned, the title is also objectionable on the ground that it needlessly and inappropriately broadcasts our faith. As to my other accusation, namely that you falsely accused me of not writing to you, what is your reply? You say: "I have answered all of the letters which you have written. If I have not written during the summer months, it is because I was at Mobile taking Father [Peter] Imsand's place and I didn't have time to write." Once again you are addressing your answers to charges I did not make. Have I ever complained that you have not written to me? The thought has never entered my mind. I merely complained that you falsely accused me of not writing to you; I did not say you did not write to me; I said you said I did not write to you. Now, what could be more clear than that! Simply to convince you of the unreasonableness of your complaint, may I invite you to compare the length of my letters with that of your own; then let us see who is indebted to whom.

Why is it that you went off on this tangent anyway? Why is it that when a person attacks you on one flank, you act as if he is attacking you on another, and instead of taking means to repulse the real assault, you spend all of your forces against an illusory onslaught? This is the way the Yankees fight. But don't put too much confidence in these tactics, for, although it is an easy matter to overcome a whole army of sham troops that one imagines he sees before him, and to route them without even flashing a sword or putting spark to a single grain of powder, it is quite another matter indeed to win the day from an army of real troops who attack from where they are, not from where you would wish them to be. Such troops are not to be repulsed by the mere thunder of rhetoric. Now then, dear Father, let us put aside once and for all these Yankee tricks; they are of no avail, neither in this world nor in the next. You asked me what I meant by saying that you were a "double-dyed Yankee." I did not think that my meaning would elude a man of your perspicacity. It is very true, of course, that, according to the philosophical dictum, the person one knows least of all is himself. This dictum, however, along with many of its kind, should be taken *cum grano salis* [with a grain of salt]. Furthermore, the reason for a lack of self-knowledge is often the result of a desire to avoid the unpleasant truth about one's self, a desire which, needless to say, I would not wish to attribute to you.

Before turning to more serious matters, I must tell you, for your consolation, that your letter, however insulting, has not really altered my feelings toward you. Furthermore, I sincerely forgave you for your offensive remarks. True, these remarks were fairly numerous and a little acidulous, but, served as they were in a bland sauce of well-turned compliments, they were not entirely unpalatable. Ah, but the weakness of human nature! In theory, you know, no one is more contemptuous of flattery than I, but in practice, I am as susceptible to it as the next man. How true it is that one always wants to believe the flatterer. I recall what Father [Joseph] de Jocas used to say: always tell the ugliest woman in the world that she is beautiful, and instead of regarding this statement as ironical and being offended by it, she will prefer to persuade herself, despite the loud protests from her mirror, that there is much truth in what you say, even though you exaggerate ever so slightly. Alas, this is the way I succumb to your compliments. In vain am I able to consider myself insignificant in every respect as long as you attribute to me, as you did in your last letter, the title of "Major." Really, how can you call me "major" without qualifications, without specification—in other words, "major" in every respect without actually believing that I am "major" in respect to something? Clearly it is impossible. Every error, as [Bishop Jacques-Bénigne] Bossuet (1627-1704) has said so well, is based on a half-truth. Oh, I beseech you then, my dear Father, put an end to these sweet lies! I may be strong enough to disbelieve them when first you utter them, but upon their reiteration I will surely succumb. But let us get on to a more serious subject.

We have just had another series of engagements along the Rappahannock, but unfortunately I did not witness any of them. When I say "unfortunately" I don't mean to imply that I am trying to get myself killed, but rather that my not being there deprived me of the pleasure of describing for you the battle scenes. I always enjoy being able to write to you about battles that I have actually witnessed. Yet, even though I cannot give you a firsthand account of the battlefields of Chancellorsville and Fredericksburg, nor recount for you the acts of valor these fields witnessed, I can tell you this much: our troops suffered more in both places than the communiques have indicated. True, we defeated and routed the enemy, and we did it in a way that ought to cover him with shame—were the Yankee capable of this sentiment. But it is also true that this victory cost us dearly. Everyone agrees that this time the Yankee's plans were better conceived and that they were executed with more energy and skill. Their soldiers fought with greater valor, their generals commanded with more intelligence and they were able to discover every one of our weak points and to take full advantage of this knowledge. In short, even though they beat a hasty retreat across the Rappahannock, even though they fled before an army numerically far inferior to their own (they who had bragged about being able to crush this army with their first charge!), at any rate, this time they did not flee in panic at the first sight of our valiant men. This time they put up resistance.

As is always the case, the Louisiana Batallions had many casualties. Before the engagements the number of men in both brigades scarcely totaled 2,500; yet the number of killed, wounded, or taken prisoner has scored to 1,100. Brigadier General [Francis] Nicholls, the commander of my brigade, had his leg, or rather his foot blown off by a cannon shot that went right through his horse. The animal, needless to say, was killed. This poor unfortunate (I'm speaking of the general, not of the horse) had lost his left arm in the battle of Harpersburg; however he does not consider this double loss sacrifice enough for he is already talking about returning to the brigade to resume his command. It won't be very long either before he's back, perhaps in a few weeks; just as soon as he gets a wooden leg, without which he can never climb back in the saddle. The surgery on his foot was successful and the wound has healed very quickly. He is here in Lynchburg now, and I go visit him from time to time. Both the officers and the men respect him very much and, despite the fact that he is only twenty-eight years old, they have the utmost confidence in him.

My regiment went into the melee with 180 strong. We lost eighty-two: fifteen killed; sixty wounded and the rest taken prisoner. Col. [John] N. Legett, who was commanding the regiment in the absence of Colonel Waggaman, at that time on a special mission in Louisiana, was numbered among the dead. The poor fellow was almost torn in two by a shell. He had just enough time to realize what had happened and to ask his men to pardon him for all his shortcomings and to assure them that he held no rancor against any of them. (There had been difficulties between him and the men and he was not a popular commander).

I don't think that any of our former students were killed during the recent battles. Stanhope Posey, presently adjutant general for his father, General [Carnot] Posey, was wounded, but not very seriously. The oldest Sims boy, a lieutenant in the 8th was also slightly wounded. You knew him, I'm sure—young Frank's brother. He's here in the hospital now; he recognized me the first time I came around to visit the sick. [Gustave] Bruyère, who is in the same company, came through the battles safe and sound, whereas Alfred Laforest, having been sent back to the hospital two days before the fighting began, on account of an old wound that had not healed properly, was not with his regiment. He came over here to see me last Sunday. He is the same boy; hasn't changed a bit: a good Christian and a good soldier, very much admired by all who come in contact with him. It's remarkable that since he's been in the army, he hasn't suffered a bit from his rheumatism, or from any other malady for that matter, and I dare say that had he not been wounded, he would never have seen the inside of a hospital.

Just yesterday I ran into the oldest Valdes boy, the one that was at Spring Hill not long ago. He's not going back to his regiment; instead, they'll put him to work here at the hospital. The poor fellow simply does not have strong enough a constitution to make the long marches. Do you remember that simple little fellow from Thibodaux named Sandy? Well, he is in Lynchburg too; has been here for the past seven or eight months as a patient. His illness, however, is not serious. The poor fellow just got himself married, and although he told Laforest that he had made his Easter duty, I don't believe that he really had. The fact is that he married a Protestant girl before a Protestant minister. I haven't heard anything about a subsequent marriage before the pastor at Lynchburg, but I'm sure that had there been one, the pastor would have informed me. *Ah, les têtes louisiannaises*—at times there is not much gray matter in them! I just finished giving a verbal thrashing to another Louisianian, a relative of Father [Gustave] de Kernion, if you please. He had gotten himself mixed up in a matter equally as foolish as Sandy's, and in a few other matters besides. But won't he be a longtime remembering what I told him! As a matter of fact, he met Doctor Duffel right after he had left my room and he said: "I just came from seeing Father Gache. My, but didn't he give me hell! I've never been bawled out like that before in my whole life. I was so 'shamed, I'd like to gone right through the floor." Paul Gusman was promoted to lieutenant in my regiment, and from what I hear he is very well liked by all. He managed to dodge all of the shots and shells of the recent engagements. Our poor regiment—we were 867 when we came to Virginia; now we're ninety-two. That in itself should indicate how little there is for me to do there now.

Oh, but do let me tell you about another one of your former gems, one that I almost forgot. The other day, just as I was passing in front of the Varieties Theater in Richmond, someone ran out from under the marquee and called out to me. "Father Gache, don't you recognize me?" "Why, yes. Wait a minute now and I'll tell you your name." "My name's Fox," he answered straightaway. "Precisely," said I. After being slightly wounded in the Maryland campaign, this amusing young man received his discharge, and not being able to find any other means of subsistence, he turned to the theater where he now acts on the stage under the name of "Mr. Browne." I lectured to him about wasting the good education he had received at Spring Hill, but again he assured me that he had not been able to find any other way to earn a living. "Well, isn't that just dandy," I said. "In order to gain a living in this world you forfeit your chances for life in the next. That's using your head." He assured me that he never played a role in an immoral performance and that he never missed his Sunday mass ("Well, well, well"—as the Holy Father [Guy] Gilles was wont to say). Then he went on to add that he wasn't the only alumnus of Spring Hill who had turned to the stage; that he knew of many others, and that as a matter of fact, the best actors in all of the South were former students of Spring Hill College. Poor Father [Francis] Lespès, did he ever suspect, I wonder, during the long hours and years of his work with the thespian group, what would come of it all!

I'm sure that as true Southerners you all mourned the death of our brave General Jackson. I don't have to tell you that our loss was a very great one; that he alone was worth 50,000 men. This you already know. Perhaps what you don't know, however, is that, in his own way, he was a very good Christian. The face of this austere Presbyterian expressed all of the characteristics of a devout member of that sect; yet, he was not a bigot—at least so far as I have heard. He often remarked publically that it was in God alone that he put his confidence, and after each victory he always ordered the chaplains under his command to offer prayers of thanksgiving. Shortly after he was wounded at Chancellorsville, he said to one of his adjutants who had offered him sympathy: "Oh, well; it was for a good and wise purpose that God has sent me this wound; I would not part with it even if I could." Finally, when it became certain that he was going to die, it was his wife who courageously told him that there was no hope for his recovery. "Very well," the general answered, "Very well. It's alright. The Lord be praised!" And many times over he expressed sorrow for his sins. Since he was probably in good faith, one can hope that his pious sentiments must have led him to an act of perfect contrition. Surely, He who so loves to bestow mercy, must have bestowed it abundantly on this man.

I've observed that these religious sentiments expressed by General Jackson are not unusual among the members of the old Virginia families. General Lee is also very religious, not in an ostentatious and wordy manner, but sincerely and genuinely. It would be hard to imagine a man of greater modesty and simplicity, though he is certainly our "Great Man" *par excellence.* I don't doubt at all that he'll be our second president, provided the good Lord spares his life and provided our republic lives beyond its infancy. Should he become president, you can be sure that his tenure in office will be memorable. He has one quality in particular which singles him out, a quality which is as estimable in a military officer as in a civil authority, and that is a certain inflexibility of purpose in the accomplishment of his duty, but at the same time without the bruskness and severity which are sometimes wont to disfigure this virtue. With him things that should be done, are done; with him politics, cliques and favoritisms are given no quarter. It makes no difference if a man is called Colonel So-and-So or General Such-and-Such—if he has failed to do his duty, he is punished just as the lowliest private would be. And if he gives evidence of being incapable, he is relieved of his command without sentiment or hesitation. The general is an Episcopalian, but at the same time he is, as are almost all of the men of his class, very favorable toward Catholics and he has the greatest esteem for them. His brother Commodore [Sidney Smith] Lee, presently in command of the fortifications at Drewry's Bluff on the James, is not so talented nor so well-known, but I happen to know him personally and I can assure you that he shares the same religious sentiments and sympathies towards Catholics. One day last summer the commodore with two or three friends paid a visit to the orphanage of the Daughters of

Charity at Richmond. Just before departing, he gave the children a little talk: "My dear girls, you must pray, you must pray hard for the army and especially for us at Drewry's Bluff. When it comes to winning battles, I rely more on the prayers of pious souls than I do on the power of our artillery. And you, even though you are still very young, you can help us more than anyone else to defeat the enemy because you are innocent and God willingly listens to your prayers."

Sister superior assured him that the girls did indeed pray for the army every day and that they prayed particularly for the troops at Drewry's Bluff because they knew that at Drewry's Bluff they had some very special friends. "Ah, ha," said the commodore, "Now I know why things have been going so well for us there and why we managed to give such a hard time the other day to that gunboat that came a little too close to our batteries. So children, continue to raise your little hands toward heaven and pray God that He will direct our artillery straight toward the target." Then, after a short pause, he turned to sister superior and said: "Sister, wouldn't it be grand if all of you—the girls and the sisters—could come up and say some prayers right there at Drewry's Bluff? I do believe that a prayer said at the very place would be specially efficacious. Besides, when your children return to Richmond, after having seen our emplacements with their own eyes, I'm sure their prayers for us would be more real and more meaningful. Come and spend the day with us. I'll send a steamer for you; it will pick you up in the morning and bring you back that same evening."

After hesitating a few moments, the sister accepted the invitation. So, when the day of the outing arrived, the steamer was there waiting for the little battalion of some fifty orphans and eight nuns. The ship's captain (evidently chosen expressly for this occasion), was a Catholic. I can't tell you how many little girls were adopted for the day by all of the officers and particularly by Commodore Lee himself, nor can I describe for you the kindness, consideration and respect everyone displayed toward the nuns. Sister superior, however, did say when they all got back to Richmond that. "the trip, Father, was rather more edifying for the soul than it was comfortable for the body." But be that as it may, after a magnificent dinner at which the officers themselves were present, and at which they helped with service, the tour of Drewry's Bluff began. The group saw the whole fort from the battlements down to the subterranean installations; they saw how the guns were loaded and fired, and finally they were led up to a plateau where they could see the length of the James along which the enemy were supposed to come, if indeed they ever would come. It was here that the little group knelt down, recited a brief prayer, then rose to chant the Litanies of the Blessed Virgin, singing, as I have frequently heard them sing, with great gusto. It was a real joy for all of the men present to see them and to hear them singing so fervently, and I think that all were impressed at the way in which Divine Providence had found such good mothers for these poor children whose lot otherwise would have been so unenviable. After the litanies they went back soon to the wharf where the steamer was already waiting to take them home. It was evident that the visit had meant every bit as much to the commodore and to the men as it had to the sisters and to the children.

As far as religion is concerned, the views of Gen. Joe E. Johnston are very much like those of Commodore Lee and his brother, though perhaps even more Catholic. And as far as prayer is concerned, General Johnston makes no bones about his belief that Catholic prayers are the only ones he has any confidence in. Of all of the generals I have ever seen, other than, of course, General Beauregard, General Johnston is the one most like a French general. His wife never meets a priest or a nun without begging them to pray that she and the general will be converted. "We're Catholics already in our hearts," she confesses. "I don't know what's keeping us from actually joining the church." This is also just about the same way matters stand with General [George Wythe] Randolph, the former Secretary of War; however, several of his relatives have already been converted. You see then, our highest officers are not ill disposed toward Catholicism. I know that you are aware of the sentiments of our worthy president, but perhaps you don't know about those of Mrs. Jefferson Davis. She is somewhat like Mrs. Johnston. When she first came to Richmond, she sought out the Daughters of Charity and asked them for prayers; then she asked them to suggest someone who would be a good governess for her children. She specified that she wanted a practicing Catholic. On one occasion, having been invited to visit the chapel in the Orphans' Asylum, she smiled and said: "It's strange, but each time I go into a Catholic church or chapel, I seem to hear a voice deep down within me saying, 'This is where you ought to be.' " I should say this attitude toward Catholicism, which is rather general among the upper classes and which was rare twenty years ago, especially in Virginia, gives great hope for the future.

You tell me that my *"frère de lait"* is bragging about our having opened up the gates to the Orient—that is to say, to Georgia. This is a part of the country where there is a great deal to be done. Although I have never been there myself, I feel I know this state because of all of the dealings I've had with the Georgia troops. If I could be the apostle of any particular state, I'd choose Georgia. But you must be tired of reading all of this; I too am growing weary. So let me close. . . .

I finally received the case of wine which Father Gautrelet so kindly sent to me. But as it was not sufficiently well-packed, only six bottles survived the trip to Lynchburg. I am most satisfied with the quality of the wine, which the journey seems to have improved. So by all means, keep sending it whenever you can do so easily and safely. I promise to pay you ten piastres a bottle for it. I use it with moderation: one bottle serves me twelve days. You didn't say anything about the masses I asked you to have said for me, but I suppose you are attending to this. *Adieu, mon bon Père.* Pray always for me, and believe that I am

As ever, yours in Our Lord
H. Gache

P.S. My best to all of Ours; to the bishop, when you see him, and to Doctoc Rohmer and Mr. Parada. Tell Father Serra that he owes me a letter and that his apostolate at Ile Mont-Louis and at Bayou Batterie will avail him naught: If he doesn't pay his debts he will no more enter heaven than did the wicked debtors. Doctor Duffel sends his best wishes to one and all. I haven't time to re-read this letter; please forgive all of the spelling and grammatical errors, if you find any, as well as my illegible hand.

COMMENTARY

Beginning with one of the casualties at Chancellorsville, Brig. Gen. Francis Redding Tillou Nicholls (b. Donaldsonville, Louisiana, August 20, 1834–d. near Thibodaux, Louisiana, January 4, 1912), Gache names a number of Louisiana soldiers in this letter to Philip de Carrière. Nicholls was graduated from West Point in 1855 and resigned his commission the following year to study law at Tulane. In 1861 he formed the Phoenix Guards, which later became Company K of the Louisiana Eighth, a regiment in which he was the lieutenant colonel. He had been wounded once before at Winchester, May 25, 1862, captured, exchanged and then appointed colonel of the newly organized Fifteenth Regiment after Charles M. Bradford's forced resignation. In the following October he was appointed brigadier general of the Second Louisiana Brigade, which included the Tenth Regiment. He recovered from the wounds which Gache described in this letter; and, as the commander of the Lynchburg Post, he was to have more dealings with the Louisiana chaplain. Major General Hill recommended that Nicholls' command be filled by Gache's friend Col. Henry Forno, but the colonel was transferred instead to Mobile. After the war Nicholls was Governor of Louisiana (1888-92), and then was appointed chief justice of the state supreme court.[118] Besides Nicholls, several Spring Hill students were casualties at Chancellorsville, the first of whom Gache mentioned was Stanhope Posey (b. Hermitage Plantation, Wilkinson County, Mississippi, September 6, 1841–d. Yazoo City, Mississippi, September 10, 1893), the oldest son of Gen. Carnot Posey (1818-63), who came to the Jesuit college in 1855. On April 15, 1861, this "man of culture and refinement, with a pleasing gift of speech rarely possessed" enlisted in Captain Todd's Louisiana Guards and was sent to Pensacola. When Rightor's Battalion was deactivated in April 1862, Posey, whose one year enlistment was completed, resigned and was then commissioned in the Mississippi Sixteenth, at that date under the command of his father. Like George Spotswood, Stanhope Posey became a Catholic at Spring Hill "remaining steadfast to his religion through all the vicissitudes of life." During the war he met Eliza Whyte (b. Petersburg, Virginia, June 16, 1840–d. Yazoo City, Mississippi, August 9, 1910), the sister of the first Mrs. William Hinton, and a member of the Hinton household at "Folly Castle" in 1850. She and Stanhope were married by Fr. Mulvey at Petersburg in 1866.[119]

The "oldest of the Sims boys" that Gache met was William (b. Napoleonville, Louisiana, April 4, 1836–d. Napoleonville, Louisiana, September 8, 1876), who came to Spring Hill a year after Stanhope Posey. Like John Duffel, he and his brothers, Robert Nicholls (1841-99) and Francois (1847-1901) were registered as "French speaking," a fact which is not surprising since they were members of the Trépagnier family which had been established in Mobile since the time of its foundation, and in New Orleans since 1728. Also, like Duffel, William Sims enlisted in Colonel Nicholl's "Phoenix Company" in June 1861. Twelve months later he was elected 2d lieutenant, and then in December 1862, 1st lieutenant in the Louisiana Eighth. Captured at Rappahannock, November 7, 1863, he remained in various federal prisons until June 13, 1865, when he took the oath of allegiance to the United States, and returned to his profession as lawyer in Assumption Parish.[120] Another enlistee in the "Phoenix Company" was Gustave Bruyère (b. Ascension Parish, Louisiana, February 4, 1842–d. near Frederick, Maryland, July 9, 1846), the son of Henry and Rosalie Melancon Bruyère. Gustave, who enrolled at Spring Hill College in 1856, was one more student whose first language was French. He and William Sims were captured the same day at Rappahannock, November 7, 1863, but unlike Lieutenant Sims, Sargeant Bruyère was exchanged and returned to his regiment in March 1864. Four months later he was mortally wounded and died behind Federal lines.[121]

Another Spring Hillian Gache reported having met among the wounded was Alfred-Job-Joseph-Aubin de Laforest et Cazeau (b. New Orleans, Louisiana, March 11, 1841–d. near Stover, Missouri, May 7, 1911), who came to Spring Hill two years before Bruyère and remained there until he received his A.B. in June 1860. The following July 7, he enlisted in Colonel Nicholls' "Phoenix Company" at Camp Moore. However, there is a letter dated April 19, 1861, which indicates that Laforest's first choice was Captain Fish's Crescent Rifles, but his application was not accepted. In January 1863, Laforest was wounded in a skirmish, and because this wound did not heal he returned to the hospital in April where he remained until the first part of May. Shortly before Gache visited him, he had been made corporal in Company E, and on the following November 7, he was to be one more Spring Hill alumnus captured at Rappahannock, and, with Bruyère, he was to be exchanged in March 1864. Captured again at Spotsylvania the following May, he remained, like Sims, a prisoner until the end of the war, spending most of the time at Point Lookout, New Hampshire.[122]

The "oldest Valdes boy" whom Gache described as not having the constitution to make long marches but who managed to find work at the hospital, was most probably Celestine, although what outfit he belonged to at the time is not clear. Seven months after Gache wrote this letter Celestine Valdes joined Capt. Price Williams, Jr.'s Company, which subsequently became Company A, First Battalion Alabama Cadets. But since he was sixteen years old at the time, and had enlisted without his parents consent, he was discharged December 31, 1863, leaving Albert Innerarity, also sixteen, to carry on in his stead.[123] If the identity of Celestine Valdes has not been confirmed, that of "Sandy from Thibodaux" is certain. This "simple little fellow" was James A. Scudday (b. Thibodaux, Louisiana, June 24, 1842–d. New Orleans, Louisiana, December 18, 1901), the son of Dr. James and Margaret Aubert Scudday, who came to Spring Hill in December 1854. Three years later he transferred to the Louisiana Military Institution at Alexandria, where, as Gache may have been surprised to learn, he received "most flattering testimonials from the professors," and here he remained until he enlisted for one year's service in the Louisiana Guards' Battery, Artillery. In the Spring of 1862 he was in Captain Giradey's Company of Nelligan's First Regiment. During this time he tried to obtain a commission, and despite the efforts of his cousin, the former commanding officer of the Grivot Guards and present Louisiana Attorney General, Judge F. S. Goode (1831-85), James Scudday remained a private throughout the war. Wounded at Cedar Mountain, he was hospitalized for more than a year at Lynchburg, returned to duty, and then transferred back to the Lynchburg Post where he remained until the end of the war. He had married Lelia Lee Walker (b.1846) in a ceremony performed by Rev. William H. Kinckle (1818-67), the Rector of Grace Memorial Episcopal Church, Lynchburg, one month before Gache brought his Jesuit brothers up to date on their former students.[124] The other young Louisianan who received a tongue-lashing would be difficult to identify, not only because a complete patients' roll for the Lynchburg hospitals is unavailable, but also because Gache's identification of this young Creole is not precise. He said that he was related to Father Huchet de Kernion, but the number of this man's relatives approached infinity, encompassing the Innerarity brothers, the Sims brothers, and others whose names appear in this correspondence. Even the identity of Father Huchet de Kernion is not certain. There are two Jesuits, brothers, and it is not clear which one Gache meant: Joseph (b. New Orleans, Louisiana, July 16, 1820–d. St. Louis, Missouri, December 30, 1900) or Felix (b. New Orleans, Louisiana, November 26, 1831–d. New Orleans, Louisiana, October 6, 1859).[125]

There was no doubt in the minds of the Jesuits at Spring Hill who read this letter about the identity of Paul Gusman (b. Covington, Louisiana, March 12, 1843–d. Florenville, Louisiana, February 6, 1907) who came to the college in December, 1859. The son of John and Matilda Barn Gusman, Paul enlisted as a private in Colonel Forno's Fifth Louisiana, May 10, 1861, and there is no record when he was transferred to the 10th, where he was elected 2d and then lst lieutenant in Company F, formerly the Opelousas Guards. Although Gache obviously admired him, he failed to inform the priests at Spring Hill that he was a patient again at Lynchburg during January and February 1864. Wounded at Martinsburg, September 18, he never recovered sufficiently to return to combat. After the war he became a captain on the vessels which traveled between Covington and New Orleans.[126] The final Spring Hill student Gache made mention of in this letter was Bernard Fox (b. New Orleans, Louisiana, October 22, 1840–d. New Orleans, Louisiana, December 6, 1898) who, in 1863, adopted the stage name "Mr. R. J. Browne" and kept it to the delight of theater goers up and down the Atlantic littoral until his death. When Bernard Fox enrolled at Spring Hill College with Alfred Laforest, both his Irish-born parents were dead. There is no record how long Fox remained at Spring Hill, but the year he arrived John Duffel was the prefect of the Thespian Society, and of its branch for the grammar school boys, the Calliope Academy. The moderator of this group was Father Francis

Lespès (b. Pau, France, September 2, 1820–d. Spring Hill, Alabama, November 14, 1872), one of the five who came with Gache from Le Havre to Mobile in 1847. The goals of the Thespians often clashed with those of the Philomatic Society, a club established in 1848 "to form style and train students in the art of public speaking," the moderator of which was Hippolyte Gache. The sympathy the correspondent manifested in this letter for "poor Father Lespès" is better appreciated in the context of this academic rivalry between societies dedicated to a mastery of the laws and art of oratory and rhetoric.[127] During the 1857 academic year, Bernard Fox was the president of the Thespian Society, and on June 7, 1861, he enrolled in Captain George Clark's Continental Guards, later Company A of the Seventh Louisiana. In the following June he was wounded at Fort Republic and during the next several months spent time in and out of various hospitals, although when Gache encountered him in Richmond he was registered on the company rolls as a deserter. Diagnosed as having contracted a disease which had been the plague of armies since the discovery of the New World, the erstwhile Thespian was discharged from the army on Columbus Day 1863.[128]

The three other Jesuits Gache mentioned for the first time in his correspondence were Joseph de Jocas (b. Carpentras, Vaucluse, France, June 29, 1807–d. Lyons, France, January 23, 1881); Guy Gilles (b. Mende, Lozere, France, December 21, 1787–d. Baton Rouge, Louisiana, August 28, 1855) and Peter Imsand (b. Viege, Valais, Switzerland, November 29, 1808–d. Pensacola, Florida, June 27, 1880). Father de Jocas was his master of novices at Avignon and, seemingly, taught him more than the principles of asceticism. Father Gilles, a member of the faculty at the Jesuit college of St. Mary's, Kentucky, was dispatched to Mobile in 1846 to welcome the first Spring Hill Jesuits to the South. Having a reputation for sanctity, as well as a love for the Greek classics, "holy Father Gilles" took Gache's place at Baton Rouge in 1855 and then promptly succumbed to yellow fever. When Father Prachensky left for the Peninsula, he turned over the keys of St. Joseph's Church, Mobile, to Father Imsand. This church and the school, which Imsand took great pains to build, contributed greatly in Americanizing Mobile's polyglot Catholic population.[129]

In this letter, in which he reflected on the religious sentiments of a number of important persons in the Confederacy, Gache gave a delightful account of his meeting with the *preux chevalier* of the Lee family, Sidney Smith (b. Camden, New Jersey, September 2, 1802–d. near Alexandria, Virginia, July 23, 1869), the older brother of the war's greatest soldier. In the priest's description of an afternoon spent at Drury's Bluff, the father of Fitzhugh Lee (1835-1901) stands out as a man of singular modesty and kindness. The sister superior of St. Joseph's Female Orphan Asylum,

Richmond, who accompanied Gache on this venture down the James was Sister Blanche, née Mary Ann Rooney (b. Dungannon, Tyronne, Ireland, August 30, 1834–d. Washington, D.C., June 2, 1884), who had entered the Emmitsburg convent in 1850, the last year of the Irish famine and the year the Maryland Sisters of Charity became the French Daughters of Charity.[130]

Lydia Sims McLane (b. Wilmington, Delaware, January 30, 1822–d. Washington, D.C., February 22, 1887), the wife of General Joseph E. Johnston, had three sisters who were converts to Catholicism: Juliette McLane Garesché (1826-85); Catherine Mary McLane (1829-53) and Mary Elizabeth Hobbins (1832-?). After the death of her husband, Peter Bauduy Garesché (1822-68), wartime owner-director of the famous Columbia, South Carolina, ammunitions factory, Juliette followed the path taken by her two surviving daughters, Catherine Milligan (1850-1940) and Lydia Johnston (1856-1932) in 1876 when she entered Mère Duchesne's St. Louis convent of the Religious of the Sacred Heart. Sent first to New Zealand and then to Paris, Mother Bauduy Garesché, R.S.C.J. ended her adventure-filled days in Mère Guinand's convent at St. Michel, now Convent, Louisiana.

Varina Howel Davis (b. "Maringo" Parish, Louisiana, May 7, 1826–d. New York, New York, October 16, 1906), was recognized as a woman of strong religious convictions who had a penchant for employing Irish Catholic nurses for her children. One year before Gache wrote this letter Varina persuaded her husband to be baptized in the Episcopal Church, and for his part the president continued to show consideration for Catholics, possibly because of his early education with the Dominican priests at St. Thomas Aquinas College, near Springfield, Kentucky.

It is difficult to judge with certainty about converts to Catholicism among the relatives of Thomas Jefferson's grandson, George Wythe Randolph (b. "Monticello," near Charlottesville, Virginia, March 10, 1818–d. "Edgehill" near Charlottesville, Virginia, April 3, 1867). The Secretary of War had ten brothers and sisters who reached maturity and his more distant Randolph kin, such as Randolph Tucker, C.S.N., the future husband of Margaret Hinton, were almost countless.[131]

In this letter Gache commented on the losses of the 10th and advised Father de Carrière of his admiration for the Georgia troops. His tally of the regimental losses at Chancellorsville is substantially the same as that given in the official report. Of the forty officers in the 10th there were only nine who were not either killed or wounded during the course of the war, and at Chancellorsville twelve regimental color bearers were killed. Moreover, this was an engagement which had long-lasting effects on the regiment's morale. During the same period the "Report of the Sick and Wounded" at

Hospital #3, Lynchburg, showed a sizeable percentage of the patients were from Georgia outfits, a fact which likely explains the chaplain's predilection for the inhabitants of the state where his *frère de lait*, Father André Cornette, had been missioned. Cornette did not remain long in Georgia, but his replacement, Anselm Usannez (1819-95) did, and achieved, in his own way, what Gache had dreamed to accomplish. When Hippolyte wrote this letter Usannez was the newly named rector at Grand Coteau, but in the following year, he too, apparently, had not given complete satisfaction to his superiors, and so was removed by Jourdan and dispatched to Spring Hill. No sooner had he arrived at the college than he was sent to Andersonville, Georgia. Here this fellow novice of Joseph Bixio attended to the Federal prisoners in the stockade where he soon became known as "Father Hosannah." Here also he became first a friend to, and later a defender of, the ill-fated Capt. Henry Wirz (1823-65) who stood trial for the atrocities at Andersonville.[132]

J.M.J.

Lynchburg
[Francis Gautrelet] June 1, 1863

Reverend and dear Father,

I have just learned that Bishop Quinlan is planning to visit Richmond in the near future. Would it be possible to ask him, or someone who will be traveling with him, to kindly bring me the notebooks containing my sermons and retreat notes. There are times when I could make very good use of them. Please warn whoever brings them, however, to be careful not to lose them. Also, it would be very good of you to pack them in such a way that no one will know what they are. If you cannot persuade the bishop or one of the members of his party to bring me these notebooks, please send them to me by some other trustworthy person such as Major Sands or Lieutenant Colonel [Michael] Nolan.

Another request. As the supply of candles made from whale-fat and the like has been exhausted, we are going to be forced, in the very near future, and to the great satisfaction of Father Serra, I would venture to guess, to imitate the early Christians in the illumination of our altars. In order to make candles myself, I have bought fifteen pounds of wax—and at 2 piastres a pound, if you please. Now I want to bleach this wax, but I don't know how. Tell me, then: is there anyone on the faculty at Spring Hill who could give me a reliable formula for bleaching wax, one which would make no exorbitant demands on money or skill? If there is, I'll certainly be indebted to him if he would send me the formula; and if this bleaching invention is original, I'll use my influence with the President of the Confederacy to obtain a patent for that man.

And now a third and final request. To my great scandal (and most assuredly to yours when you hear what I have to say) there are Catholic army chaplains here in Virginia, and indeed even a bishop, who have made an agreement with the "Protestant chaplains" to take turns in conducting a daily funeral service for all of the military dead brought to the cemetery, whether they be Catholic, Protestant, Jew or Turk. So as not to violate the laws of the [Catholic] church in this respect they recite not the prayers of the Latin ritual, but other prayers, and in English. They also insist that they do not read these prayers for the dead, but rather for those who are present at the funeral service. The pastor at Lynchburg is one of these priests. They have asked me to cooperate too. They had even hoped that I would be forced to do so by an order from the commandant of the post. But I made them understand that they were dealing with a Catholic who for many years had been inspired by the philosophy of Father Serra!

I went to work by first of all dethroning a Presbyterian minister who, without inquiring whether he had the right to do so or not, assumed the title of "senior chaplain" on the post, and who then claimed that the other chaplains should be subject to his orders. The first time he sent me an order, I took it to the commandant and made him look at the date of my appointment. It was I, and not the Reverend Presbyterian minister, who should have been "senior chaplain." The commandant took a look at the document and immediately saw that I was right. Next, I drew attention to the fact that I could not carry out his order concerning the burials. "When I entered the service of the Confederacy," I said, "I did so as a Catholic priest, and naturally with the understanding that I would be expected to render only those services which were in accord with the laws and customs of my church. Moreover," I went on to add, "among the dead, which the order I have received obliges me to bury, there are many Protestants and Jews, who, while they were alive, not only disbelieved in Catholic prayers and ceremonies, but even regarded this form of worship as an abomination. Why then, after they are dead, should we bury them with a ritual which, as long as they were alive, they rejected with indignation and horror? If they were sincere in their distrust of all things Catholic, we should respect their sentiments, as well as the sentiments of their families and friends who would be horrified if such an order were carried out. If they were not in good faith, then they don't deserve any religious service at all."

"Your first objection concerning the laws and customs of your church had occurred to me," the commandant replied. "But it was the pastor at Lynchburg himself who assured me that this would be no problem. I had never considered your second objection that such a service might seem wanting in respect toward the dead as well as toward their families and friends. Had this thought occurred, of course, I would never have issued the order. I shall now revoke it."

The good colonel, who is a Methodist, could not have been more reasonable, could he? But would you believe it: the pastor at Lynchburg, who is now called upon to conduct only Catholic services for the Catholic dead, persists in believing that there was nothing wrong about the concessions that were made in the first place! He even went to tell the commandant (no doubt to justify his previous action) that a Catholic priest may indeed do what was ordered; that it is not contrary to faith or custom. That a priest can do so under certain extraordinary and weighty circumstances, I will agree. But that he can do so without losing his dignity, without acting contrary to the spirit of the laws of the church—well, that is simply something which I cannot understand. These priests just don't want to forfeit their $80 a month compensation—that's the heart of the matter.

Now, I'd like to know the mind of the fathers at Spring Hill on the question. And so, if you understand the problem, I would be very happy to receive any further arguments you could send me to bolster up the right side against these priests and this bishop who have been too accommodating. *Adieu*, Reverend Father; don't forget me on the great feast days during the month of June.

Yours,
H. Gache, S.J.

My best regards to all of Ours.

COMMENTARY

General Nicholls was not appointed to the Lynchburg Post command until August, 1863, and therefore the commandant about whom Gache wrote in this letter was Maurice Scarsbrook Langhorne (b. Cumberland County, Virginia, March 27, 1823–d. Lynchburg, Virginia, March 28, 1908), the 1861 organizer and captain of the Lynchburg Grays which became part of the Eleventh Virginia Regiment. Hospitalized after Seven Pines and then failing to win reelection in his regiment, Langhorne remained in Lynchburg until he was relieved by the convalescing Nicholls. The colonel's dealings with Gache confirm a subsequent description of him as one whose "manners were polished and courtly, following the regime of the school of old Virginia gentlemen, of which he was a splendid type." Moreover, the colonel was "charitable to all in word and deed, and was rarely, if ever, heard to speak harshly of anyone; he loved his neighbor and did his best at all times to make the world better and happier by his daily precept and example." Undoubtedly, he tried to make Hippolyte Gache's world better and happier, a world which the chaplain saw threatened by the laxity of Bishop McGill and Father Sears on the one hand, and on the other, by the chicanery of Reverend Jacob Duche Mitchell, D.D. (b. Pennsylvania, November 2, 1806–d. Alexandria, Virginia, June 28, 1877). Doctor Mitchell had been the pastor of Lynchburg's Second Presbyterian Church since 1830, a dedicated Mason and a prominent champion of the temperance cause, two reasons why Gache may not have seen in him "a gentleman of rare accomplishments, literary and scientific, which made him a delightful conversationalist." But he was also a man "burning with patriotism," with two sons in the army, and if he had fifty, he stated, "they would be given up to the service of the state in such a contest." Soldiers, he believed, should "show themselves men, and in the day of battle put their trust in God and never turn their backs upon the enemy"[133]

It may have surprised Gache to learn that two months after he wrote this letter to Spring Hill, the reasonable Colonel Langhorne addressed a letter to General Cooper recommending that one of the two Catholic chaplains at Lynchburg be reassigned. Since Sears was also the pastor of the Catholic parish, it was obvious that the colonel thought Gache, whom he listed as the second Catholic chaplain, was expendable, and that his place would be better served by two additional Protestant chaplains. Langhorne complained that "the only duty (Sears and Gache) perform is to visit the few members of their church that are inmates of the hospital—the number being always small. There are five general hosps. here, making an aggregate of thirty hospitals, to be visited by three (3) Prot. Chaplains." Cooper's office wanted clarification, but General Nicholls was appointed post commandant on August 11, and the question was not pursued.[134]

The bishop of Mobile did not come to Virginia during the war and consequently Lt. Col. Michael Nolan (b. County Tipperary, Ireland–d. Gettysburg, Pennsylvania, July 1, 1863) acted as courier for Gache's precious notebooks. Nolan had left New Orleans as a sergeant in the Louisiana First, and after his arrival in Virginia, rose rapidly to colonel. At Sharpsburg, where he was wounded, he assumed command of the Louisiana Brigade after the death of Brig. Gen. William Edward Stark (1814-62). His own commission as brigadier general had not yet reached him when he was killed at Gettysburg. John Rapier, a distinguished soldier himself, recalled: "When I was a little boy around New Orleans, I used to collect bills for sugar at a small grocery, right opposite Charity Hospital in that city. The owner of the store was a young, blue-eyed, light-haired Irishman, named Mike Nolan. Mild and polite and friendly in his manners; and I am sure it is no shame to my foresight that at that time I did not recognize in him to be the best, bravest and grandest soldier I ever met."[135]

J.M.J.

Lynchburg

[Rev. Father de Carrière] September 7, 1863

Reverend and dear Father, P.C.

Thank you for your good letter of August 28 which I received the day before yesterday. But most especially, thank you for having remembered my feast day [August 13] as you did. It had almost slipped my mind; I was in Columbia, South Carolina, on that day, buried away in a retreat—not my own but one I was giving to the Ursulines. Hence, I had little time to think either of myself or of my feast day.

I'm not telling you for the first time about this trip; you knew that I was going, I'm sure. I left Lynchburg on the evening of July 31 and the next morning I arrived in Petersburg where, at the insistence of the pastor, whom I know well and who is an excellent priest, I stayed over Sunday and preached a sermon that evening. My pronunciation was so excellent that everyone in the congregation realized that I was speaking English. General Blanchard, who had served my mass that morning, was among those present, and on the next morning, Monday, he was my companion on the journey as far as Warrenton, North Carolina, where he was going to visit his family who had been living there for some time. What a wonderful Catholic the good general is! But like most of the just, he has his trials and tribulations. Last year, after the Battle of Seven Pines, just before those engagements which are now called the Battles of Richmond, he was relieved of the command of his brigade an sent to Louisiana as a commander of a training camp. The reasons given for his new assignment were designed to prevent the suspicion that he had been considered unfit for the command. It appears, however, that he was so considered; he himself is convinced of it, and the difficulty he has in obtaining another command is a rather strong indication of it. There has never been any charge made against him, and neither he nor his friends can guess what he had done wrong. For my part, I wouldn't be surprised if it is not a case of pure and simple bigotry. The general is a very zealous Catholic. As he is a convert from Protestantism, he knows what his former co-religionists are, what they are worth, and he values them accordingly. For this reason, he never loses the occasion to join battle with them, and when he lets them have it, it is with both barrels—even though delivered with a winsome smile. I wouldn't be a bit surprised if, during a religious discussion in which the general is wont to speak rather sharply, he offended a superior officer, who, in order to punish him for his excess of theological acumen, decided to find fault with his military savoir-faire. That's the world for you! Happily, the general knows well that *omnes qui pie volunt vivere in Christo Iesu, persecutionem patiuntur* [”anyone who wants to live a godly life in Christ Jesus can expect to be persecuted” *2 Tim. 3:12*]—and he has his share of it. Still, this does not lessen the humiliation he feels when his many friends question him on his new post, and he is forced to answer that he does not have any. By way of parenthesis—you know, I presume, that Colonel Nolan was killed at Gettysburg. A great loss for Father Hubert! But back to my trip to Columbia.

General Blanchard and I parted company, as I said, at Warrenton. No sooner had he gotten out of the carriage, than a young soldier who was being sent home to some place in South Carolina because of illness, approached me and said: “You don't know me, Father, but I know you very well. I saw you many times last year on the battlefields near Richmond, or as you rode alongside our ranks on that black horse of yours, encouraging us and saying: ‘Boys I am here. If you have need of me you'll not have to go far to find me; I'll be with you. Be of good heart!' and I," he went on to say, "How often did I want to speak with you, if only long enough to ask for your blessing. Yet I never found the opportunity. But that's alright; it was always a great consolation for me to realize that a Catholic priest was with us. And because I was sure that you blessed us in your heart—all of us who wanted to be blessed—I felt that I had received your blessing even though we never met."

Words like these will tell you that this young man was not a Protestant, or even a run-of-the-mill Catholic. He had been converted to the faith four years ago and then, after two years in a seminary in Angers, France, he decided, because of a misdirected patriotism (misdirected, that is, if he had a true vocation, but I suppose I ought not to presume to judge), that he would return home and fight for his country. But the poor boy will never be of much use to his country: he was returning home with consumption and diarrhea. His frail constitution had not withstood the hardships of camp life; but he is such a good youngster and he has accepted God's Will so wholeheartedly. I am certain that when death does come, it will simply mean the blessings of heaven. Needless to say, the time passed quickly in his company, while I was taking care of him and sharing with him Sister Pacifica's delicious cakes, as well as the brandy, the sugar, and the other tidbits which Sister Rose had so providentially packed in the "good Father's" valise. As I say, the time passed quickly, so quickly in fact that I hardly realized on Wednesday morning, August 5, we had already reached Columbia. Here we said good-bye, knowing that we would never see one another again—at least not in this world. I then hurried over to the rectory (I already knew one of the priests there) and washed up a bit after the trip. Next I went over to the convent where I said Holy Mass and where I made the acquaintance of the sisters whom I was supposed to convert.

The good nuns had known of me for a long time, and last year they had hoped that I would come and give them their retreat. A little misunderstanding, however, (one which has been a source of considerable amusement to Father Hubert and me), deprived them of this "treat." This is what happened. During my first year in Virginia, I met a Catholic gentleman who had formerly been an Episcopalian minister. This man discovered in me a quality that you, with your limited range of perception, had never guessed that I possessed. I mean to say he found me a man of singular worth, particularly in regard to spiritual matters. (I do hope that President Davis will give that man a patent for his discovery, should he happen to apply for one). Now, like all great discoverers, eager to share their knowledge with the world, my friend hastened to tell his sister, an Ursuline nun in Columbia, about the treasure he had found, and he persuaded her to do all she could to procure my ministrations for the next convent retreat. Even though your acquaintance with convent life is more limited than my own, surely you can imagine the flurry of excitement with which the sisters greeted this news. Their imaginations painted my virtues in colors ten times brighter than those depicted by the charitable ex-minister. There wasn't one of the nuns who doubted that if she could but see and hear me she would become forthwith a thaumaturge. It was decided, therefore, to move heaven and earth to get the Louisiana chaplain. Consequently, when the time for the retreat drew near, the mother superior, who is the sister of Bishop [Patrick Neeson] Lynch of Charleston, wrote a letter to her brother requesting that he invite me to come to Columbia to give the retreat. The bishop, who on one occasion had met Father Hubert, but who had never heard of Father Gache (a fact which should not be too surprising), and never dreaming that there would be two Louisiana Jesuits with the army in Virginia, assumed that it was Father Hubert that she wanted as retreat master.

Accordingly, he wrote to Father Hubert; then thoughtfully informed his sister of *her* mistake.

Father Hubert scarcely had any burning desire to give the retreat. He doubted, moreover, that he would be able to get a long enough leave to do so. Consequently, he asked me to go in his stead, arguing that I was better qualified to preach a retreat to nuns, and that, seeing that I was still convalescing (all of this took place right after the Battles of Richmond), I might more easily be able to obtain a leave of two or three weeks. "What," I cried, "You ask me to go to Columbia when it was you they requested! Do you take me for a fool—a presumptuous fool? I know myself too well to think that I could fill your shoes. Moreover, it would be an insult to the bishop to appear at the convent without ever having received an invitation. You, however, might possibly write to the bishop, explaining to him that you are not able to accept his kind invitation, but that there is another poor chaplain here, a man named Gache, likewise a Jesuit; who, although he has been known at times to slaughter the English language, would be very delighted indeed to go in your place—if His Excellency should so desire." Father Hubert suited his action to this council, and when the bishop read the letter and realized that it was he and not his sister who had made the mistake, he laughed heartily, but at the same time, he braced himself against the sort of explosion which can be launched only by an enraged mother superior whose target is her episcopal brother.

Unfortunately, it was much too late to remedy the situation. While Father Hubert was employing all of the resources of his rehetoric to persuade me to go and evangelize the good nuns, I, with the possibility of my being the object of their apostolic desires as far from my mind as was the possibility of my being the Emperor of China, was overwhelming his eloquence with protestations of my own abject unworthiness, and while letters were passing back and forth between Father Hubert, the bishop and the Reverend Mother, the time had run out. Father Hubert and I were obliged to leave for the Maryland campaign and it was already too late to give the retreat. The sisters were obliged to make it without a director, which they did. The following winter when Bishop Lynch encountered Father Hubert at Richmond, he gave him all of the details of this little drama and asked him to pass them on to me. You will not be surprised, therefore, to learn that when I finally arrived in Columbia, I was greeted like an angel from on high. The bishop himself came over to see that I was welcomed with suitable pomp, and to install me in the home of his brother, Doctor [John] Lynch, the guardian of the temporal health of the good Ursulines. During my stay with the doctor and his family, I never once felt that I was with strangers, for they received me from the minute that I arrived as if I had been a dear friend of long standing; they couldn't have made me feel more at home. To tell you all about the kindnesses they showered upon me during the twelve days I was their guest, or to describe in detail the choice attentions of which I was the object—all of this would simply be demanding the impossible of me. As far as the retreat was concerned, I'll merely say that its success came up to my most optimistic expectations; in fact, it even surpassed them. Every nun without exception was converted, and all admitted that my points were excellent, magnificent, and often even original. They were terribly sorry to see me leave, and each one expressed the most sincere hope that I would one day return to them. At least this is what they told me, and I would like to believe that they meant it.

Columbia is a pretty spot; the atmosphere of aristocracy and refinement which is a characteristic of South Carolina, is very much in evidence here. The Protestants who have the ascendancy, as they have in almost every other place, are extremely liberal and tolerant.

I have never heard of Catholics having to suffer any sort of persecution, and today they are accepted by everyone. Columbia would be an ideal place for us to build a college: it is centrally located between our schools to the north and those to the south, and it offers great opportunities to do apostolic work with the students as well as with their parents. I don't know of any other place where the Protestants seem so well-disposed for conversion. Apropos of this subject of conversions, do you recall having met at Spring Hill a young gentleman named Caldwell? He used to come from time to time to visit with his brother-in-law, Charles Montague, who was one of our students at the college. Young Caldwell was a writer of sorts who had already published a small volume of poems. Well, one afternoon while I was visiting the cemetery at Columbia with one of the parish priests, a Father [Jeremiah J.] O'Connell, I was attracted by a small tombstone, of a rather odd shape, bearing the name Caldwell. The name, together with certain information mentioned on the stone, immediately brought to mind the Caldwell gentleman whom I had not thought of since I had last seen him at Spring Hill. I mentioned all of this to Father O'Connell and asked him if he had ever known Mr. Caldwell. "And isn't it the same who's in the grave? Read everything it says on the epitaph." I did; and I recognized that this indeed had been our guest at Spring Hill, the husband of Miss Agnes Montague. He died three years ago of consumption. Father O'Connell also told me that, after giving evidence for a long while of leanings toward Catholicism, Mr. Caldwell had finally made a public and formal profession of faith just three months before his death. As there are many people in Columbia like Mr. Caldwell, I hope that Bishop Lynch will take the necessary means to establish a college for us there and that it will prosper.

The schools, the schools—this is where the most good can be done, and where it can be done most effectively.

True, it can be wearisome to watch over the young and to prepare classes for them; true, it can be more pleasant and more satisfying in some respects to give retreats, to preach missions and to be pampered in parishes or coddled in convents. But if a man wishes to give the greatest glory to God; if he wishes to do the most efficacious work for the good of souls, he should stay in the school room. If I were the father confessor of all the priests in this country, I would advise every single one of them to be a school master, while continuing, of course, to remain a parish priest.

I left Columbia on the sixteenth of August, taking the long way home, as they say. That is, I returned by way of Charleston. When the bishop was in Columbia he urged me to pay a visit to his episcopal see, and then while I was giving the retreat, I received a letter from him in which once again he insisted that I come to pay him a visit. Meanwhile, his brother, the doctor, and his sister, the reverend mother, were pleading with me to accept the proffered invitation. So, despite the fact that the good Daughters of Charity in Lynchburg were impatiently awaiting my return, so overwhelming was all of this insistence on my going to Charleston that I simply could not return to Lynchburg by the direct route.

I was in Charleston on the eighteenth and nineteenth, during which time I visited Fort Sumter, Fort Moultrie and all of the batteries on Sullivan Island. It was too hot to go see Morris Island. While I was on Sumter, I imagined I could hear the first roar of cannon and the first whistling of shells, and from the steeple of St. Michael's (Episcopal) Church, I saw with my mind's eye the battle between the ironclad, which had attacked the fort, and two monitors. When the captain of one of these monitors was killed, they both retired and thus the battle was terminated. But the final result of my visit was to convince me that sooner or later Charleston will fall. Nothing since then has led me to alter this opinion. They say there was no way to prevent it, but in trying to conserve our strength, we've made the enemy no less certain of success. Before leaving Charleston, I had occasion to meet the French consul who is at the same time the commandant of the warship, *La Granade.* He is a charming Parisian whose modest reserve is in pleasing contrast to the bluff ways of the Americans. I also visited with Delphin Bienvenu who is ill and lodged with a private family. He recognized me as I was saying mass at the Sisters of Mercy, and he came to see me afterwards at the bishop's residence. He told me that all of the Creoles who were on Morris Island the day of the assault went to confession to Father [Léon] Fillion, a French priest who had gone to Morris Island for precisely that purpose. Even Cyrille Villeré, of scarcely pious memory, made his confession along with the others, and ever since then his conduct has indicated that he was really quite sincere. Another example of the effect of a good education! I got the impression that the Louisianians are well liked in Charleston, and particularly by the bishop who told me that he was very impressed with my Creoles.

I was distressed that you took into your head to send the notebooks containing my sermons and retreat notes at a time when they might so easily have been lost. I had asked you to send them only at such time as you might be very sure of my receiving them. Not for all the world would I suffer these notebooks to be lost; the loss of Mobile itself would afflict me no less sorely. If you have not yet sent them, please hold on to them until you have moral certitude that they will reach me. I have had no news from Father Hubert since his return from Pennsylvania; however, someone told me that he is not very well. Sincere regards to our fathers and brothers; to Mr. Parada and to Doctor Rohmer. Please tell [Ramon] Oriel and [Octave] Légier that I am shocked that they are at Spring Hill, seeing that their post is in the army. Be sure to remember me to Mr. de Armas and to Edward Bermudez when you see them.

Yours sincerely in our Lord,
H. Gache, S.J.

COMMENTARY

Fortified with tidbits and other delicacies suppled to the "good Father" by Sister Rose, née Margaret Noyland (b. Castlebar, Mayo, Ireland, 1834–d. Emmitsburg, Maryland, March 14, 1909) and Sister Pacifica, née Mary Josephine Ulrich (b. Baltimore, Maryland, February 15, 1843–d. La Salle, Illinois, April 1, 1905), Gache traveled to South Carolina in August, 1863, to give a retreat to the Ursuline nuns in Columbia.[136] In this letter to Philip de Carrière he gave an account of his trip, beginning with a summary of the conversation with his traveling companion, Brig. Gen. Albert Blanchard (b. Cambridge, Massachusetts, September 10, 1810–d. New Orleans, Louisiana, June 21, 1891). It is possible, as Gache surmised, that anti-Catholic sentiment may have played a role in the general's treatment by superiors; there is no proof that such was the case. On the other hand, there is substantial evidence that, even at this date, Blanchard's ability as a military commander was called into doubt by his peers. There is also evidence that the nagging Blanchard problem was handled with more than mere consideration for the feelings and the honor of the loyal and conscientious general who seems to have bungled every command and who showed such little insight into the limitations of his talent. The Wednesday before Gache met him at St. Joseph's Church, Petersburg, Blanchard had written President Davis one of his many letters begging for a new command. This letter implies yet another reason, besides the desire to visit his family in Warrington, why he decided to quit Richmond in August. "I thought that when I was relieved. . . ," he stated, referring to his having been replaced at Alexandria, Louisiana by General Kirby Smith, "that it meant that I should be actively employed, else I preferred to be doing something for the cause, however little. Instead, I have been *loafing* around Richmond for two months. I ask employment—Please, Sir, save me from this mortifying idleness."[137]

The identity of the former seminarian who approached Gache after the train left Warrenton has been impossible to confirm. Although there were some South Carolinans enrolled at the *grand sêminaire* of Angers before and during the Civil War, there is no record of any one of these students leaving France to enlist in the Confederate Army. The most likely candidate is a certain James Geraty of Charleston whose name appears once on the lists of students at the nearby *petit sêminaire* of Cambrée. However, there is no record of a Geraty in any South Carolina regiment that fought in Virginia in 1862-63.[138]

"The Catholic gentleman who had been an Episcopalian minister," and who arranged Gache's trip, was Ambler Weed (b. Richmond, Virginia, 1826–d. Norfolk, Virginia, March 17, 1871), the brother of Sister Charles, née Mary Otis Weed (b. Richmond, Virginia, 1829–d. Villa Crucis, Columbia, South Carolina, March 16, 1889). Ambler Weed was ordained for the diocese of Virginia in 1846 and served for the most part in Accomack County until 1858 when he entered the Roman Catholic Church in which he was ordained a priest after the war and was assigned to Staunton where he directed the thriving school founded by his notorious predecessor, Joseph Bixio.[139]

Mother Baptista, née Ellen Lynch (b. Cheraw, South Carolina, November 2, 1832–d. Charleston, South Carolina, July 28, 1887), was the superior of the convent which the Civil War diarist, Mary Boykin Chesnut (1823-86), had visited in 1862 and which was also the object of Gache's travel the following year. The nun's brother, Patrick Neeson Lynch (b. Clones, Monaghan, Ireland, March 10, 1817–d. Charleston, South Carolina, February 26, 1882) was ordained third bishop of Charleston on March 14, 1859, and another brother, John (b. mid-Atlantic, January 8, 1809–d. Columbia, South Carolina, October 20, 1881) and his wife Elizabeth Steele Macnamara (b. Salisbury, North Carolina, December 18, 1823–d. Columbia, South Carolina, May 4, 1903) provided the Jesuit with hospitality during his stay in Columbia.[140]

In this letter Gache recounted that one of the local priests, Jeremiah J. O'Connell (b. County Cork, Ireland, November 21, 1821–d. Belmont, North Carolina, October 23, 1894), the author of *Catholicity in the Carolinas and in Georgia*, walked him through St. Peter's cemetery where he recognized the grave of a man well known to the Spring Hill Jesuits.[141] This was Howard Haine Caldwell (b. Newberry, South Carolina, September 20, 1831–d. Columbia, South Carolina, February, 1859), son of Chancellor James J. Caldwell (1817-50). Howard had been married to Agnes Montague (b. Wade, Fayetteville, North Carolina, August 13, 1837–d. Columbia, South Carolina, November 28, 1921), whose brother

Charles, Jr. (b. Wade, Fayetteville, North Carolina, April 10, 1845–d. Bandera, Texas, April 25, 1916), enrolled at Spring Hill in 1858.

Shortly before the war the Montagues moved to Texas and Charles, Jr. recalled that when that state seceded and was raising troops, "I asked permission of my father to enlist. He refused, owing to my age . . . In July of that year (1861), however, I ran away and joined Company C, Texas Second Regiment and was sent to guard the long road from San Antonio to El Paso and New Mexico." This sixteen year old soldier, according to one account, was credited as having been the one who fired the first shot of the war in Texas, not against an insolent Yankee, but against an Indian who tried to steal some Confederate Army horses he was assigned to guard at Fort Davis. Recalling this incident in later years Montague described himself as being "for my age, a pretty tough Texas cowboy," a fact which did not save him from being mustered out of the regiment and told to return home. But, as he further recalled, he was also the descendant of two South Carolina governors, and so he determined to make his way back to Columbia where he enlisted in the South Carolina Sixth Cavalry, and in this regiment he served the Confederacy until General Johnston's surrender in April 1865. Although his brother-in-law, Howard Haine Caldwell, had been admitted to the South Carolina bar in 1855, his chief interests were teaching and writing. His two published volumes of poetry suggest that if death had not overtaken him, he might have earned an enviable reputation as a celebrated Southern poet. In 1857 he joined the faculty of the ill-fated St. Mary's College, Columbia, an institution which enjoyed a brief, precarious toehold in the academic world. In 1859, Caldwell founded *The Courant*, a literary magazine of quality—one more harbinger of the coming renaissance of letters in the South at the very eve of the war.[142]

In the Fall of 1862 the French consul at Charleston was summoned to Paris leaving the provisional exercise of consular functions to another agent whose credentials were accepted by the Confederate Government. Fearing that the Federal Navy was about to shell Charleston, this new official hastily and without authority left his post, turning over the office to a clerk then at the New York Consulate. Secretary of State Judah Philip Benjamin (1811-84) protested this action "of delegating to functionaries, who reside among our enemies," the power to act in the name of Napoleon III. A response from the Quai d'Orsay assured the Confederate Government that the incumbent would receive orders to resume the position he had abandoned in panic.[143] When Gache arrived in Charleston, therefore, there was no council of His Imperial Majesty who had official accreditation, but seeing that this port city had long had strong ties with France, it was natural that the commanding officer of the warship *La Granade* assume the responsibility of keeping the consulate functioning on an ad hoc basis. This

Frenchman, whose civility was such a contrast to inurbane American ways was Julien-Sosthènes-Joseph Bayot (b. Ouessant, Finistère, France, May 31, 1831).[144] Also prominent in the French colony since his arrival there in 1850, was the Reverend Léon Fillion (b. Cholet, Maine-et-Loire, France, August 17, 1817–d. Charleston, South Carolina, February 21, 1865), the father confessor to the Louisiana Creoles whose conduct had so impressed Bishop Lynch.[145]

In this letter Gache names two Creoles who were Spring Hill alumni: Delphin Bienvenu (b. St. Bernard Parish, Louisiana, December 23, 1834–d. New Orleans, Louisiana, September 2, 1917) and Cyrille Villeré (b. St. Bernard Parish, Louisiana, 1830–d. New Orleans, Louisiana, January 29, 1886). The former enlisted in Captain Surgi's Sappers and Miners Company of the Louisiana Militia in April 1861, was wounded at Shiloh and discharged from the army. In June 1863 he reenlisted at Mobile in Company D, Maningault's Battalion of the South Carolina Artillery and in the following February he was transferred to the South Carolina Siege Train. Shortly after Gache visited him he received confirmation, signed by General Beauregard, to an assignment at the Soldier's Relief Hospital, Charleston, where he remained until he was paroled. Doctor Bienvenu gained a certain amount of attention in 1882 during the Labadieville Affair when he wrote a tract encouraging Louisiana Catholics to have recourse to the pope against Archbishop Napoleon Perché who had refused to take action against a priest of doubtful morals. Bienvenu's kinsman, Cyrille Villeré, was one of the first pupils to enroll at the Jesuit Alabama college, transferring there from St. Charles, Grand Coteau, in the fall of 1847. This grandson of the first Creole governor of Louisiana, Jacques-Phillipe Villeré (1761-1830), enrolled in Captain Delery's St. Bernard Horse Rifles Company of the Louisiana Militia, April 29, 1861. Then, three days before Bienvenu enlisted in Company D of Maningault's Battalion, Villeré enrolled in Company A. Transferred the same day as Bienvenu to the South Carolina Siege Train, he remained in the headquarters of this outfit until the end of the war.[146]

Also in this letter Gache named a number of other former Spring Hillians. One of these, like Bienvenu and Villeré, had roots in St. Bernard Parish. This was Ramon Oriel (b. November 16, 1839), the son of Dr. Francisco and Incarnación Collantes Oriel. Another was Octave Légier (b. New Orleans, Louisiana, January, 1846–d. New Orleans, Louisiana, February 11, 1905) who had been a student at the college when the war began. Although his obituary noted that "as a soldier in the army of Tennessee, his record was second to none," and "that for four years he carried a musket and proved himself a brave and true soldier," the facts of his service have not been fully recorded. What is known is that as a seventeen-year-old lad he enrolled, on July 10, 1863, at Mobile in a Louisiana artillery company, but, as Gache's letter testified, he was still at Spring Hill in the fall. However, seeing that he was paroled in North Carolina on April 26, 1865, one day before Charles Montague, it is obvious that he had seen some service before the end of hostilities. After the war Légier became a well known steamboat clerk along the Mississippi. Research has not uncovered any facts about Oriel beyond 1865.[147]

Edward Bermudez (b. New Orleans, Louisiana, January 20, 1832–d. New Orleans, Louisiana, August 22, 1892), scion of another of Louisiana's most illustrious Creole families, came to Spring Hill in March 1848 and received his A.B. in 1851. In 1860 this relative of General Beauregard was a delegate to the secession convention, and after much agonizing signed the ordinance which severed the ties between Louisiana and the Federal government. This same year he enlisted as a private in the Orleans Guards, but there is no record of his having gone to Virginia in his cousin Charles Dreux's battalion. At the time when Gache wrote this letter, the unhappy Bermudez had settled down to being an army clerk in Mobile where he tried to obtain a position in the Assistant Adjutant General's Office. In the following January he was still writing desperate letters to the Assistant Secretary of War in a vain attempt to obtain a position commensurate with his talent and training. Elected an assistant city attorney in New Orleans after the war, he was removed by General Sheridan as "an impediment to reconstruction," and so he went to New York where he obtained a LL.D. at the Jesuit college, Fordham. After this period of his life his fortune changed, and a most successful career was crowned in 1880 when he was named chief justice of the Louisiana supreme court, a position he bequeathed twelve years later to General Francis T. Nicholls. His idyllic marriage to Armanda de Maupassant (1829-97) tied his family closer to France and offered a wealth of anecdotes to romancers of the Creole legends. Bermudez' father, Judge Joachim (1796-1866) was one of the two signatories for the State of Louisiana of the Charter of the "Catholic Society for the Diffusion of Religious and Literary Education" in 1847, the other being the notary public Octave de Armas (1804-89). It is not clear from his letter who the "Mr. de Armas" was that Gache wished to be remembered to along with Edward Bermudez. Most probably it was Arturo Christoval Léon de Armas (b. New Orleans, Louisiana, February 24, 1824–d. New Orleans, Louisiana, September 6, 1904) who had brought his son Arthur, Jr. (1853-89) to enroll at Spring Hill College in July 1863, a fact that Father Cornette noted in the vice president's diary. But it is also possible that Gache was referring to Arturo's cousin, his old friend Octave.[148]

Lynchburg, Va.
December 27, 1864

Rev. Father de Carrière
Spring Hill College

Reverend and dear Father, P.C.

During the first few weeks of October, I received a letter from Father Gautrelet in which he told me that I would soon receive one from you containing all of the news that has recently been brought to Spring Hill. Ever since that moment I have been looking forward to the arrival of that precious missive; but always in vain, and so, I have finally concluded that either the letter has never been written or that it has gone astray. In either case, I have decided that I should wait no longer. It would seem also that you did not receive the two or three letters which I wrote to you in the course of this past summer. And you know how it costs me to write long letters! The last time I wrote to you was toward the end of September, but as I didn't say anything much of interest in that letter, you didn't miss much by not having it delivered. Really, there is only one reason why I write to you at all: to give you a visible proof that I haven't forgotten you—you or the others in the community.

Since September I haven't done anything or haven't seen anything worthy of special mention. There was just one retreat which I gave to the Sisters of Mercy which broke the monotony of living from day to day. Apart from that I've done very little. I don't mean to say that I've been idle, for besides the sermon which I write out in English and deliver every Sunday, I have found many other little occupations which fill up the days, and which even make them pass rather quickly. But despite all of this, I am not accomplishing very much that is worthwhile, partly because for a long time now we have not had many sick here and partly because among the sick we do have there are very few Catholics. In town there is hardly enough work to keep one priest busy; furthermore, the parish priest at Lynchburg is not eager that his parishioners have much to do with me. I certainly can't say, after all of this, that *messis quidem multa operarii autem pauci* ["the harvest is rich but the workers are few," *Luke 10:2*]. If anything, there are too many workers for this harvest. Would you believe it?—the post here at Lynchburg is blessed with five, no six chaplains: two Catholics and four Protestants! And for some curious reason almost all of the Protestant chaplains want to work right here where I am. They have filled the hospital with an assortment of sectarian books and newspapers which are used by the sisters and myself for lighting our fires, and the patients now find themselves with a plethora of paper for various household purposes.

Sometime ago one of these ministerial individuals had the impertinence to establish himself right here at the college. I answered that I had great difficulty understanding that, inasmuch as the commandant of the post knew very well that one man was enough for this assignment, and that I had scant need of assistance. "Yes," he replied, "But you appreciate that not all men have the same religious opinions." "Oh, as far as that is concerned," I said, "I have not as yet met a single patient who failed to receive from me anything that you yourself might have given him—friendly words, encouraging words, and, if you will, some prayers. Should I ever find anyone who wishes to see you, however, you will be duly informed. Finally, there is no room here at the college."

He was visibly taken aback at this, and without another word, he rose, took his hat, and left, assuring me, certainly with very little sincerity, that he would be delighted were I to come and pay him a visit sometime. Unwilling to acknowledge complete defeat, he then sought out the Chief Surgeon of the Division and requested his permission to preach and so forth in the wards. The surgeon, who is far from being a Catholic, but who is nevertheless a man who despises all Protestant ministers, told him that he was unable to grant that permission as it was against regulations; however, he would give him permission to hold religious services in the hospital yard. Obviously, this did not amount to much, and it was very far from what the ambitious preacher had envisioned, but not being able to do any better, he had either to content himself with the yard or consent to receive a salary which he would do nothing to earn—an alternative which his delicate conscience would not permit. So, it was arranged that he would come to preach twice a week at about 4:30 p.m. This would be just a few minutes before supper; however, we took care not to mention this detail.

On the following Wednesday, our apostle arrived at about 4:45 with two or three books tucked under his arm. Once again he announced the purpose of his visit, and followed by four or five neophytes, he headed toward a corner of the yard where he was soon joined by about twenty others. He began the service with the singing of a hymn; then, getting up on a small grass mound and raising his eyes to heaven (imploring the Holy Spirit, I presume), the evangelical gentleman began to distribute to his hearers the bread of the Word. Up to this point there was nothing extraordinary. Eloquence was gushing forth in great torrents from his Presbyterian lips. *Conticuere omnes intendique ora tenebant* ["All were hushed and held their gaze bent upon him," *Virgil, Aeneid II, 1*], when behold!—a naughty refectorian, a wily rogue from Erin's green shores, who had been silently watching the proceedings and slyly waiting the precise moment to throw the meeting into confusion, suddenly sounded the supper bell. Before the clock had struck five, all of the congregation was at the table and the preacher was left alone, his arms outstretched and his mouth gaping, still standing on the grassy mound.

You ought to have seen the dismay and astonishment of that disciple of Calvin as he picked up his books, put on his hat and walked away. I am certain he would have given a good part of his month's salary to have been able to suffer his mortification unseen, but unfortunately he was not even to have this small consolation, as he had to endure the shame of observing a crowd of both whites and colored—standing in the doorways and at the windows—shamelessly he-hawing at his plight. You may be sure that his humiliation tended to tame his zeal, and not once since then was he ever seen on the accursed little grass mound. From then on he was satisfied to bring a few tracts and newspapers and distribute them to those who were confined to their beds.

Not long after our minister's disgrace, a Presbyterian was appointed head doctor at Ferguson, a hospital which is in our division and which is under the care of our sisters. This fact seemed to offer the aforesaid chaplain the opportunity to recoup his losses. So, a few weeks after his ordeal here, he went over to Ferguson and asked the new doctor, his co-religionist, for permission to preach in the wards. As the doctor was not yet aware of the terms of the understanding between the sisters and the army, he readily granted the requested permission. This in itself was already a triumph for the minister and the glory that seemed to be in store for him at Ferguson was enough to make him forget his loss at the college. Now he could preach to the bed-ridden, who would have no possibility to escape, and he could be sure that every member of the congregation would be present at the end of his sermon. But, alas and alack, how vain are the plans of mortal man! The sister in charge at Ferguson is also a child of the Emerald Isle—a sweet and timid dove who scarcely dares to open her eyes or to speak above a whisper in her day to day dealings with the world, but, a dove who shows the boldness and the courage of a lioness as soon as there is a question of defending the

Faith; a dove who would box the ears of the Sultan on his throne if by this gesture she might prevent a blasphemy. As soon as she heard that on the following Sunday there was to be a sermon in Ward 2, she immediately sent for the doctor in charge and asked him if he had given permission for preaching in the wards. When he replied that he had, she said: "Doctor, this is forbidden by Division Regulations, and no exceptions have heretofore been made. I must ask you kindly to revoke your permission. And if the permission is not revoked, we ourselves will be forced to leave. You must make the choice."

The doctor was flabbergasted. He couldn't very well have said to the nuns: "Pack your bags," for that is exactly what the Surgeon General would have said to him on the following day. Consequently, he promised to revoke the permission. But then for several days, either because he was ashamed to speak to the preacher about it, or for some other reason, he said nothing at all. On the following Sunday, therefore, the minister came armed, as was his wont, with two or three books to inaugurate a series of sermons. It was about three o'clock in the afternoon when the sisters, who were in their quarters, were suddenly startled by a Protestant hymn booming forth from the ward on the other side of the street. There could be no doubt about it: in spite of everything, the preacher had indeed arrived!

Immediately the serving sister sent a ward master to tell the minister that it was absolutely forbidden to sing or to preach in the wards. But the preacher was in no mind to heed this behest. Whereupon, she herself went down, fearlessly threw open the door to the ward and from this vantage point made signs to the preacher of a nature so unambiguous as to leave no doubt of her intention. The minister, who at that moment was reciting a prayer, begging God "to let me know my sinfulness" (for these are the words that the sister heard), pretended not to notice her presence and went blithely on. The sister, by now thoroughly indignant, walked right through the ward, straight up to him, and said: "Sir, this place is a hospital; not a meeting house. Please cease your preaching and praying. Otherwise I shall report you to the chief doctor of the division. He has forbidden the holding of all religious services in this hospital."

Seeing such a tiny woman laying down the law to him with such force, the preacher merely said, almost inaudibly: "The good sister wants to do what is right. I too wanted to do what is right, to do my duty as I saw it." And without saying another word, he once more closed his books, put on his hat and walked away, looking for all the world like the proverbial fox caught raiding a chicken coop. We've never seen him since. In fact, he has left Lynchburg.

Well, my intention was to write only a few lines, and here my story of the preacher has covered four whole pages. I'll entrust them now to God's keeping for I do not know if you will ever receive them. Good-bye dear Father. My regards to all of our Fathers and Brothers there and to all of the externs who are our friends. Happy New Year to all!

Devotedly yours in Our Lord,
L.H. Gache, S.J.

COMMENTARY

Just about the time the Daughters of Charity and their chaplain arrived in Lynchburg in November 1862, a soldier from the Mississippi Second died, in Christian's Factory Hospital, Division #1 of General Hospital #2, from small pox. During the course of the next nineteen months ninety-eight more men died from this dreaded disease and many others suffered from its ravages. To cope with the epidemic at Lynchburg, army surgeon, John Jay Terrell (1826-1919), set up a small pox camp at Darrington, then just outside the city limits and today the site of the Methodist cemetery, Lynchburg.[149] Sister Rose was asked to take charge of this hospital, so the Daughters of Charity, in addition to their duties at the College Hospital and at Ferguson's Factory, nursed the sick and dying here until the summer of 1864. When the camp was first set up Terrell considered asking the Jesuit chaplain to visit the quarantined patients, but he hesitated to do so because of the danger involved. "But Father Gache himself proposed it and did much to relieve the suffering of the patients . . . (Gache and the sisters) just had to segregate the patients and soothe their sufferings and let the disease take its course."[150] The fact that Father Hippolyte, the only Lynchburg chaplain to serve at the fever hospital, never mentioned Darrington might suggest that beneath his studied bravura there was a certain modesty, but unquestionably Doctor Terrell's testimony places the Jesuit in the ranks of other heroic chaplains like Reverend George W. Dame at Danville and Gache's better known confrere Father Anselm Usannez at Andersonville.[151] By December 1864, when he wrote the preceding letter, the epidemic had all but run itself out, an actuality which might explain why he found he now had so much time on his hands. As the weary war stretched on, not only had tension grown between himself and the Protestant chaplains, but his relationship with Father Oscar Sears, which never seemed more than cordial, was now decidedly strained. Sears' objections to Gache socializing with the parishioners of Holy Cross parish, however, had not prevented the Louisiana chaplain from sending one of the local students to Spring Hill.[152] The retreat he preached that broke the monotony of these colorless days was begun in early December; the retreatants were seven sisters of Our Lady of Mercy, nurses at the Confederate Hospital, White Sulpher Springs, Virginia, who were from the Charleston convent where he had met Delphin Bienvenu the year previously. These sisters had come to Greenbriar White Sulpher Springs in December 1861 with Reverend Jeremiah J. O'Connell's brother, Chaplain Lawrence P. O'Connell, C.S.A. (1826-91), and when that hospital was forced to relocate to Montgomery County in May 1862, the sisters moved with it, serving with little or no monetary compensation until the end of the war when they found themselves stranded and without means to return home. After a series of harrowing experiences these refugees on the rim of the Confederacy were at last united with the Charleston Sisters of Mercy three months after the war was over.[153]

On September 2, 1864 Reverend Jacob Duche Mitchell resigned from the army[154] and on October 28, Reverend William McGee (b. Richmond, Virginia, December 23, 1821–d. Betheny Station, Virginia, April 2, 1891), whose candidacy as a replacement for Gache had been sponsored by Mitchell the year previously, received his official army appointment and assignment to the Lynchburg hospitals where he had functioned as a civilian chaplain since 1862. McGee, who was a convert at nineteen to the Methodist church—from atheism or Catholicism (it is difficult to specify from his curriculum vitae)—never deviated until the day of his death from the strict line Methodist itinerant preacher, and was no doubt responsible for distributing some of the tracts which Gache found so abhorrent.[155]

The second Protestant chaplain at the Lynchburg hospitals at this date was a Baptist minister, the complex and controversial Reverend John Lipscomb Johnson (b. Spotsylvania County, Virginia, August 12, 1837–d. Clinton, Mississippi, March 2, 1915). After the war Johnson, a professor of English at the University of Mississippi, Oxford, was an author of the state's harsh Jim Crow law, an accomplishment in which he took great pride. Educator, editor, politician, duelist, Johnson was destined to become one of the most energetic preachers in the South, a man whose forceful personality and powerful oratory elicited varied and strong reactions, oftentimes contradictory, from his hearers.[156]

The third Protestant chaplain at Lynchburg during this period was a minister of a far different temperament from Johnson, Mitchell, and McGee. This was Reverend William Venable Wilson (b. Prince William County, Virginia, January 18, 1818–d. Lynchburg, Virginia, January 22, 1908), who had been compelled by the exigencies of the war to leave Moorefield, which had been incorporated into West Virginia, for Lynchburg, where he had been licensed to preach for the first time in 1843. A quiet man, Reverend Wilson served in various Virginia Presbyterian churches for more than fifty years before and after the war.[157]

Records do not indicate any other Protestant chaplain serving at the Lynchburg Post at the time Gache wrote the preceding letter, although it is possible that an itinerant preacher or some minister from Lynchburg visited the patients on the wards of the many hospitals in the city. But this fact does not help for a positive identification of the unnamed Presbyterian minister who had played the principal role in the cruel anecdote that Gache took such pleasure in recounting, and had the man been a non-resident of the town Gache would have noted the fact. The most likely candidate, therefore, is Reverend Jacob Duche Mitchell, "a revivalist and never so happy as when conducting a meeting of that description," with whom Gache had clashed in 1863 and whose retirement had made him less conspicuous in the wards toward the end of 1864.[158]

Other members of the cast that participated in the drama Gache described in this letter are easier to distinguish, but not all are as easy to identify. The chief surgeon of Hospital #3 who was reputed to have had such a poor opinion for all Protestant ministers, was Thomas H. Fisher (b. Fauquier County, Virginia, 1822). He had come from Danville with the sisters and was put in charge of the college hospital in November 1862. Fisher, a most elusive man, was also responsible for Ferguson Hospital, a former tobacco factory consisting of two frame buildings, one two stories high and the other three, at 13th and Main Streets. Sister Aloysius, née Margaret Kane (b. County Wexford, Ireland, September 10, 1828–d. Emmitsburg, Maryland, May 20, 1871), was the head matron there, the "sweet timid dove" of Gache's report.

In November, Doctor Joseph William Akin (b. Bowling Green, Kentucky, June 17, 1830–d. Louisville, Kentucky, June 19, 1904) was appointed surgeon in charge at Ferguson's. Akin, who had settled at Natchez, Mississippi, before the war, enlisted in Posey's 16th in July 1861 and resigned the following February. There is no further record of his assignments until November 1862, when he is listed as the surgeon of the Alabama Fifteenth Regiment. Finally, records reveal the identity of the "naughty refectorian: who broke up the prayer meeting by ringing the supper bell." He was Private Felix Muldoon (b. Ireland, 1839–d. Washington, D.C., April 7, 1904) and on July 17, 1861 he had enlisted in Capt. William Thornton's Company, the Prince William Cavalry, subsequently Company A, Fourth Virginia Cavalry Regiment. In December, 1862, Muldoon was admitted to the Danville hospital and was then transferred to Lynchburg. In December still a patient, his name was removed from the list of cooks and placed on that of hospital stewards.[159]

Charleston
July 18, 1865

Rev. P. de Carrière
Spring Hill

Reverend and dear Father, P.C.

Let at long last the silence be broken! It has been ages, hasn't it?, since last I wrote to you. And so much has happened in the interim: I have visited so many places; met so many people and have seen so many remarkable things. As a result, I have so much to tell you that I scarce know where to begin.

Toward the middle of last February, by a very special dispensation of Divine Providence, I was transferred, along with the Daughters of Charity, from Lynchburg to Richmond. For the sake of brevity, I shall not speak to you about the tears which our departure set flowing. The good people of Lynchburg (smile at their simplicity, you who have more knowledge of the world!) seem to have regarded me, rightly or not, as a thaumaturge, and attributed to me the power of curing the sick, believing that I had, in fact, cured many, especially among the children. When they learned of my departure, there was heard in Lynchburg weeping and loud lamentation, comparable perhaps, to what was heard in Ars when the villagers learned that *their* sainted *cure* was no longer in their midst. But as I have said, I'll pass over all of this in silence, and I'll merely mention that three weeks after my departure, the sights and sounds of mourning were everywhere yet in evidence. Ah friend, how easy life might be if one's presence were not so essential to those about him. But on to Richmond! As you probably already know, I was there when the Confederates abandoned the city and the Federals took it over. President Davis and his cabinet fled about seven o'clock on the evening of April 2, and the last groups of our soldiers had followed by midnight. At the hospital where I was stationed, we were given the order to remain at our posts until the Federal troops arrived. After that we were to carry on as circumstances would permit. This is exactly what we did.

After the departure of the President and before all of the troops had left, a fire broke out which utterly destroyed the richest and the most beautiful part of Richmond, and which ruined the fortunes of so many families. What a spectacle this poor city presented on the third, fourth, and fifth of April, and especially on the third. Imagine, if you will, the fire which had completely consumed some of the houses, and which, meeting with no resistance, was rapidly spreading; the ominous murmur of the advancing flames, broken at intervals by the crashing of walls and roofs; the thick, choking billows of black smoke; and in the midst of such a scene, imagine great surging throngs of all classes filling the streets; some carrying whatever they managed to snatch from the flames—bolts of cloth, provisions of meat, boxes of shoes, sacks of flour; others, empty handed, coming out to see if the fire was moving toward their property; others, standing helplessly in front of their houses, contemplating the already certain ruin; still others were there who had come from different parts of the city merely to watch the progress of this terrible spectacle. And among all of these people no one spoke; everywhere there was grim silence, drawn faces and a sense of hopelessness and horror. Except for an occasional exclamation from a child or from a Negro who had salvaged something from the flames, no human voice was heard. This very silence was all the more impressive for being suddenly broken again and again by the detonation of whole arsenals as the fire spread. Each explosion hurled blazing embers sometimes as far as a half-mile; thus further spreading the conflagration. Then, like phantoms against the background of the burning city, the sudden appearance of the first Yankee cavalry scouts: they came galloping sword in hand and pistol in belt giving the impression, as they looked neither to the left nor to the right, that they were even more frightened than frightening.

If you can imagine all of this you'll have some idea, but a very inadequate one, of what Richmond was like during those three days—three days which seemed like three months. By the sixth the fire had all but spent itself and a semblance of order returned to the city. At last toward the middle of Holy Week, General [Edward Cresap] Ord, the commandant of the newly created Department of Virginia, arrived. He is the son of a man who was at one time a scholastic in the Maryland Province, and, as you might suppose, he is a Catholic, although he does not practice his religion. However, his brother and adjudant general, Lieutenant Colonel [Placidus] Ord, is a good Catholic as are his general Provost Marshall, Lieutenant Colonel [John] Coughlin, and several members of his staff. Moreover, the surgeon who was sent to the hospital where I had been stationed was a good practicing Catholic. All of this augured well for the future and, in fact, the citizens of Richmond were in no time convinced that they had fallen into the hands of the *best* of enemies. Fortunately, there were no gestures of protest, no violent outbursts; everything went off as well as could possibly have been expected under such circumstances. I don't know whether the Protestants of Richmond realized to what extent the kindly attitude of the conquering army was due to the Catholicism of its leaders, and that consequently it is to Catholicism that the conquered are beholden.

For me personally the greatest joy was that Father O'Hagan was with General Ord's Division. It was Father O'Hagan, as you recall, who was taken prisoner three years ago with Father Tissot on the banks of the Chickahominy. It was only natural that this good Father wished to enter Richmond with the victorious Yankee army—Richmond, a city into which three years ago he had been led as a prisoner of war by a band of truimphant rebel soldiers. He had now returned not only for the reason I have indicated, but also to offer the Catholics in the area the opportunity to make their Easter confessions. The day he arrived was Wednesday of Holy Week, and you can imagine my joy when I learned of his coming! I went directly to him and promised to surrender myself on condition that he would take me with him back to Georgetown. The condition for the surrender was accepted easily enough; he had not forgotten that I had done everything possible for him during his captivity, and he was now happy to have the opportunity to repay me. We embraced one another and laughed at the reversals of our roles—as if it were the funniest thing in the world.

During the next few days he introduced me to General Ord, Lieutenant Colonel Ord, Lieutenant Coughlin and to many others of his friends in the army, among whom, it seems, he is quite popular. He was able to accomplish a great deal of good for people in dire need thanks to the many concessions he obtained from the general and from other officers. General Ord released me on parole (and I am still a paroled prisoner); his brother, the colonel, himself gave me a transportation ticket for Washington, and on Easter Monday I sailed from Richmond in the company of Father O'Hagan and many other acquaintances. I had done everything possible to persuade Father Hubert to come along with us, but this did not fit with the plans he had made; moreover, he had friends in Richmond whom he did not want to leave at that time. The fact that he stayed behind certainly did not turn out to his advantage; he has been seriously sick since that time and probably would not have been had he come with us. The change of climate, the food and the rest would most assuredly have done him good.

On Tuesday morning I arrived in Washington and then at Georgetown, where I was warmly welcomed by our fathers. My health was far from excellent at this time; during the five preceding months I had been always more or less sick since the hospital diet and my stomach were engaged in a little war of their own. By the way, I often laughed at a remark you once made in one of your letters. You wrote saying that for several days such and such a thing was no longer served at table. "Bah," I said to myself, "this and many more besides have been absent from my table, not merely for several days, but every day for the past two, three or even four years, and somehow I'm still alive." But then I had to admit that, although I didn't die as a result of these privations, my health had indeed suffered. However, once at Georgetown, thanks to the attentions of the good fathers, the walks, and the little promenades in the carriage; thanks even more to my visits to some dear "rebel ladies" who had wanted to meet and talk with the "rebel chaplain" (and who never failed to have goodies on hand for him); and thanks most especially to my abstemiousness in respect to undiluted water (for whatever you may think—you and those teetotaling sermons of yours—it was precisely the excess of this appallingly pure beverage, unmixed with that saving grace of wine so earnestly recommended by the apostle, that had reduced me to such a pitiable state)—thanks to all of this, I say, I soon found myself feeling chipper, and once again capable of doing great things.

I had been at Georgetown for almost five weeks when the Provincial, Father [Angelo] Paresce, came there on some business. Thinking that I might be in danger of boredom at Georgetown, or rather, feeling that a little more variety would be better for me, he invited me to accompany him to Baltimore to spend a week there with our fathers at Loyola College. As his proposal was not that sort which one can accept or decline with equal grace, I immediately thanked him and began making preparations for the trip. As we were leaving the house, I was handed a letter that had just arrived from Father Jourdan. It was his reply to a letter which I had written to him at the beginning of April informing him of the fact that I was still alive and telling him that I was at Georgetown. In his letter Father Jourdan requested that Father Hubert and I put ourselves at the disposal of Archbishop [Martin John] Spalding of Baltimore for the diocese of Charleston where two very badly needed priests had just died. This order, which came right out of the blue, far from presenting an obstacle to the proposed journey, now made it imperative. So I left with Father Provincial, stopped for dinner at Gonzaga College, Washington, and arrived at five o'clock that same evening in Baltimore.

I remained ten days in this noble city because I had to wait both for my pass from Washington and for an interview with the archbishop who was busy putting the finishing touches to a diocesan synod by preaching a retreat to his clergy. But these ten days did not seem long in passing as they gave me the opportunity to become acquainted with Baltimore. It is a city which I like very much, and of all the cities in the United States, it is the most Catholic both in appearance and in reality. I don't know how many churches exist there, but there are more religious orders there than in any other place that I know. There are Jesuits, Redemptorists, Vincentians, Sulpicians and Christian Brothers; there are at least five convents of Daughters of Charity; two convents of Visitation nuns, one Carmelite convent; a Good Shepherd convent, a convent of Notre Dame sisters, a convent of German nuns, a convent of Negro nuns—and all of these convents are thriving, and most are under the spiritual direction of our fathers. But it seems to me where Catholicism shows itself in a most striking manner is in the faces of the people themselves—faces which are friendly, cheerful and kind. A priest walking down the streets of Baltimore is hailed at practically every step he takes. I don't mean by a few Irish servant girls who sometimes make rather grotesque curtsies, but by men of quality who tip their hats with a *savoir-faire* that would do credit to any French gentleman. Another feature that speaks eloquently for the state of Catholicism in Baltimore is the fact that there are presently sixty diocesan seminarians studying philosophy and theology at the Major Seminary. This seminary, you know, is under the direction of the Sulpicians. These good men are the same the world over. One day Father Provincial and I paid them a visit—and such hospitality! Without exaggeration, they wanted me to remain with them the whole day, and naturally Father Paresce felt we could not refuse.

But of all the enchantments of Baltimore, nothing so captivated my heart as Loyola College. I know of no other house in the Society so agreeable—it is the most ideally situated, the most convenient, the cleanest, the most elegant (without, however, being elaborate), the most comfortable and the most spacious (relative to the number of Jesuits in the community). It has everything necessary; yet nothing is in excess; everything is where it ought to be and as it ought to be. If only there were a large courtyard with a garden, it would be *the ideal* city residence and college. But our fathers there are so busy, I'm afraid they'd never have time to enjoy such an amenity. This one drawback, therefore, is scarcely noticed. The number of students, all of whom are day scholars, is not exceptionally large—there are only about one hundred—but they are the most admirable young men. I was really astonished to see the order, the discipline, the silence which reigned so perfectly outside of times of recreation. I was most impressed too, by the good manners and the respect the boys show toward their masters. One could see at a glance that they were from the best families in town. And their piety! It is no less remarkable than their other qualities. There are about eight or ten who come voluntarily at the crack of dawn every morning to serve mass. They dress in surplices and black cassocks and it does one's heart good to see them in the sanctuary. In no noviceship could one hope to see the Divine Services more suitably performed. The scholastic who trains these young men certainly achieved very creditable results: his efforts have been crowned with the most remarkable success. Four of these acolytes made application to go to the noviceship while I was there; their talents and piety will win them eager acceptance, I am sure. In general I was quite impressed by the Maryland Province Jesuits, and particularly by the scholastics. The Jesuits there, I believe, are different from those in our part of the country; there they seem to be better adapted to the American ministry. They do a great deal of good and they have a considerable influence—even in political matters in Washington, although they do not deliberately seek this.

Father [Aloysius] Roccoffort is in Washington; still the same and working just as hard as ever. Oh, but look—I've already covered eight whole pages. If shame did not restrain me, I could double the length of this letter with an account of my three days in Philadelphia and my eight days in New York. But you would not have the patience to read all of this; you've done well to have read so much as it is. So, I'll content myself in telling you that I saw Fathers [Isadore] Daubresse and [Henry] Duranquet in New York and Father Prachensky at Fordham (he has grown monstrously fat), and that I'm now in Charleston where I shall stay until September. *Adieu, mon bon Père. My best regards to all of Ours.*

Yours always,
H. Gache, S.J.

P.S. If you write to me address your letters in care of Rev. J [ohn] Moore, D.D. Excuse my scribbling. I have written this letter in the late afternoon and the light is now so poor I can scarcely see the words I am forming.

COMMENTARY

It will be remembered that Hippolyte Gache was dispatched to Danville in August 1862 to replace Egidius Smulders who had gone off to North Carolina in search of his lost health. Now in March 1865, it was the peregrinating chaplain of the Louisiana Eighth who arrived in Lynchburg to attend to the flock that Gache, parodying the style of Jeremiah the Prophet, had so ironically compared to the citizens of the village Ars, near Lyons, who wept when their cure, St. John Vianney (1786-1859) was taken from them to enjoy his eternal reward. The Dutch Redemptorist came to Lynchburg at the invitation of Oscar Sears, arriving there after he completed an experiment which was as ambitious as it was curious. In October he had written to Jefferson Davis: "I understand that there are now in our hands a large number of Irish Catholic prisoners of war, who I think may be induced to enlist in the Confederate Army." He then proceeded to outline his recruiting plan, concluding that "I respectfully request that (these prisoners) may be collected in one locality, that facilities may be offered me and some other Catholic Priest for conducting religious exercises amongst them and for holding other incourse (sic) with the view of bringing them over to the Confederate cause."[160] Seemingly intrigued, the President wrote that he approved of the idea of separating Catholic from Protestant prisoners of war, but in November Brig. Gen. William M. Gardner (1824-1901), commander of military prisons east of the Mississippi, could not implement this plan "because I have found it impossible, for the time, to get either a place to confine or guards to watch" segregated Roman Catholic prisoners.[161] But what Gardner found impossible Brig. Gen. Zebulon York (1819-1900), the commander of what was left of the Second Louisiana Brigade, was able to accomplish. He saw to it that a special camp was set up some eight miles from Salisbury, North Carolina, to accommodate 700 foreign born Catholic prisoners of war, and these were turned over to Father Smulders. "I gave them an eight days mission, heard all of their confessions and they received Holy Communion," he recalled, but "to join our army few availed themselves of the opportunity," and so they were ordered to return to the Salisbury Prison, where the inmates "died between twenty and thirty every day," and those that survived were finally paroled and sent across the lines.[162] Although not facile with the pen, Smulders was a resourceful person. In Monroe, Michigan, before the war, he had founded a religious community of women, one of the few American congregations which has managed to survive and even thrive to this day: the Sisters Servants of the Immaculate Heart of Mary. But that in North Carolina, at the end of the war, he managed singlehandedly, and in eight short days, to preach for God and recruit for the army; to hear 700 confessions and distribute as many communions, must mean that Smulders was in fact the thaumaturge Gache was in fancy. His mission accomplished, the inspired recruiter then accompanied the Louisiana troops back to Virginia. At the time of Lynchburg's surrender, when all the "Confederate authorities had left," he was preaching another mission at Father Sears' church. His description of the last days of the city is graphic: "A few cavalrymen had orders to burn all the bridges, one RR bridge was burning. Father Sears and myself, we took command, being the only officers left, and stopped the burning. A few days after, when the federals entered the city with orders to burn public buildings, we saw the officer in command, told him how we had prevented the burning of bridges and wished him to do likewise. An answer by telegram from Grant saved the courthouse, etc."[163]

Gache's part in the destruction of Richmond was not so dramatic; yet he too reported having met obliging Union officers, most of whom were — predictably — Catholics, such as the Ord brothers, General Edward Cresap (b. Cumberland, Maryland, October 18, 1818–d. Havana, Cuba, July 22, 1888) and the less famous Lieutenant Colonel Placidus (b. Sault Ste. Marie, Michigan, December 25, 1821–d. San Antonio, Texas, July 9, 1876). These were the sons, as Gache reported, of a former Jesuit scholastic, James Ord (b. England, January 7, 1789–d. Omaha, Nebraska, January 25, 1873), a man of a mysterious and intriguing background. He was reputed to have been the son, from the lawful and morganatic marriage of King George IV (1762-1830), and Mrs. Maria Anne Fitzhubert (1756-1837), who had been whisked away to the New World shortly after his birth. In October, 1806, he entered the Society of Jesus at Georgetown and left in May 1811 to become a midshipman, a position he held until April 1813 when he resigned to accept a commission of 1st lieutenant in Capt. Joseph Nelson's Company, Thirty-Sixth U.S. Infantry, after which he was stationed as a recruiting officer in Georgetown, D.C. Peace again being established, James Ord resigned from the army in February 1814 and married Rebecca Ruth Cresap (1794-1860) of Cumberland County, Maryland. The career of his son Edward Ord is well known; that of Placidus was cut short by his accidental death, at which time he was a major in the army, despite the fact he had been brevetted colonel during the war while serving as the assistant adjutant general to Edward.

Another brevetted officer that Gache met in Richmond was John Coughlin (b. Williamstown, Vermont, c. October 5, 1837–d. Washington, D.C., December 4, 1911), brigadier general when he was mustered out of the army in June 1865. Twice wounded during the war, at Port Walthall, Virginia, in May and at Petersburg in July 1864, this officer who paroled

Hippolyte Gache, April 14, 1865, was a recipient of the Congressional Medal of Honor. After the war he settled in Washington, D.C. where, never married, he owned and managed a downtown drug store.[164]

Records do not reveal the name of the "good practicing Catholic" surgeon who took charge of the Stuart Hospital where Gache, Doctors Fisher and Akin, steward Muldoon and the Daughters of Charity had been housed since February 13. Whoever this individual was, he was quickly replaced by Doctor William H. Palmer (1829-1912), a native of Woodstock, Connecticut, surgeon in the Third New York Cavalry, who was not a Catholic.[165] But the Jesuits whom the paroled chaplain named in this letter are easier to identify. Angelo Paresce (b. Naples, June 3, 1817–d. Woodstock, Maryland, April 9, 1879) was, as Gache reported, the provincial of the Maryland Province, an area which included all of the Atlantic seaboard states north of South Carolina. Aloysius Roccoffort (b. Marseilles, France, March 15, 1819–d. Philadelphia, Pennsylvania, May 31, 1904), had been Hippolyte's classmate at Vals and was one of his shipmates to Mobile in 1847. Roccoffort had also accompanied Gache to Grand Coteau in the spring of that year and replaced Henry Duranquet (b. Chalus, France, December 18, 1808–d. Woodstock, Maryland, December 30, 1891), Joseph Desribes' uncle, who had been teaching at St. Charles since its foundation by Joseph Point. Isadore Daubresse (b. Vervick, Belgium, April 23, 1810–d. Frederick, Maryland, August 17, 1895) had been one of Roccoffort and Gache's teachers at Vals. During the great Jesuit exodus from France in 1848, Daubresse landed in New York where he and his traveling companion Peter Tissot joined the faculty at the Jesuit *collège*, Fordham.

At Baltimore, Gache informed de Carrière, he had met a scholastic who greatly impressed him. This was Jeremiah O'Connor (b. Dublin. Ireland, April 10, 1841–d. New York, February 27, 1891) the young man who looked after the Loyola College acolytes, three of whom entered the Society that year: Charles Doizé (b. Baltimore, Maryland, February 14, 1847–d. New Orleans, Louisiana, March 28, 1873); Jerome Daugherty (b. Baltimore, Maryland, March 25, 1841–d. Philadelphia, Pennsylvania, May 24, 1914) and Henry J. Shandelle (b. Reuthen, Westphalia, Germany, September 21, 1848–d. Washington, D.C., November 27, 1925). Gache was destined to live at a later date with Shandelle and Daugherty, two men whose personal qualities seemed to reflect more the communities in which they lived rather than the training they had been given by Jeremiah O'Connor. The former was described as "the Lord Chesterfield of the Georgetown (University) faculty;" the latter as "a lubricant for creaking machinery, an oil reservoir for settling troubled water."[166]

In 1864 Bishop Lynch had been dispatched to Rome as commissioner of the Confederate States to Pius IX and did not return to Charleston until

November 1865. For this reason the Archbishop of Baltimore, Martin John Spalding (b. Rolling Fork, Kentucky, May 23, 1810–d. Baltimore, Maryland, February 7, 1872) became a type of overseer for the Charleston diocese, Father John Moore (b. Castletown-Devlin, Westmeath, Ireland, June 27, 1835–d. St. Augustine, Florida, July 30, 1901), being the unofficial vicar general. When two priests of the diocese died shortly before the end of the war—Gache's compatriot Léon Fillion and Patrick O'Neill (b. Thomastown, County Kilkenny, Ireland, March 17, 1810–d. Charleston, South Carolina, February 15, 1865)—Spalding wrote to Odin for substitutes. The Archbishop of New Orleans in turn appealed to the Jesuit mission superior, and for this reason the two paroled Louisiana chaplains were ordered to Charleston. Hubert, "that wonderful man who never left his regiment," was yet confined to a Richmond hospital and was not able to leave Baltimore on May 30 with the reinvigorated Gache.[167]

In the Fall, when Darius Hubert was strong enough to travel, it was not to Charleston where he went, but to New Orleans. There, as chaplain to the Benevolent Association Army of Northern Virginia, he continued to dedicate more years of his life to the memory of this adopted, defeated country, and there he preached the eulogy at the funeral of its first and only President.[168]

Finally, there is the matter of identifying the "dear rebel ladies" of Georgetown who lavished attention and "goodies" on the languishing rebel chaplain. Their names will never be known with certainty. But in the Spring of 1862, after the President's House at William and Mary had been entrusted to the Southall family and after Williamsburg had fallen, Rebecca Ewell joined her sister Elizabeth, the erstwhile nun, in Georgetown. Very likely she was accompanied by their niece, Miss Lizzy. So, it is not unreasonable to conclude that in the Spring of 1865 the convalescent found himself once again pampered by the two gentle ladies who had, three years previously, been so solicitous for his welfare. Nor is it fanciful to conclude that on one of these salubrious drives through Georgetown with Rebecca and Lizzy, he met, for the first time, the woman whose conscience he would direct for almost two score years, Rebecca's sister—Elizabeth Stoddert Ewell.[169]

EPILOGUE

Hippolyte Gache arrived in Charleston on June 1, "not a day too soon," bringing with him for Father John Moore's comments Archbishop Spalding's historic petition to the Holy See regarding the Fenian Brotherhood. Moore, who confessed being overwhelmed by the number of sick and dying in the city, tried to get the Jesuit to undertake the reparation of war-ravaged St. Joseph's Church, but Gache begged off giving the excuse that he did "not understand such matters," and left in August for Columbia to conduct once again the *Spiritual Exercises* for the Ursulines.[170] In February the Columbia convent had fallen prey to the flames which followed in the wake of the conquering Federal Army, and General Sherman issued a special order housing the nuns and their pupils in the Methodist Female College. After Appomattox the girls were allowed to return to their families, but the nuns remained to greet the paroled chaplain, who, as the convent's scribe recorded, had the "goodness to pay his own expenses, and to travel over rugged roads in a Government Ambulance, the railroad having been torn up by the Federal Army in its famous "March to the Sea'." The scribe further editorialized that Gache's visit had been a high point in the history of the convent, "truly a very remarkable time." The reason was that "some thirty or forty Protestant families were living at the same house, among whom were Episcopalians, Methodists, Presbyterians—who all united in respect even reverence to the Religious and the Rev. Jesuit Father."

During the preceding four years, marvels had indeed multiplied. Now the same attention the Protestants in Williamsburg had lavished on him was now repeated in Columbia. Moreover "a parlor on the second story was assigned to his use, in which he sat— when not engaged in the Chapel." If in 1862 he had seen humor in the proximity of his Lynchburg quarters to the chapel—reminding his *frère de lait*, the saintly Andrew Cornette, that he himself was "not religious enough" to comprehend such mysteries—there is reason to suspect that the paroled retreat director must now have seen in the makeshift parlor cause to tickle his fancy. The scribe continued: "And while he would be in the chapel opposite giving meditations, or hearing confessions, the Protestant ladies would most kindly have on his table fruit (and) milk." Might such a gesture have brought him back to his earliest days? A blurb, published in 1713, informed the parents of youngsters enrolled at Bourg-Saint-Andéol that, besides the ordinary fare of salted lard and vegetables, the seminarians at the *petit sèminaire* were given generous amounts of "garden fruit, chestnuts and tempered wine of the region to insure thay they would become hale and hardy and able to serve better the parishes where one day they would be sent." Philip de Carrière might well disagree, but to a man who worked so hard at remaining French, milk from South Carolina cows must have compared poorly to the product from those all but forgotten vineyards of the Côte de Rhône; yet anything was better than water, "that appalling pure beverage . . . that had reduced me to such a pitable state" during the war. Ever ready to mock himself, Gache was yet profoundly touched by the delicacy and kindness of others, and so it was not surprising now, as the scribe recounted, that "The Reverend Father expressed himself as being greatly edified by the amiable charity of those Protestant ladies."[171]

This retreat to the Ursulines in the Methodist Female College suggests a scene which moves smoothly from something close to caricature to something very near pathos, and yet in his war letters Hippolyte Gache often testified that for him there was no better corrector of intellectual extravagance and religious prejudice than a personal love of friends.

Father John Moore expressed genuine sorrow when Gache left Charleston for New York on October 5, and added that his "stay amongst us will not soon be forgotten."[172] The reason why he went to New York rather than to New Orleans is not clear, nor is it recorded how long he stayed there. Meanwhile, he had been reappointed a trustee at Spring Hill, where presumably he was expected to return. Sometime before January he was in New Orleans, but then shortly after this date he was assigned to Loyola College, Baltimore, and in 1868 was appointed superior at Holy Trinity Church, Georgetown, D.C., where Bixio had brought his trunkfull of Confederate script in 1865.[173]

Like Prachensky, Smulders and Sheeran, Gache never returned to the South for further assignments. The future for the Catholic Church seemed part of the spoils that belonged to the victor. What he had not been able to accomplish at St. Peter and Paul's in Baton Rouge and what he had no heart to begin at St. Joseph's in Charleston, he achieved in Georgetown where Holy Trinity rectory, completed in 1870, stands to this day as a tasteful and dignified monument to the erstwhile Louisiana chaplain's imagination and ingenuity.[174]

Between 1872 and 1904 he served in a number of Jesuit colleges and parishes from Maryland to Massachusetts, retiring at the age of 86 to the novitiate at St. Andrew-on-Hudson near Hyde Park, New York. As a boy at Bourg-Saint-Andéol the scholar of promise would watch the Rhône rushing on its course, past Avignon, down to the sea; now, some seventy years later he could see, from the palasades, the less urgent waters of the Hudson flow in the same southerly direction, past the point where the Yankee James Bigler laid the first telephone cable under its waters, to the same sea which had terrified him so as a young scholastic at Vals.

His memory and physical strength began to fail. The days passed and he did not distinguish them one from another. He became more confused. Novices were assigned to read to him and give him loving care, but the present receded more and more into the background and he remembered only the past. His powers of expression in English, which were never strong, quietly faded, like some Languedoc tune lost on the breeze, and although he did not know it, there were few ears left to hear when he spoke French. Finally he was brought to the hospital of Saint-Jean-de-Dieu, near Montreal, and there looked after by French-speaking nuns. He died, October 8, 1907, in the 91st year of his life. A French Jesuit who notified his niece of his death wrote: "In spite of his infirmities and his advanced age, the Reverend Father right up to the end was a faithful companion of the Lord Jesus to whom he had committed his youth . . . and he edified everyone by his great devotion to the Blessed Sacrament."[175]

The remains of Father Hippolyte were buried at St. Andrew-on-Hudson, far from the resting place of Confederate veterans, but beside Jesuits, many of whom like himself had been sent as exiles from their native lands to achieve great deeds in a new world. There is no greater edifice built to the ideal of these men than the triumphant house of studies commanding the Hudson valley—granite, like the men buried in the cemetery, and with a vital personality, rich, complex, bracing and generous. The cemetery remains yet today, but the living Jesuits have since departed, and the building has become a school for gourmet chefs that specialize in French cooking. The chaplain to the Louisiana Tenth would have liked that too. His humor was heavy, at times arch, but he did enjoy ironic endings and he did prefer civilized cuisine.

LOUIS-HIPPOLYTE GACHE

June 18, 1817	Born Beaulieu, Ardèche, France
1826-36	Attended seminary at Bourg-Saint-Andéol, Ardèche, France
1836-37	Attended Jesuit college, Chambéry, Savoy—rhetoric studies
1837-40	Attended Jesuit college, Mélan, Savoy—philosophical studies
September 8, 1840	Entered the Lyons Province of the Society of Jesus at Avignon, France
1840-42	Novitiate, Avignon
1842-46	Theology studies at Vals, Haute-Loire, France
March 28, 1846	Ordained to the priesthood at Vals
October 27, 1846	Left France for Mobile, Alabama, with five companions
January 17, 1847	Arrived in Mobile
September 1, 1847	Spring Hill College opens under Jesuit direction
1847-48	Minister of the house and prefect of studies at St. Charles College, Grand Coteau, Louisiana
1849	Master of Novices and chaplain at Spring Hill College
1850-52	Vice Rector, fund raiser, treasurer and President of Saints Peter and Paul College, Baton Rouge; Pastor of St. Joseph's Church, Baton Rouge
1852-61	Director of the seminarians, lecturer in philosophy and theology, chaplain to the lay students at Spring Hill College, Mobile, Alabama
August 15, 1858	Pronounced final vows as a Jesuit, Spring Hill College, Alabama
April-June 1861	Chaplain to the Confederate troops, Pensacola, Florida
July 19, 1861	Received chaplain's appointment, Confederate States Army, and three days later assigned to the Tenth Louisiana Volunteer Regiment

July 29, 1861	With the Tenth Louisiana Regiment, assigned to Virginia
April 14, 1865	Made a paroled prisoner at Richmond, Virginia
1866-67	Spiritual father to the Jesuit community, Loyola College, Baltimore, Maryland
1867-68	Professor of philosophy, Loyola College, Baltimore, Md.
1868-70	Pastor, Holy Trinity Church, and superior of the parish community, Georgetown, D.C.
1870-72	Professor of philosophy, Holy Cross College, Worcester, Mass.
1872-74	Curate, Gesu Church, Philadelphia, Penn.
1874-78	Curate, Old St. Joseph's Church, Philadelphia, Penn.
1878-81	Pastor, St. John's Church, Frederick, Md.
1881-84	Curate, Gesu Church, Philadelphia, Penn.
1884-86	Spiritual father to the Georgetown College Jesuit community, Georgetown, D.C.
1886-87	Spiritual father to the Fordham College Jesuit community, Fordham, N.Y.
1887-1900	Curate, St. Joseph's Church, Troy, N.Y.
1900-04	Spiritual father to the Jesuit community, Old St. Joseph's Church, Philadelphia, Penn.
1904-07	"House confessor" to the Jesuit community, St. Andrew-on-Hudson, N.Y.
October 8, 1907	Died, hospital of Saint-Jean-de-Dieu, near Montreal, Canada

NOTES

1 • Names and biographical information on Gache's family supplied by his great grand niece, Mme. Roselyne Laffont, "Les Rosiers," Salindres (Ardèche), France. Citation from Robert Labrély, *Le vieux Bourg-Saint-Andéol* (Viviers [Ardèche], France: 1960), p. 158. Resumé of the history of the *Petit Séminaire* up to 1853 contained in Labrély's book, pp. 159-62. For Gache's academic career: "Obit. H. Gache," *Litterae Annuae Provinciae Lugdunensis, S.J., a die 1 Octobris 1907 ad dieum 15 Augusti, 1908* (Bruxellis: typis Josephi Polleunis, 1909), p. 51; hereinafter cited as "Obit. H. Gache." For the *collège-en-exile* of Chambéry: Pierre Delattre, S.J., *Les Establissements des Jésuites en France depuis quatres siècles* (5 Vols.; Enghien, Belgium: De Meestre, 1949), Vol. I, pp. 1258-70; and John W. Padberg, *Colleges in Controversey: The Jesuit Schools in France from Revival to Suppression, 1815-1880* (Cambridge, Massachusetts: Harvard University Press, 1969), pp. 66-7.

2 • For the suppression of the French Jesuit *collèges*, see Joseph Burnichon, S.J., *La Compagnie de Jésus en France: Histoire d'un siècle, 1814-1914* (4 Vols.; Paris: Beauchesne, 1916), Vol. II, pp. 82-91. For the *collège* at Mélan, see Pierre Delattre, S.J., *Les Establissements des Jésuites en France*, Vol. III, 207-11. For an overall view of the whole period, see John W. Padberg, *The Jesuit Schools in France*, pp. 49-67. For Gache's career during this period, see "Obit. H. Gache," p. 51.

3 • Joseph Burnichon, *La Compagnie de Jésus en France*, Vol. II, pp. 99-106, 164-65; and "Obit H. Gache," p. 51.

4 • *Litterae Annuae Provinciae Lugdunensis, Soc. Jesu a 1 octobria 1840 ad 1 octobris 1841* (5 Vols., Lyons Province Society of Jesus, n.p.), Vol. II, pp. 24-26.

5 • For a sketch of Maisounabe, see Joseph Burnichon, *La Compagnie de Jésus en France*, Vol. II, pp. 256, 261-64; Vol. III, 143-48; and Michael Kenny, S.J., "Jesuits in the Southland," typewritten Ms. in Archives of the New Orleans Province of the Society of Jesus, Grand Coteau, Louisiana, p. 44. Hereinafter cited as Michael Kenny, "Notes." For Gautrelet, besides the references above, see Joseph Burnichon, *La Compagnie de Jésus en France*, Vol. IV, pp. 110-113; Pierre Delattre, *Les Establissements des Jésuites en France*, Vol. III, pp. 610-15, Vol. IV, pp. 1400-04, Vol. V, pp. 1-11. Joseph Burnichon has also written a biography which gives a wealth of information on the matter treated above: *La Vie du Père François-Xavier Gautrelet*, (Paris: Retaux, 1896). Also, Henry Ramière, S.J., *The Apostleship of Prayer* (New York: The Apostleship of Prayer Press, 1898) is of value, as is Michael Kenny, *Catholic Culture in Alabama* (New York: The America Press, 1931), pp. 41-43 which describes the importance of Pauline Jaricot's work in the South. A more detailed sketch of Jaricot can be found in

Katherine Burton, *Difficult Star: The Life of Pauline Jaricot* (New York: Longmans, Green & Co., 1947).

6 • Joseph Burnichon, *La Compagnie de Jêsus en France*, Vol. III, p. 18. Michael Kenny, *Catholic Culture in Alabama*, pp. 31-131, gives a confused but thorough history of these events.

7 • Michael Kenny, "Notes," p. 47. Joseph Burnichon, *Le Compagnie de Jêsus en France*, Vol. III, p. 18.

8 • Hippolyte Gache to Louis Boisson, June 17, 1885, in possession of Mme. Roselyne Laffont, Salindres (Ardèche), France.

9 • Jean Jordan to Anthony Blanc, October 26, 1846 in Blanc Papers, New Orleans Collection, Archives of Notre Dame University, Notre Dame, Indiana.

10 • Robert Ignatius Burns, S.J., *The Jesuits and the Indian Wars in the Northwest* (New Haven: Yale University Press, 1966), p. 36. Michael Kenny, "Notes," p. 40.

11 • Julien Jordan to Francis Abbadie, April 28, 1847 cited in Michael Kenny, "Notes," p. 44.

12 • Albert H. Biever, S.J., *The Jesuits in New Orleans and in the Mississippi Valley: Jubilee Memorial,* (New Orleans: Hauser Printing Co. 1924), pp. 88-90.

13 • *Ibid.*, p. 93: Michael Kenny, "Notes," pp. 48-9.

14 • Nicholas Point to Johann Roothaan, February 17, 1837, cited in Michael Kenny, "Notes," p. 34.

15 • John Baptist Les Maisounabe to Johaan Roothaan, October 5, 1846, cited by Joseph Burnichon in *La Compagnie de Jêsus en France*, Vol. III, p. 302.

16 • J.J. Moore to Martin J. Spalding, July 12, 1865 in Spalding Papers, Archdiocese of Baltimore Archives, Baltimore, Maryland. The memory of the rigors of that summer were still vivid many years later.

17 • "House Journal" (Archives of the Convent of the Sacred Heart, Grand Coteau, Louisiana), August 1847.

18 • Maisounabe to Blanc, February 16, 1848 in Blanc Papers.

19 • Moore to Spalding, October 4, 1865 in Spalding Papers.

20 • Michael Kenny referred to Vitalis Gilles as "the Master of Novices" at Spring Hill in 1847, but this was an acting appointment. Gache was the first official Master of Novices according to the *Catalogus Sociorum et Officiorum Provinciae Lugdunensis*, (1849), p. 71. The reference to Kenny is *Catholic Culture in Alabama*, p. 132.

21 • Hippolyte Gache, "Our College in Baton Rouge, Louisiana," *Woodstock Letters*, XXVII (1898), 2. Michael Kenny gives some background information on the establishment of the college in "Notes," pp. 53-7.

22 • George Blackney to Blanc, February 21, 1851 in Blanc Papers.

23 • Hippolyte Gache, "Our College in Baton Rouge," *Woodstock Letters*, XXVII, 2. The college property was on the north side of North Street between Uncle Sam, presently North 5th, and St. Mary's, which today is North 7th. The nefarious St. Hipolite Street has become North 6th Street. See Reverend Lyle F. Hitzman, "St. Joseph Church, Baton Rouge (1792-1893): The First One Hundred Years" (M.A. thesis, Notre Dame Seminary, New Orleans, Louisiana, 1973).

24 • Adine Guinand to Blanc, February 26 and April 6, 1851 in Blanc Papers.

25 • Citation from Louise Callan, R.S.C.J., *Philippine Duchesne: Frontier Missionary of the Sacred Heart, 1769-1852* (Westminister, Maryland: Newman, 1957), p. 668. Resumes of the lives of the Religious of the Sacred Heart mentioned above were obtained from the Archives of the Sacred Heart, Grand Coteau, Louisiana, and the Istituto del Sacro Coure, Rome.

26 • Guinand to Blanc, December 5, 1855; Sister Emily to Blanc, January 6, 1850; Gache to Blanc, January 28, February 4, 26, 1851—all in Blanc Papers.

27 • H. Gache, "Our College in Baton Rouge," p. 5.

28 • François-Xavier Gautrelet to Blanc, December 5, 1855 in Blanc Papers.

29 • S. Spencer Semmes, class of 1855, the son of Admiral Joseph Bernard Raphael Semmes, C.S.N., cited in Michael Kenny, *Catholic Culture in Alabama*, p. 250.

30 • News clipping dated April 11, 1861, from an unknown date of the New York *Tribune*, cited in John E. Jones, *Florida During the Civil War* (Gainesville, Florida: University of Florida Press, 1963), p. 47.

31 • "Philip de Carrière Obit.," *Woodstock Letters* (1913), XLII, p. 228: Michael Kenny, "Notes," p. 82; *Catholic Culture in Alabama*, p. 223.

32 • STEPHEN MALLORY: Michael Kenny, *Catholic Culture in Alabama*, p. 98. For the date of the Pensacola trip, see John B. Jones, *A Rebel War Clerk's Diary* (2 Vols.; New York: Old Hickory Bookshop, 1935), Vol. I, p. 40.

• PIERRE GUSTAVE TOUTANT DE BEAUREGARD: T. Harry Williams, *P.G.T. Beauregard: Napoleon in Gray* (Baton Rouge: Louisiana State University Press, 1955), pp. 63-4.

• JOHN QUINLAN: Code, *Dictionary of the American Hierarchy, 1789-1964* (New York: Joseph F. Wagner, 1964), p. 244. Hereinafter cited as *DAHier*. John Quinlan to John Mary Odin, May 22, 1861 in Odin Papers, New Orleans Collection, Archives of Notre Dame University.

• CHAPLAINS: *The War of the Rebellion: A Compilation of the Official Records of the Union and Confederate Armies*, (130 Vols., Washington, D.C.: Government Printing Office, 1880-1901), Ser. IV, Vol. I, p. 257, hereinafter cited as *Official Records* unless otherwise noted. James Moscoe Matthews, ed., *Statutes at Large of the Provisional Government of the Confederate States* (Richmond: R.M. Smith, 1864) p. 99.

• PENSACOLA CHURCHES: Oscar Hugh Lipscomb, "The Administration of John Quinlan, Second Bishop of Mobile, 1859-1883," *Records of the American Historical Society of Philadelphia*, LXXVIII (1967), p. 23.

• PATRICK COYLE: Compiled Service Records of Confederate Soldiers who served in Organizations from the State of Florida (CSR); Compiled Service Records of Confederate Generals and Staff Officers, and Nonregimental Enlisted Men (CSRO&M); Register of the Appointment of Chaplains (Appointment Book), Ch. I, Vol. 132, no entry; Indices, Entries Pertaining to Chaplains Appointments (Indices), Ch. I, Vol. 86, p. 365, in Adjutant and Inspector General's Office (A&IGO), Record Group (RG) 109, National Archives (NA), Washington, D.C.; Dom Aidan Henry Germain, *Catholic Military and Naval Chaplains 1776-1916* (Upper Darby, Pennsylvania: Dougherty Printing, 1929), pp. 113-14. Coyle at Corinth: William Henry Elder to John Mary Odin, May 13, 1862 in Odin Papers. Biographical Records of Diocesan Personnel, Archives of the Diocese of Nashville,

Nashville, Tennessee. See also Special Order (S.O.) #51, April 30, 1862, A&IGO in RG 109, NA. Quotation in text: Julien C. Young, "Pensacola in the War for Southern Independence," *Florida Historical Quarterly*, XXXVIII, (1959), p. 369. Citizenship—Naturalization Entries: Patrick Francis Coyle, Irish alien, entered country as minor, 1848; given citizenship, July 21, 1852, United States Circuit Court, Mobile, Alabama, 1852-1854, p. 481. Oscar Hugh Lipscomb, "The Administration of John Quinlan, Second Bishop of Mobile, 1859-1883," passim, and by the same author, "Catholics in Alabama, 1861-1865," *Alabama Review*, XX (1967), p. 95.

33 • CHARLES LE BARON: LeBaron file, Pensacola Historical Museum; Le Baron file, Historical Pensacola Preservation Board, Pensacola, Florida; Thomas M. Owen, "Brief Memoranda Concerning a Southern Line of the Sands Family," *The Gulf States Historical Magazine*, I (March 1903), p. 353.

• HENRY ST. PAUL: Obituary, New Orleans *Daily Picayune* (February 21, 1886), p. 4. Thomas M. Owen, *History of Alabama and Dictionary of Alabama History*, hereinafter cited as *DAH* (4 Vols.; Chicago: S.J. Clarke, 1921), Vol. IV, p. 1906; CSR (Louisiana), Company E, Confederate States Zouaves and also Seventh Louisiana Battalion. Appointment of Beauregard as Captain and A.Q.M. at Alexandria, Louisiana, S.O. 243/7, Adjutant General's Office (AGO), Ch. I, Vol. 86, p. 195, RG 109, NA. Andrew B. Booth (comp.) *Records of Louisiana Confederate Soldiers and Louisiana Commands* (New Orleans: 1920), III, Bk. 2, p. 672, hereinafter cited as Booth, *RLCS*, unless otherwise noted. Herman de Bachelle Seebold, M.D., *Old Louisiana Plantation Homes and Family Trees* (2 vols.; n.p.: Published privately 1941), Vol. II, pp. 21-22. Alfonso Conlan, C.S.C., "A Study of the Trustee Problem in the St. Louis Cathedral of New Orleans, Louisiana, 1842-1849," Louisiana Quarterly, XXIII (1948), pp. 1064-67; XXXI (1948), pp. 897-972. Michael Kenny, *Catholic Culture in Alabama*, pp. 227-8. Cemetery Record, St. Louis #2, New Orleans, Louisiana.

34 • VICTOR GIRADEY: CSR (Louisiana) Richtor's or Dreux Battalion; resignation tendered and transferred to Blanchard's Louisiana lst, Ch. I Vol. 47, p. 166; killed in battle, Ch. I, Vol. 42-1, p. 696, RG 109, NA. Booth, *RLCS*, Vol. III, Bk. 1, p. 30. Ezra J. Warner, *Generals in Grey: Lives of Confederate Commanders* (Baton Rouge, Louisiana: Louisiana State University Press, 1959) p. 105.

• CHARLES M. BRADFORD (b. Pennsylvania, 1826–d. New Orleans, Louisiana, Sept. 26, 1867): Adjutant General M. Grivot noted, in the *Annual Report of the Adjutant General of the State of Louisiana* (Baton Rouge: 1894) for the years 1860-62, that Bradford resigned his commission July 23, 1861 (p. 245). But in Ch. 8, Vol. 170, p. 11, his date of resignation is given as May 4, 1861; that is, before Gache wrote this letter. CSR (Louisiana) 15th Regiment; CSRO&M; Texas Regiment, Ch. I, Vol. 94, p. 222. See also Ch. 8, Vol. 157, RG 109, NA; Marcus J. Wright and Colonel Harold B. Simpson, *Texas in the War, 1861-1865* (Hillsboro, Texas: Hillsboro Press, 1965), pp. 29, 123; Eldon Stephen Branda (ed.), *The Handbook of Texas* (Austin: Texas State Historical Association, 1976), (3 Vols. plus Supplement), Supplement pp. 103-4. Typescript of Tablet Inscription of Tombs (Girot Cemetery, New Orleans, La. Prepared by D.A.R., Chapter "Spirit of '76" in Tulane University, New Orleans, La.

35 • JOURDAN, also written Jourdant: Obit. *Woodstock Letters*, XVI (1887), pp. 99-101. Michael Kenny, *Catholic Culture in Alabama*, p. 209, and particularly "Notes," pp. 54, 60-61.

36 • JOSEPH MONTAGNAN: Michael Kenny, *Catholic Culture in Alabama*, p. 225; "Notes," p. 94.

37 • Eleven letters written by Michael Nash, S.J., each entitled "Letters from a Chaplain," were published in *Woodstock Letters* between 1887 and 1890. The account of the destruction of the dry dock cited above is in Vol. 17 (1888), pp. 146-8. The citation describing the destruction of St. John the Evangelist Church is in Vol. 18 (1889), p. 163. Nash was also a contributor to the New York *Tablet* during the war. See his obituary in *Woodstock Letters*, XXVI (1897), pp. 334-46.

38 • JOHN RAPIER: Obit., *Mobile, Register*, May 8, 1905, p. 3; May 9, 1905, p. 1. *DAH*, Vol. IV, p. 1314. Patrick Walsh, "The Irish in South Carolina, Georgia, Alabama, Louisiana and Tennessee," *Journal of the American-Irish Historical Society*, Vol. III (1900), pp. 106-7.

• FRANCIS B. ROHMER: "Synopsis of an Autobiographic History of Dr. Francis John Bte. Rohmer," a twenty-five page typed document compiled from personal notes of Dr. Rohmer by his grandson Stephen Mallory LeBaron, March 1955, and other memorabilia in the private collection of Mrs. Edward O. Cain, Jr., Mobile, Alabama; "Bell Genealogy Notes," *Deep South Genealogical Quarterly*, VIII (1970) p. 243. Michael Kenny, *Catholic Culture in Alabama*, p. 343; Francis Rohmer changed the spelling of his name to Romer shortly after arriving in Louisiana, and that was the spelling of the name until after the war. In these edited letters the corrected version *Rohmer* has been used, although Gache consistently used the preferred spelling of the 1860's: *Romer*.

39 • ANDRÉ CORNETTE: Michael Kenny, *Catholic Culture in Alabama*, p. 256; "Notes," pp. 70-71. Raymond B. Schmandt and Josephene H. Schulte (eds.), "Spring Hill College Diary, 1861-1865." *Alabama Review*, XV (1962), pp. 213-35, and "Civil War Chaplains: A Document from a Jesuit Community," *Records of the American Catholic Historical Society of Philadelphia*, X (1962), pp. 58-64.

• JOHN SERRA: Obit., *Woodstock Letters*, XVI (1887), pp. 97-99. Michael Kenny, *Catholic Culture in Alabama*, pp. 224-5.

40 • General Grivot's Report to the Louisiana Legislature, November 22, 1861 in the *Annual Report*, p. 241. For a summary of De Leon's account of President Davis and the Zouaves, see Hudson Strode, *Jefferson Davis* (3 vols.; New York: Harcourt, 1959), Vol. II, pp. 82-84.

41 • Letters dated New Orleans, April 17, 1861 and Spring Hill, June 1861 appeared in *Etudes*, VII (1862), pp. 808-12. The sentiments of these French Jesuits should be judged in the light of those expressed by Napoleon Perché in the *Propagateur catholique* (See Willard Wright, "Bishop Elder and the Civil War," *Catholic Historical Review*, XLIV (1958), pp. 291-92). Because the College Baptismal Records for this period were destroyed by fire, it is impossible to identify the Alabama captain who received baptism from the unnamed Spring Hill Jesuit. But significantly, Michael Kenny stated that Father Serra, despite his atrocious accent, made "numerous converts among army officers and highly educated men" during the war years, having

"mastered a readier medium of reaching the intelligence of the heart than fluency of speech." "Notes," p. 113.

42 • CHAPLAIN SELECTION: Letter of Giles Smulders to his Provincial, September 26, 1865, Fort Jennings, Georgia, Redemptorist Provincial Archives, Brooklyn, New York. Letter of Colonel Henry B. Kelly to Archbishop John Mary Odin, July 12, 1861 in Odin papers, Archives of Notre Dame University, Indiana. Sidney J. Romero, "The Confederate Chaplain," *Civil War History*, I (1955) 127-28.

• HIPPOLYTE GACHE: Date of appointment given in Appointment Book, Ch. I, Vol. 132, #33, and in Indices, Ch. I, Vol. 86, pp. 366-433 as well as in Vol. 82, p. 269 and Vol. 96, p. 81. Gache file in CSR and in CSRO&M in RG 109 NA. Gache is not mentioned in Booth, *RLCS*, and the information about him in Aidan Germain, *Catholic Military Chaplains*, p. 117, is misleading and sometimes incorrect.

• MANDEVILLE de MARIGNY: Óbit., New Orleans *Daily Picayune*, June 4, 1890, p. 8; quotation in text taken from this obituary. J. W. Cruzat, *Biographical and Genealogical Notes Concerning the Family of Philippe de Mandeville, Ecuyer, Sieur de Marigny*, 1709-1910 (Louisiana Historical Society Publications, Vol. 4, p. 1911).

• Commission in Ch. I Vol. 82, p. 269, Register of Commissioned Officers in the Provisional Army of the Confederate States (RCO in PACS). Marigny file in CSR (Louisiana) Tenth Regiment in RG 109, NA; *Dictionary of American Biography* (New York: Scribner & Sons, 1935), Vol. XII, pp. 282-83 hereinafter cited as *DAB*. Grace King, *Creole Families of New Orleans* (New York: Macmillan, 1921), pp. 23-58. Stanley C. Arthur and George C. Huchet de Kernion (eds. & comps.), *Old Families of Louisiana* (New Orleans: Harmanson, 1931), pp. 316-20. Herman Seebold, *Old Louisiana Plantation Homes*, Vol. I, pp. 55-56; Vol. II, pp. 131-32.

• STATISTICS ON TENTH LOUISIANA REGIMENT: Ella Lonn, *Foreigners in the Confederacy* (Gloucester, Massachusetts: Peter Smith, 1965), p. 109. Ordered to Virginia and assigned to Magruder: Official Records LI, Pt. 2, pp. 174, 234.

43 • HENRY D. MONIER: *Biographical & Historical Memoires of Louisiana . . . & a Record of the Lives of Many of the Most Worthy and Illustrious Families and Individuals* (Chicago: Goodspeed Publishing Co., 1892), Vol. II, pp. 261-62. Hereinafter cited as Goodspeed, *BHML*. Monier's journal was published as part of "A Soldier's Story," in Napier Bartlett (ed. and comp.), *Military Record of Louisiana: Biographical & Historical Papers Relating to the Military Organizations of the State* (New Orleans: J. Graham & Co., 1875) pp. 24-56; hereinafter cited as Henry Monier, "Journal." Andrew Booth, *RLCS*, III, Bk 1, p. 1013.

• JOHN LEGETT: Some genealogical data collected in *Stars and Bars*, Chapter 69, Children of the Confederacy, Mobile Alabama, Chapter Book 43; Quarterly Abstracts of Passenger Lists of Vessels Arriving at New Orleans, 1820-75. "Ship Hope" from Liverpool, November 11, 1844 in RG 36, NA. Legett file in CSR (Louisiana) Tenth Regiment. RCO in PACS, Ch. I, Vol, 82, p. 269. Promotions: July 28, 1862, August 30, 1862 in Ch. I, Vol. 86, p. 70. Register of Officers and Soldiers of the Army of the Confederate States who were killed in battle or who died of wounds or diseases (RKorD), Ch. X, File 6, p. 142 in RG 109. Andrew Booth, *RLCS*, II, Bk. 1

p. 417. The book *Exercises et Manoeuvres de l'Infanterie: Ecole du Soldat, Ecole du Peloton, Ecole des Guides, Service des Places, Service en Campagne* (Nouvelle-Orléans: L. Marchand, Imprimateur: 1861) containing the notes scratched out by John Legett is in the Collection of Manuscripts and Printed Materials Relating to the Participation of Specific Confederate Soldiers in the Civil War, 55-C, Manuscripts Division, Howard-Tilton Library, Tulane University, New Orleans, Louisiana. Following Legett's brief notes there is this entry in another hand: "I found this book on the battlefield of Williamsburg a day or two after that terrible fight, and probably the owner with the slain was numbered."

44 • HENRY MARKS: Goodspeed, *BHML* Vol. II., pp. 261-62, New Orleans *Daily Crescent*, March 3, 1867, p. 8. CSR (Louisiana) Tenth Regiment. RCO in PACS, Ch. I, Vol. 82, p. 269 in RG 109 NA. Andrew Booth, *RLCS* III, Bk. 1, p. 876.

• THOMAS POWELL: Age, place of birth, occupation as student of medicine given in CSR (Louisiana) Tenth Regiment. Although questioned, Powell's rank as major was supported by the troops and by General Francis Nicholls, as correspondence in his personal file indicates, RG 109 NA. This fact is not reported by Andrew Booth, *RLCS*, III, Bk. 2 p. 186. Henry Monier, "Journal" gives the account of Powell's death on p. 55.

• EDWARD SETON: Reverend Donald J. Hebert, *Southwest Louisiana Records*, IV, p. 450. Seton's place and date of birth appear on p. 588. The Eighth Census of the United States, 1860, Louisiana, Calcasieu Parish, Lake Charles, p. 119, shows that he was a resident of that town at the time of his enlistment. His military records generally list him as *Edward A. Seaton*: CSR (Louisiana) Tenth Regiment. RCO in PACS Ch. I, Vol, 82, p. 269. "Prisoners of War Captured at Wilderness, May 10, 1864," Register, Fort Delaware, 4, p. 53; "Prisoners who died at Fort Delaware," Register, Fort Delaware, 65 p. 116 in RG log NA. Andrew Booth, *RLCS*, III, Bk. 2 p. 503.

• GASPAR BALLAND: The Eighth Census of the United States, 1860, Alabama, City of Mobile, Southern Division, 132, RG 29, NA. Father Cornette noted in the Vice President's Diary on July 7, 1865 "our old servant Gaspar" was sent to Grand Coteau, presumably for retirement.

• HENRY J. MILLER: Baptismal Record, St. Peter's Church, Richmond, August 12, 1838; CSR (Virginia) 3d Artillery, RG 109, NA. James S. Ruby, (ed.), *Blue and Gray: Georgetown University and the Civil War* (Washington, D.C.: Georgetown Alumni Association, 1961), p. 88. Schockoe Cemetery, Richmond, Virginia, Index to Interments, 1822-1955, folio 332.

• HENRY MILLER, SR.: Obit., Richmond *Daily Dispatch*, July 24, 1883, p. 1 from which citation in text has been taken. After the death of his Saarborn wife, Magdalena (1804-79), Miller remarried. Marriage Records, St. Peter's Church, Richmond, Virginia, June 8, 1880. Hustings Court, Richmond, Virginia, Index to Interments, 1822-1955, folio 412, 434.

46 • HENRY FORNO: Obit., New Orleans *Daily Picayune*, February 2, 1866, p. 6. New Orleans *Deutsche Zeitung*, April 26, 1866. CSR (Louisiana) 5th; CSRO&M. "Louisiana Militia," Ch. VIII, Vol. 170, p. 48. RCO in PACS, Ch. I, Vol. 82, p. 264. List of killed, wounded or missing in Ewell's Division, August 22 to September 20, 1862, "Series I, Vol. 12, Pt. 1, p. 810 in RG 109, NA. Andrew Booth, *RLCS*, II, p. 898. Alison Moore, *Louisiana Tigers, or*

the Two Louisiana Brigades of the Army of Northern Virginia, 1861-1865 (Baton Rouge, Louisiana: Ortlich Press, 1961), p. 173.

- L.H. BALDWIN: Baldwin file in the New Jersey Historical Society Library, Newark, New Jersey. CSR (Louisiana) 5th; CSRO&M; Ch. I, Vol. 132 #160 (Chaplain Appointment Book). Ch. I, Vol. 86, p. 373 (Indices). Ch. I, Vol. 82, p. 264 (Resignation) in RG 109, NA. Despite Baldwin's letter to McClellan, dated Sharpsburg, October 13, 1862, the chaplain's name appeared on the Roll of Prisoners of War, September 17, 1862, indicating that he had been captured at Antietam and paroled November 6, at Fort Henry, Maryland. There is an obvious discrepancy here. Sidney Romero, "Louisiana Clergy and the Confederate Army," *Louisiana History* II (1961), p. 291.

47 • See Charles W. Turner (ed.), "Major Charles A. Davidson: Letters of a Virginia Soldier, " *Civil War History*, XXII, 1976, p. 19 for Magruder's problems with de Coppens' Zouaves at this period.

48 • CHARLES MONBAR: Company roles indicate that this sergeant died August 21, 1861. CSR (Louisiana) 1st special RG 109, NA.

- SAMUEL TODD: Obit. New Orleans *Daily Picayune*, February 2, 1905, p. 16. No extant rolls give significant information about Todd's military career, a fact which is not exceptional for personnel assigned to Dreux's (Rightor's) Battalion. Andrew Booth, *RLCS*, III, Bk. 2, p. 841.
- NICHOLAS RIGHTOR: Obit. New Orleans *State*, August 12, 1900, p. 11; August 13, 1900, p. 8. RCO in PACS, Ch. I, Vol. 96, p. 275. Ch. I, Vol. 86, p. 62 (Appointment). He resigned June 11, 1862 and during the Teche campaign was captured at Lafourche, July 15, 1863, in RG 109, NA. Andrew Booth, *RLCS*, III, Bk. 2, p. 322.
- EUGENE WAGGAMAN: Obit. New Orleans *Daily States*, April 25, 1897 p. 6. CSR (Louisiana) 10th. RCO in PACS, Ch. I, Vol. 82, p. 269 (Appointment). Ch. I, Vol. 96, p. 81 (Register of Commissioned Officers) in RG 109, NA; Andrew Booth, *RLCS* III, Bk. 2, p. 952. Clement A. Evans, *Confederate Military History* (Atlanta: Confederate Press, 1899), Vol. X. *Louisiana* by John Dimitry, pp. 610-11. Stanley C. Arthur & George Huchet de Kernion, *Old Families of Louisiana*, pp. 83-95. Alison Moore, *Louisiana Tigers*, p. 173. Henry Monier, "Journal," p. 25. St. Louis #1 Cemetery Records, New Orleans.

49 • JOHN WINSTON: CSR (Alabama) 8th; RCO in PACS, Ch. I, Vol. 86, p. 15 (Appointment, June 11, 1861; Resignation June 6, 1862) in RG 109 NA. *DAH*, IV, 1790. *DAB*, XX, pp. 404-05.

- PATRICK LOUGHRY: CSR (Alabama) 8th; RCO in PACS, Ch. I, Vol. 83, p. 8 (Appointment May 20, 1861) in RG 109, NA. Age and some background given in "Naturalization Entries, Circuit Court Minutes, 1837 and 1840," p. 55, Circuit Court, Mobile, Alabama.
- CORNELIUS LYONS: "Register Books of the Prefect of Classes and Studies," 1849-77, Archives, Spring Hill College, Mobile, Alabama, (4 bound ms. volumes), Vol. III, p. 107, hereinafter cited as SH Register Book. Incomplete record which contains some erroneous information in CSR (Alabama) 8th, RG 109, NA. Historical record roll, dated January 1, 1865, entitled "Cornelius Lyons," State of Alabama, Department of Archives and History, Montgomery, Alabama hereinafter cited as *DA&H, Alabama.* Lucille Mallon and Rochelle Ferris, comps., *Burial Records: Mobile County,*

Alabama (2 vols., Mobile: Mobile Genealogical Society, Inc., 1971), II, p. 155.

- JOHN LYONS: SH Register Book, II, p. 190, Muster rolls show that Lyons enlisted May 4, 1861 at Pensacola, but there is no record of him after December 31, 1863, *DA&H, Alabama.*
- LYONS FAMILY: The Eighth Census of the United States, 1860, Alabama, City of Mobile, 4th ward, p. 8; 2d ward, p. 45. Kate Cumming, *Kate: The Journal of a Confederate Nurse*, ed. Richard Barksdale Harwell, (Baton Rouge, Louisiana: Louisiana State University Press, 1950), pp. 19-22, 212.

50 • DOMINIC YENNI: sketch in *Woodstock Letters*, 18 (1889), pp. 211-218; 262.

- JOHN MAGRUDER: Ezra J. Werner, *Generals in Gray*, 207-208.

51 • DARIUS HUBERT: CSR (Louisiana) 1st; CSRO&M: Ch. I, Vol. 86, p. 365 (Indices). Ch. I, Vol. 132 #6 (Appointment). RCO in PACS, Ch. I, Vol. 82, p. 260. Hubert accompanied Blanchard from Louisiana to Virginia: letter from Blanchard to General Cooper, March 26, 1865, A&IGO in RG 109, NA. Andrew Booth, *RLCS*, III, Bk. 1, p. 184. Aidan Germain, *Catholic Military and Naval Chaplains*, pp. 129-30. T.S. King, S.J., "Letters of Civil War Chaplains," *Woodstock Letters*, 43 (1914), pp. 24-34; 168-180. Michael Kenny, *Catholic Culture in Alabama*, p. 216; "Notes," pp. 72-75.

- JOSEPH PRACHENSKY: Obit., *Woodstock Letters*, 20 (1891), pp. 120-21; CSRO&M. Ch. I, Vol. 86, p. 367 (Indices). Ch. I, Vol. 132 #45 (Appointment); Quotation in text from a letter of Patrick N. Lynch to John McGill, August 23, 1861 in Archives of the Diocese of Richmond, Virginia. Aidan Germain, *Catholic Military and Naval Chaplains*, pp. 129-30.
- FRANÇOIS MINORET: The Eighth Census of the United States, 1860, Alabama, City of Mobile, Southern Division, 123, in RG 29, NA.

52 • EGIDIUS SMULDERS: Joseph Wuest, C.SS.R., *Rev. Giles Smulders, C.SS.R.* (Ilchester, Maryland: St. Mary's College Press, 1909). Obit., CSRO&M. Ch. I, Vol. 132, #32 (Appointment). Ch. I, Vol. 86, p. 366 (Indices) in RG 109, NA. Quotation in text from a letter of Giles Smulders to his Provincial, September 26, 1865, Redemptorist Provincial Archives, Brooklyn, New York.

53 • Z. Lee Gilmer Diary (Ms. at the University of Virginia Library, Charlottesville, Virginia), December 9, 1861. Gilmer was in Company B, Nineteenth Virginia Regiment.

54 • OSCAR SEARS: Obit. notice, *Sadlier's Catholic Directory, Almanac and Ordo* (New York: Sadlier, 1878), p. 240, hereinafter cited as *Sadlier's Catholic Directory*. CSRO&M, Ch. I, Vol. 132, #119 (Appointment). Ch. I, Vol. 86, p. 371 (Indices). Sears to George W. Randolph, June 12, 1862, in A&IGO in RG 109, NA. "Dimissi" notebook, Archives of the Maryland Province of the Society of Jesus, Baltimore, Maryland, January 13, 1852. Francis Joseph Margi, *The Catholic Church in the City and Diocese of Richmond* (Richmond: Whittet and Shepperson, 1906) pp. 83, 96.

- DAVID WHELAN: Obit. notice, *Sadlier's Catholic Directory*, (1866), p. 421; Oscar Hugh Lipscomb, "Administration of John Quinlan," p. 41.
- THOMAS MULVEY: "Register of Students," Archives of All Hallows College, Dublin, Ireland, no. 114 gives the proper place of birth but not the date. R.J. Purcell, "Missionaries from All Hallows (Dublin) to the United

States, 1842-1865," *Records of the American Catholic Historical Society of Philadelphia*, 53 (1942) p. 244. James Henry Bailey II, *A History of the Diocese of Richmond: The Formative Years* (Richmond: Chancery Office, (1956), pp. 154-56. James Henry Bailey, *Jubilee, (1842-1942) St. Joseph's Church, Petersburg, Virginia* (Petersburg, Virginia: N.P., 1942).

• MICHAEL O'KEEFE: Certificate of death, Department of Health and Mental Hygiene, State of Maryland, Baltimore, Maryland. CSRO&M: Ch. I, Vol, 86, p. 370 (Indices). Ch. I, Vol. 133 #130 (Appointment): letter from Blanchard to Mahone, March 22, 1862, Norfolk, Virginia, A&IGO. On December 2, 1862, Albert Blanchard, then stationed at Headquarters, Monroe, Louisiana, requested that Father Hubert be appointed brigade chaplain, but with no reference to O'Keefe as a precedent, the request was not granted by order of the Secretary of War: "There is no such officer as brigade chaplain. The nominee may be appointed for a post or a regiment only," A&IGO, in RG 109, NA. Aidan Germain, *Catholic Military & Naval Chaplains*, pp. 126-27. Thomas J. Hogan, *The Golden Jubilee of the Church of St. Mary's of the Immaculate Conception with a Resumê of Catholic History of the City of Norfolk, Virginia* (Norfolk, Virginia: Burke & Gregory, 1909), p. 38. George Theodore Maioriello, "History of Tidewater Catholicism," The Catholic Virginian, February 29, 1952.

• CHURCH OF THE IMMACULATE CONCEPTION. Cambiaso's church was begun in 1851 and completed in 1857. It was demolished in 1928 and rebuilt in 1930. Hilton L. Rivet, S.J., *The History of the Immaculate Conception Church in New Orleans (Jesuits)*, n.p., 1978.

55 • ROBERT KELLY: Michael Kenny, "Notes," p. 63. John R. Grene, S.J., "A Contribution Towards a History of the Irish Province of the Society of Jesus," *Woodstock Letters*, 16 (1887), p. 224.

• JOSEPH DESRIBES: Obit., *Woodstock Letters*, 33 (1904), pp. 94-95; Michael Kenny, *Catholic Culture in Alabama*, pp. 221-22.

56 • WILLIAM E. HINTON: Obit., Petersburg *Daily Index-Appeal*, June 23, 1894, p. 1. Baptismal Register, St. Joseph's Church, Petersburg, Virginia, December 4, 1855. Monument, Square #163, Blandford Cemetery, Petersburg, Virginia.

• ELLEN COXE MCGOWAN HINTON: Obit., Petersburg *Daily Index-Appeal*, July 24, 1892, p. 4. Marriage, Petersburg *South-Side Daily Democrat*, p. 2. Marriage Records, St. Joseph's Church, Petersburg, Virginia, September 4, 1856. There are no records of Ellen McGowan having been a student at a convent of the Sacred Heart on the Atlantic seaboard. Since some of the records at Manhattanville College, New York City, were destroyed by fire, she could have attended that institution, but because her daughter, Margaret, was a student at Eden Hall, Philadelphia, where the records are not extant before 1854, it is probable that it was here where Ellen was educated.

• MARY JANE WHYTE HINTON: Edward A. Wyatt, IV, (ed. & comp.), *Checklist for Petersburg, 1786-1876 (Virginia Imprint Series, 9)* (Richmond: Virginia State Library, 1949), pp. 242-43. Index to Marriage Register, Hustings Court, Petersburg, Virginia, 1784-1865, Circuit Court, Petersburg, Virginia, January 1841. Tombstone, William E. Hinton section Blandford Cemetery, Petersburg, Virginia.

- MARY ELLEN HINTON THOMPSON: Register of Marriages, Hustings Court, Petersburg, Virginia, 1854-90, Circuit Court, Petersburg, Virginia, I, p. 44. Student Records, Georgetown Visitation Convent, 1843-45, Washington, D.C. Family Bible in possession of Mrs. Norma Tucker, Shreveport, Louisiana, has biographical data on members of the Hinton-Thompson families.
- WADDY THOMPSON: Obit., New Orleans *Daily Picayune*, December 12, 1916, p. 2. File in Waring Library, Medical University of South Carolina. *South Carolina Historical Magazine*, Vol. IV (1903), p. 360. Burial place of Mary Ellen and Waddy Thompson: Thompson plot, Greenlawn Memorial Cemetery, Hammond, Louisiana.
- HUGH SMITH THOMPSON: *DAB*, 18, pp. 458-9.
- JENNY HINTON DUNN: Student Records, Georgetown Visitation Convent, Washington, D.C., 1860? Register of Marriages, Hustings Court, Petersburg, Virginia, 1854-1900, Circuit Court, Petersburg, Virginia, I, p. 112. Burial records, Cemetery, Scotland Neck, North Carolina.
- ALDEN S. DUNN: of "Dunn's Hill," Chesterfield County, Society of Mayflower Descendants (General) #26239. Burial records, Cemetery, Scotland Neck, North Carolina.
- MARGARET HINTON TUCKER: Attendance Records, Eden Hall, Convent of the Sacred Heart, Philadelphia, 1870-75. Archives, Religious of the Sacred Heart, St. Louis, Missouri. Register of Marriages, Hustings Court, Petersburg, Virginia, 1854-1900. Circuit Court, Petersburg, Virginia, Vol. I, p. 148. Tombstone, William E. Hinton section, Blandford Cemetery, Petersburg, Virginia.
- RANDOLPH TUCKER: Obit. Petersburg *Progress-Index*, June 10, 1928. Tombstone, William E. Hinton section, Blandford Cemetery, Petersburg, Virginia.

57 • For possible reasons why anti-Catholicism was not as virulent in Petersburg as it was in the urban centers of the North, see Philip Morrison Rice, "The Know-Nothing Party in Virginia, 1854-1856," *Virginia Magazine of History and Biography*, LV (1947), p. 66. Letters of Anthony M. Keiley to John McGill, April 10 and 26, 1860 in Diocesan Archives, Chancery Office, Richmond, Virginia.

- ANTHONY M. KEILEY: *National Cyclopaedia of American Biography* hereinafter cited as NCAB, XIII, p. 433. James H. Bailey, "Anthony M. Keiley and the 'Keiley Incident,'" *Virginia Magazine of History and Biography*, LXVII (1959), pp. 65-81 gives an account of Keiley's aberrant career as minister to Austria and Italy. Benjamin Keiley (1848-1925), the younger brother Anthony threatened to pull out of St. Joseph's Church in 1860, became bishop of Savannah, 1900-1922. For the attitude of Protestants toward Mulvey, John Herbert Clairborne, *Seventy-Five Years in Old Virginia* (New York: Neale, 1904) p. 66 and James Henry Bailey II, *A History of the Diocese of Richmond*, p. 100.

58 • SOUTHALL FAMILY: Family Bible of Mary Fish Southall Jones in possession of Mrs. James H. Stone, Richmond, Virginia; family Bible of Elizabeth Bouche Southall Turner in possession of Mr. C.B. League, Tampa, Florida. Baptismal, Marriage, and Birth Records of Bruton Parish Church, Williamsburg, Virginia, 1868-1907 contain considerable biographical information on the Southall family which was not published in a sketch of

this family by James P.C. Southall, "Concerning the Southalls of Virginia," *Virginia Magazine of History and Biography* 45 (1938), 277-302 and by Robert J. Travis, *The Travis (Travers) Family and its Allies: Darracott, Lewis, Livingston, Nicholson, McLaughlin, Pharr, Smith and Terrell* (Savannah, Georgia: printed privately (1954) p. 69. Eighth Census of the United States (1860) p. 1, City of Williamsburg, Virginia and Ninth Census (1870), p. 25, RG 29, NA. The account of the arrest of Travis Southall in August 1861 and letters of Virginia Southall and John Tyler to President Davis in *Official Records*, 2, Vol. 2, pp. 1365-66. George Washington Southall Papers and unclassified "William and Mary College Papers," both in the Swem Library show that in the 1860's Albert Southall was a printer and a supplier of stationery. For his relationship to John Tyler, *William and Mary Quarterly*, 2nd series, III (1923) p. 164. After the evacuation of the President's House in 1862 the Southall family took possession until the Spring of 1864 when it became the headquarters of the Federal Army, and it was here presumably where Albert died. *Ibid.* p. 222. The military record of Travis is in CSR (Virginia) 3rd Cavalry, RG 109, NA. Some biographical material on various members of this family is found in the obituaries of Rev. Joseph Wilmer Turner, *Southern Churchman*, April 25, 1908, p. 21.

59 • BENJAMIN S. EWELL: Obit., *William and Mary College Quarterly Historical Magazine* (1st series), III, (1859). *DAB* (6) pp. 228-29. James S. Ruby, *Georgetown University and the Civil War*, p. 47.

• REBECCA LOWNDES EWELL: Gache's letter to Rebecca's sister Elizabeth Ewell August 29, 1867, indicates that Rebecca died about the first of the month; Ewell Papers, Swem Library, College of William and Mary, Williamsburg, Virginia. Unfortunately the death records for Williamsburg, James City, and York County for 1867 are not extant, and there are no Willliamsburg newspapers available to the researcher for this period.

• ELIZABETH STODDERT EWELL SCOTT: Obit., Williamsburg *Virginia Gazette*, June 8, 1911, p. 2. Gache's last known letter to "Miss Lizzy" is dated February 15, 1901. In 1867 she had married Beverly Seymore Scott (1844-1906) of Prince Edward County, whom Gache did not know, "but it is enough for me to know that he is your husband, in order (for him) to be the object of my profound esteem and respect." Ewell Papers.

• BEVERLY SCOTT: CSR (Virginia) 34th Infantry; Ch. VI, File 41, p. 317 (list of wounded) in RG 109 NA. Copy of Ewell Family Bible, Earl Gregg Swem Library, College of William and Mary.

• FANNY BROWN: Many references in Ewell Papers. Citation in text found in Folder 23.

• EWELL FAMILY: The Eighth Census of the United States, 1860, James City, Virginia, p. 48. Horace Edwin Hayden, *Virginia Genealogies* (Wilkes-Barre, Pennsylvania: E.B. Yordy, Printers, 1891), pp. 348-49. Percy Gatling Hamlin (ed.), *The Making of a Soldier: Letters of General R.S. Ewell* (Richmond, Virginia: Whittet & Shepperson, 1935). Mrs. Robert A. Ryland (comp.), "Family History of Ewell-Ford-Gulick-Hixson-Humphrey-Hutchison-Marks-Purcell," compilation of the Genealogical Records Committee, Daughters of the American Revolution, 1945, Virginia State Library, Richmond, Virginia, pp. 142-43.

• THOMAS AMBLER: Obit. *Southen Churchman*, February 23, 1907, p. 8; *Journal of the One Hundred and Twelfth Annual Council of the Diocese of*

Virginia (Richmond, Virginia: Medical Journal, 1907), pp. 55-56; quotation in text taken from page 56. RCO in PACS: Ch. I, Vol. 132, #66 (Appointment). Ch. I, Vol. 86, p. 368, RG 109 NA. Mary Frances Goodwin (ed.), *The Record of Bruton Parish by Rev. William Archer Rutherford Goodwin* (Richmond, Virginia: Dietz Press, 1941), p. 51.

60 • *Official Records*, Vol. IV, p. 669.

61 • THOMAS CURTIS: Eighth Census of the United States, 1860, Warwick County, Virginia, in RG 40, NA. Will of Thomas Curtis, December 11, 1879, probated March 11, 1880, County of Warwick, Circuit Court, Newport, Virginia. For a sketch of the Curtis farm and its proximity to Lee's Mill, see Brigadier General A.A. Humphreys (comp.), *Campaign Maps, Army of the Potomac Prepared by Command of Major General George B. McClellan, U.S.A.*, (Bureau of Topographical Engineers, April 1862), Map #1, Yorktown to Williamsburg.

62 • MARTIN SANDS: Thomas M. Owen, "Brief Memoranda Concerning a Southern Line of the Sands Family," pp. 352-54. CSR (Alabama) 3rd; CSRO&M; Ch. I file 82, p. 209 (Promotions); retired from 3rd Regiment, G.O. #34, October 19, 1864, and reassigned to Hq. Dist. of the Gulf, S.O. #311, November 6, 1864, A&IGO, RG 109, NA; *DAH*, IV, 1500. Michael Kenny, *Catholic Culture in Alabama*, pp. 113-14. Helen A. Thompson (comp. & ed.), *Magnolia Cemetery, 1828-1971* (New Orleans, Louisiana: Polyanthos, 1974), p. 358.

• HENRY HOTZE: Quotations in text from Henry Hotze, *Three Months in the Confederate Army*, ed. Richard Barksdale Harweck, (Tuscaloosa, Alabama: University of Alabama Press, 1952), pp. 29, 54. John L. Wakelyn, *Biographical Dictionary of the Confederacy* (Westport, Connecticut: Greenwood Press, 1977), pp. 239-40.

• JOHN BELL ROHMER: Obit., Bay St. Louis, *The Sea Coast Echo*, August 26, 1922, p. 1; quotation in text taken from this obituary. SH Register Book, Vol. III, p. 104; CSR (Alabama) 3rd; discharged from 3rd Battalion, S.O. #50/5, March 1, 1864; appointed Hospital Steward, S.O. 117/13, May 16, 1863, and assigned to Byrnes Hospital, Mobile until April 11, 1865, date of parole, in RG 109, NA; Marriage Records, Prince of Peace Catholic Church (formerly St. Vincent's), Mobile, Alabama, April 9, 1865. His certificate of death gives date of birth 1842; other documents give 1841, State of Mississippi, Hancock County file 12790, #39.

63 • JOHN BURNS: Obit., *Mobile Daily Register*, September 2, 1875, p. 4. SH Register Book, III, p. 136; CSR (Alabama) 3rd; discharged by S.O. #308, December 21, 1861, Ch. V., Vol. III, p. 28, RG 109 in NA.

• BURNS FAMILY: Eighth Census of the United States, 1860, Alabama, City of Mobile, where Robert's age is incorrectly given, p. 832, RG 24, NA. "Naturalization Entries, City Court Minutes, Mobile, Alabama," abstract made by a W.P.A. Project (n.d.), May 15, 1845. Robert: Records, Catholic Cemetery, Stone Street, Mobile, Alabama, March 15, 1861.

64 • HENRY MULDON: Obit., Mobile *Daily Register*, October 7, 1871, p. 2; November 8, 1871, p. 2; November 10, 1871, p. 2; SH Register Book, III, p. 133. CSR (Alabama) 3rd; captured, Ch. VI, file 204, p. 228, in RG 109, NA. Immaculate Conception Catholic Cathedral, Mobile, Alabama, Burial Records, #2477, November 8, 1871. Helen Thompson, *Magnolia Cemetery*, p. 122.

- JAMES MICHAEL MULDON: Obit., Mobile *Daily Register*, June 13, 1886, p. 2. SH Register Book III, p. 91. CSR (Alabama) 3rd, an incomplete record; discharged S.O. #379, from the 3rd, November 12, 1861, in RG 109, NA.
- MULDON FAMILY: Eighth Census of the United States, 1860, City of Mobile, p. 392 in RG 40, NA.

65 • JOHN DAILY: SH Register Book, III, p. 139. CSR (Alabama) 3rd, an incomplete record in RG 109, NA. A Final Statement by John J. Huggins, Captain, 3rd Alabama, March 1, 1865 on the death and military career of John Daily in the DA&H, Montgomery, Alabama. Vice President's Diary, SH College Archives, December 14, 1861.
- DAILY FAMILY: Eighth Census of the United States, 1860, City of Mobile, Alabama, 4th Ward, p. 34.

66 • JAMES HUGH MASTERSON: Baptismal Record, Catholic Cathedral, Mobile, Alabama, #483, October 21, 1849. SH Register Book III, p. 137. CSR (Louisiana) 1st Special. His record does not appear in Andrew Booth, *RLCS*.
- MASTERSON FAMILY: Certificate of Marriage, Luke Masterson & Anne Dufee, December 1848, Holy Spirit Catholic Church, Tuscaloosa, Alabama; will of Luke Masterson, Mobile County Court House, Probate, Bk. 2, p. 313. Obit., Luke Masterson, The Mobile *Daily Register*, November 6, 1850 p. 3. Records, Catholic Cemetery, Stone Street, Mobile, Alabama, gives date of death of Anne Masterson (August 12, 1850), Luke Masterson (November 1, 1850), and the uncle of James, Hugh Masterson, (April 17, 1854).

67 • JOHN INNERARITY: SH Register Book III, p. 48; CRS (Alabama) 3rd, in RG 109, NA. List of Casualties, Montgomery *Advertiser*, July 1862, in DA&H.
- INNERARITY FAMILY: Panton-Forbes-Innerarity-Hulse Papers, University of West Florida, Pensacola, Florida. Genealogical details in private papers of Jorge de Villier, Pensacola, Florida, and of H. Innerarity, Edmond, Oklahoma. Stanley Arthur & George Huchet de Kernion, *Old Families of Louisiana*, p. 225. Marie Taylor Gleenslade, "John Innerarity, 1783-1845," *Florida Historical Quarterly*, IX (1930), pp. 90-95. Obit., James Innerarity, Mobile *Commercial Register*, p. 3.

68 • JOHN AUGUSTINE: Obit., New Orleans *Daily Picayune*, February 6, 1888, p. 4. CSR (Louisiana) 1st Special in RG 109, NA; Andrew Booth, *RLCS* I, p. 89. SH Register Book II, p. 95. Michael Kenny, *Catholic Culture in Alabama*, 166, pp. 300-01. *Louisiana Historical Quarterly*, 24, (1941), pp. 765-67.
- THOMAS RABY: CSR (Louisiana) 1st Special, Ch. VI, Vol. 267, p. 18 in RG 109, NA. Andrew Booth, RLCS. III, Bk 2, p. 267. SH Register Book, III, 41. Married Louisa Bufford, September 17, 1867, Marriage Records, Terrebonne Parish. Succession, December 31, 1888, Nineteenth District Court, Terrebonne, Louisiana.

69 • MICHEL PRUD'HOMME (MICHAEL PRUDHOMME in Army records): SH Register Book, III, p. 143. CSR (Louisiana) 10th; the letter of resignation addressed to William H. Spencer, December 30, 1861, clearly shows that Prud'homme's first language was not English (letters received A&IGO, January 3, 1862) in RG 109, NA. Andrew Booth, RLCS, III, Bk

2, p. 212. Donald Hebert, *Southwest Louisiana Records*, VII, gives date and place of death.

70 • Clifford M. Lewis, S.J. & Albert J. Loomie, S.J., *The First Spanish Mission in Virginia*, 1570-1572, (Chapel Hill, North Carolina: University of North Carolina Press, 1953), pp. 36,62.

71 • Pay voucher #72, December 4, 1861 in the Gache file, CSRO&M, in RG 106, NA. For chaplains' salaries, Arthur Walker, Jr., "Three Alabama Baptist Chaplains, 1861-1865," *The Alabama Review*, 16 (1963), pp. 174-75. Bell Irvin Wiley, "'Holy Joes' of the Sixties: A Study of Civil War Chaplains." *The Huntington Library Quarterly*, 16 (1953), p. 288.

• ALOYSIUS CURIOZ: Obit., *Woodstock Letters*, 33 (1904), pp. 96-98; Michael Kenny, *Catholic Culture in Alabama*, pp. 228-29.

72 • See Willard Wright, "Bishop Elder and the Civil War," p. 296. Michael Kenny *Catholic Culture in Alabama*, p. 213; "Synopsis of an Autobiographic History of Dr. Francis John Bte. Rohmer," Additional Notes, 1.

73 • An English Combatant (lieutenant of artillery on the field-staff), *Battlefields of the South, from Bull Run to Fredericksburg, with Sketches of Confederate Commanders, and Gossip of the Camps* (2 vols., London: Smith, Elder and Co., 1863) I, p. 280.

74 • Alexandre Dumas (ed.), *The Memoirs of Garibaldi*, trans. R.S. Garnett (London: E. Benn, 1931), p. 313. G. Guerzoni, *La Vita di Nino Bixio* (Firenze: G. Barberà, 1875) p. 22.

75 • Peter Tissot, "Lettre d'un autre Père de la Compagnie de Jesus," *Annales de la Propagation de la foi*, XXXV (1863), p. 284.

76 • George Clark, *A Glance Backward, or Some Events in the Past History of My Life* (Houston, Texas: Rein & Sons, 1920), pp. 23-24. Clark's experience is briefly noted by Ella Lonn in *Foreigners in the Confederacy*, p. 264. GEORGE CLARK: Dayton Kelly (ed.), *The Handbook of Waco and McLennan County, Texas* (Waco, Texas: Texan Press, 1972), p. 61; *Biographical Souvenir of the State of Texas* (Chicago: F.A. Battey Co., 1889), p. 171. Clark's statement about the priest's experience in the "Italian" army during the war between France and Austria presents a problem. If the captain meant the last war between these two powers (1814) the unnamed priest would have had to have been seventy or more, which seems unlikely. I suggest that Bixio referred to the Piedmontese army during the 1848 uprising against the Austrians. Clark's recollection of the conversation took place many years after the actual event, and he could easily have been mistaken on this small detail.

77 • James B. Sheeran, C.SS.R., *Confederate Chaplain: A War Journal*, ed. Joseph T. Durkin, S.J. (Milwaukee: Bruce, 1960), pp. 100-02; 153-56; 160.

78 • Benjamin Francis Musser, "The Lion of Winsted," *The Provincial Annals*, V (1945-56), pp. 264-65. *Woodstock Letters*, XVIII (1889), 247. Some details of the consequences of theft by the unnamed "Confederate spy" to Father Leo were noted in the recollections of Reverend Cherubino Viola, O.F.M., Manuscript, Archives of the Franciscan Institute, St. Bonaventure University, St. Bonaventure, New York.

79 • JOSEPH BIXIO: Obit., *Woodstock Letters*, XVIII (1889), p. 247; Richard L. Carne, *A Brief Sketch of the History of St. Mary's Church, Alexandria, Virgina* (Alexandria: J. Merriot Hill & Co., 1874, p. 17.

- NINO BIXIO: Alberto M. Ghisalberti (ed.), *Dizionario biografio degli Italiani* (Roma: Istituto della Enciclopedia Italiana, 1960), Vol. X, pp. 727-34.
- LEO RIZZO DA SARACENA: Biography in the *Provincial Annals*, a publication of the Franciscan Fathers, New York, V (1945-46), pp. 260-73; 341-49. Aidan Germain gives an incomplete record of his military career, *Catholic Military and Naval Chaplains*, pp. 93-94.

80 • JAMES BIGLER: Obit., Newburgh, New York, *Journal*, July 16, 1910, p.2. *Portrait and Biographical Record of Orange County, New York: Containing Portraits and Biographical Sketches of Prominent and Representative Citizens of the County Together with Biographies and Portraits of all the Presidents of the United States* (New York: Chapman Publishing Co., 1895), pp. 1007-08. York County (Virginia) Deed Book 15, 1849-54, pp. 353-54; 358-60; Deed Book 16, 1854-66, pp. 117-18; 221-22; 294-99; 315-18; 325-26; 328-29; 335-36; 339-44; 347-48, Virginia State Library.

- SIR EDWARD JENINGS: *N C A B*, XIII, P. 387.
- LANDON CARTER: "Landon Carter of Sabine Hall," *Tyler's Quarterly Historical and Genealogical Magazine*, XIII (1932) pp. 246-256.
- RIPON HALL: *William and Mary College Quarterly and Historic Magazine* (1st series), I (1892), p. 83, XX (1912), p. 173. Mary Stuart Young, *The Griffins: A Colonial Tale* (New York: Neal, 1904).

81 • Eighth Census of the United States, 1860, Virgina, York County, pp. 58-60, RG 29, NA.

82 • Eighth Census of the United States, 1860, Virginia, James City, p. 48, RG 29, NA.

- WILLIAM MARTIN: Obit., George Braxton Taylor, *Virginia Baptist Ministers: Fourth Series* (Lynchburg, Virginia: J.P. Bell, Inc., 1913), pp. 26-27. Taylor made no mention of Crandal whose name appeared as "Crandoll" in the unprinted minutes of the 76th and 77th meetings of the Dover Baptist Association, Virginia Baptist Historical Society Library, Richmond, Virginia.

83 • Gache to Elizabeth Ewell, August 29, 1867; Elizabeth Stoddert Ewell (1785-1859) to Rebecca Ewell, December 3, 1843, and Gache to Elizabeth Ewell Scott, February 15, 1901 in Ewell Papers.

84 • JAMES WILCOX JENKINS: Private Jenkins' name appears on the roll of Captain Todd's Louisiana Guards, Dreux Battalion, but there is no record of him after October 1861. He enlisted on April 15, and was with Gache in Pensacola, CSR (Louisiana) 1st Special, RG 109, NA. Magruder mentioned the fact of Jenkins' death, but like Gache did not give his name. *Official Records*, XI, Pt. 1, pp. 403-04. A manuscript written by Private Jenkins' brother, Edward Courtney Jenkins, Jr., in the Manuscript Section of the Archives of the Archdiocese of Cincinnati, Ohio, identifies James Willcox and confirms the fact that he was the soldier to whom Gache made reference in this letter. This manuscript also contains biographical material on Juliana (Elder) Jenkins.

85 • JAMES TIERNEY: Obit., Mobile *Daily Register*, September 28, 1899, p. 8. Naturalization Entries, December 2, 1858, Mobile City Court Minutes, 130. Deed #45, May 11, 1881, Mobile County Court House, Probate. Funeral Book, St. Joseph's Catholic Church, Mobile, Alabama, September 27, 1899, p. 45.

86 • In February 1862, the Holy See extended a number of special faculties to chaplains, one of which was the power to dispense combatants from the laws of fast and abstinence. But, as Gache wrote in his letter of September 11, 1861, he had been given permission to excuse himself, and presumably others, from dietary laws. Such permission was granted by Archbishop Odin.

87 • Willard Wright, "The Bishop of Natchez and the Confederate Chaplaincy," *Mid-America*, XXXIX (1957), pp. 68-69.

• WILLIAM HENRY ELDER: *DAH*, p. 82.

88 • *Official Records* XI, Pt. 1, p. 407.

89 • WILLIAM A.W. SPOTSWOOD: Obit., Mobile *Daily Register*, September 8, 1891, p. 4. Textual citation from a letter to Colonel Bledsol, September 12, 1861, contained with his war record in Ch. VIII, Vol. 289, pp. 3-12 in RG 109, NA. Helen Thompson, *Magnolia Cemetery*, p. 358. Cammie East, "Dr. Spotswood's close shaves, straight blades and narrow escapes," Mobile *Press Register*, September 12, 1976, Sect D, p. 4. H. Cunningham, *Doctors in Gray: The Confederate Medical Service* (Baton Rouge: Louisiana State University Press, 1958), pp. 32, 57.

• JOHN GAYLE: DAB, VII, pp. 197-98.

• JOSIAH GORGAS: Ezra J. Werner, *Generals in Gray*, p. 112.

• GEORGE SPOTSWOOD: Obit., Mobile *Daily Register*, December 29, 1908, p. 5; December 30, 1908, p. 5. SH Register Book III, 41, "Vice President's Diary," gives April 7, 1860 as the date of George's baptism. CSR (Florida) 2nd and (Alabama) 53rd in RG 109, NA. The record of George as a clerk in the C.S. Navy Department, Richmond, is noted in *Register of the Commissioned and Warrant Officers of the Navy of the Confederate States to January 1, 1863* (Richmond: MacFarlane & Fergusson, 1862), p. 3. Will, January 8, 1908, in the Mobile County Court House, Mobile, Alabama, 9, p. 617. Helen Thompson, *Magnolia Cemetery*, p. 391.

90 • ALEXANDER JENKINS SEMMES: Obit., New Orleans *Daily Picayune*, September 21, 1898, p. 2. CSR (Louisiana) 8th where he is described as "a good man and excellent Doctor," RCO in PACS in RG, NA. Andrew Booth, *RLCS*, III, Bk. 2, p. 513. Napier Bartlett, *Military Record*, p. 36. Marriage witnessed October 24, 1864, in Chatham County by Right Reverend Stephen Eliott (1806-66), Episcopal Bishop of Georgia; Marriage Records, Chatham County, Georgia. *DAB*, XVI, p. 578. Herman Seebold, *Old Louisiana Plantation Homes*, II, pp. 102-110. Harvy Wright Newman, *The Maryland Semmes and Kindred Families* (Baltimore: Maryland Historical Society, 1956), p. 84.

• SARAH BERRIEN SEMMES: lot 494 Laurel Grove Cemetery, Chatham County, Georgia.

• THOMAS JENKINS SEMMES: *DAB*, XVI, pp. 582-83.

• RAPHAEL SEMMES: *Ibid.*, pp. 579-582.

• JOHN MCPHERSON BERRIEN: *Ibid.*, II, pp. 225-26.

91 • JOHN FORBES INNERARITY: Eighth Census of the United States, 1860, Alabama, City of Mobile, 4th Ward, 189 in RG 29, NA. Private papers concerning the genealogy of the de Villiers family in the possession of Jorge de Villier, Pensacola, Florida. Index to Alabama Wills, 1808-70, Mobile County Court House, Mobile, Alabama, II, p. 233. Lucile Mallon & Rochelle Ferris, *Burial Records, Mobile County*, II, p. 220. Marriage of Pierre or Pedro Troullet to Marie Isabella Norbonne, Marriage Book I,

p. 237; of Isabella Troullet to Juan Forbes, Baptism Book II, (Sophia Forbes) December 10, 1797. Catholic Cathedral, Mobile, Alabama.

92 • EDWARD LIVINGSTON: Obit., New Orleans *Times Democrat*, November 24, 1898, p. 2. CSR (Alabama) 3rd and 2nd Militia. Letter to Christopher Gustavus Memminger (1803-88), January 30, 1863, A&IGO. Discharge, S.O., April 23, 1863, A&IGO, in RG 109, NA. Baptismal Records, Christ Episcopal Church, Mobile, Alabama, January 28, 1838. He married Robina H. Russell, April 20, 1869, Marriage Records, Trinity Episcopal Church, Mobile, Alabama.

93 • LEMUEL LINCOLN, generally known as *L.L. Lincoln*: Obit., New Orleans *Daily Picayune*, March 26, 1900, p. 4; p. 12. CSR (Alabama) 2nd Militia, 3rd Regiment; (Virginia) Captain Henley's 3rd Infantry; enlistment in the Alabama Volunteer Militia, Ch. V, file 111, p. 300, in RG 109, NA. Lincoln's name did not appear on the rolls of the Louisiana 5th. Stanley Arthur and George Huchet de Kernion, *Old Families of Louisiana*, p. 71.

• CHARLES W. DORRANCE: Obit., Mobile *Daily Register*, February 12, 1873, p.3. Place of birth given in rolls of 1st Regiment, Mobile Volunteers, which he joined August 8, 1863, and from which he was discharged by reason of a disability, February 25, 1864, Ch. I, Vol. 84, 46-D, in RG 109, NA. Baptism record, Catholic Cathedral, Mobile, Alabama, July 2, 1840, #902; funeral record, *Ibid*., February 11, 1873, #2490. Marriage to Lisa Durand, June 25, 1866, Mobile County Marriages, Court House, Mobile, Alabama, Bk. 22, p. 100. Records, Catholic cemetery, Mobile, Alabama, R3-L58. Quotation in text taken from *Deep South Genealogical Quarterly*, III, (1965) p. 509.

94 • SENECA SIMMONS: Francis B. Heitman, *Historical Register and Dictionary of the United States Army from its Organization, September 29, 1789 to March 2, 1903* (2 vols., Washington, D.C.: Government Printing Office), II, p. 887. Year of birth in "Cadet Records," United States Military Academy Archives, West Point, New York. *Official Records*, XI, Pt. 1, 112-13; XXV, p. 187. His day of death is given as June 30 in the records of the Surgeon General, but it would seem he died the day after the Battle of Fair Oaks. Pension Application #7922, May 23, 1863. Surgeon General's Office, N. A.

95 • Napier Bartlett, "A Soldier's Story," *Military Record*, pp. 28-29. John Dimitry, *Louisiana*, pp. 222-23. *Official Records*, XI, Pt. 2, p. 978. Register of Prisoners of War, Vol. I, p. 86 (July 9, 1862) in RG 109, NA.

96 • PETER TISSOT: Obit., *Woodstock Letters*, 14 (1890), pp. 407-08. Aidan Germain, *Catholic Military and Naval Chaplains*, pp. 102-04. Tissot's diary was translated and published as "A Year in the Army of the Potomac," *Historical Records and Studies*, III (1904), pp. 42-87; citations in text, pp. 78-79. "Extraits de plusieurs lettres du P. Tissot, de la compagnie de Jésus, a son frère," *Annales de la Propagation de la foi*, XXXV (1863), pp. 278-79. F. Gazeau, "L'Apostolat catholique aux Etats-Unis pendant la guerre," *Etudes*, VII (1862), pp. 813-28. P. Toulemont, "L'Apostolat catholique aux Etats-Unis pendant la guerre," *Etudes*, VIII (1863), pp. 863-86.

97 • JOSEPH O'HAGAN: Obit., *Woodstock Letters*, VIII (1879), pp. 173-83. Aidan Germain, *Catholic Military and Naval Chaplains*, pp. 90-92. "Two Letters from Father Joseph B. O'Hagan," *Woodstock Letters*, XV (1886),

pp. 111-14. *Ibid.*, XIV (1885), pp. 375-80. Citations in text taken from William L. Lucy, "The Diary of Joseph B. O'Hagan, S.J., Chaplain of the Excelsior Brigade," *Civil War History*, VI (1960), pp. 402-409.

98 • THOMAS SCULLY: Obit., Boston *Pilot*, September 20, 1902, p. 1. Massachusetts Adjutant-General's Office, *Massachusetts Soldiers, Sailors and Marines in the Civil War* (Norwood, Massachusetts: Norwood Press, 1931), I, p. 617 lists Scully and notes that he was discharged for disability, October 31, 1862. Aidan Germain, *Catholic Military and Naval Chaplains*, pp. 94-95. For an account of his capture at Savage Station, July 1862 see the Boston *Pilot*, August 2, 1862, p. 2. Quotation from Higginson in Boston *Evening Journal*, April 16, 1899, p. 1. For the school controversy and Scully's part in it, see Robert H. Lord, John E. Sexton, and Edward T. Harrington, *The History of the Archdiocese of Boston* (3 vols., Boston: Pilot Publishing Co., 1944) III, pp. 81, 269. Account of the release of the prisoners in Peter Tissot, "A Year in the Army of the Potomac," p. 81. Burial Records, Holy Cross Cemetery, Malden, Massachusetts, September 15, 1902.

• THOMAS HIGGINSON: *DAB*, IX, pp. 16-18.

• ALONZO MINER: *Ibid.*, XIII, pp. 21-22.

99 • Report of Colonel Leroy A. Stafford of Operations, August 31-October 5, 1862, *Official Records*, 19, Pt. 1, p. 1014. Report of Major General Ambrose P. Hill, *Ibid.*, 12 Pt. 2, p. 214. Henry Monier, "Journal" in Napier Bartlett's *Military Record*, p. 30.

100 • MURRAY TAYOR: Obit., "Captain Murray F. Taylor," *Confederate Veteran*, July 1910, p. 82; Richmond *Times-Dispatch*, November 28, 1909, p. 8. CSRO&M, Ch. I, file 86, p. 156 (Appointments); unaddressed letter of A.P. Hill with endorsement from General J.E. Johnston, September 19, 1861, in RG 109, NA. "Colonel William H. Palmer," Richmond *Times-Dispatch*, November 28, 1909, p. 8. Letter from Murray F. Taylor to Joseph R. Anderson, March 8, 1904, Archives Virginia Military Institute, Lexington, Virginia. Butler-Bayne Thornton Franklin, "History Summary of Fall Hill" (Ms. in archives of Virginia Historic Landmarks Commission, Richmond, Virginia). Murray Forbes Taylor to Phoebe Apperson Hearst, January 16, 1908, Phoebe Apperson Hearst Collection, 72/204 ctn. 1, The Bancroft Library, University of California, Berkeley, California; Fremont Older, *George Hearst: California Pioneer* (Los Angeles: Westernlore, 1966), pp. 169-72. Oliver Carlson and Ernest Sutherland Bates, *Hearst, Lord of San Simeon* (New York: Viking, 1936), pp. 14, 52.

101 • WILLIAM PEGRAM: Report of Lt. Col. R.L. Walker of the Light Division, *Official Records*, 12, Pt. 2, p. 226. Report of Maj. Gen. Ambrose P. Hill, *Ibid.*, p. 214-216. J. William Jones, D.D., "The Morale of the Confederate Armies," in Evans' *Confederate Military History*, XII, p. 173. Thomas C. De Leon, *Belles, Beaux and Brains in the Sixties* (New York: G.W. Dillingham, 1907), pp. 168-69.

• WILLIAM SPENCER: CSR (Louisiana) 10th; Ch. I, Vol. 82, p. 269 (casualties). List of casualties in the 2nd (4th) Louisiana Brigade in the Battles of Manassas, Virginia and Sharpsburg, Maryland, August 28 to 30 and September 17, 1862, Series I, Vol. 12, pt. 2, p. 668 in RG 109, NA.

102 • Gache to Boisson, June 17, 1885, Laffont family papers. Quartermaster General's Office, Ch. V, April 26, 1862, contained in Gache file, CSRO&M, in RG 109, NA. A law passed on January 22, 1864, permitted chaplains to

draw forage for one horse, Bell Irvin Wiley, " 'Holy Joes' of the Sixties: A Study of Civil War Chaplains," p. 288.

103 • "Annals of the (Civil) War," Archives of the Daughters of Charity, St. Joseph's Provincial House, Emmitsburg, Maryland, p. 60. Henry Monier in his "Journal" states that the 10th was assigned to the old Stonewall Division on August 11. Napier Bartlett's *Military History*, p. 30; *Official Records*, XIX, pt. 1, p. 1401. Smulders to Provincial, September 26, 1865, Redemptorist Archives. Smulders to Judge Henry B. Kelly, March 1897, Tulane University Collection, 55-C.

104 • Gache file in CSRO&M; S.O. #202, Richmond, November 29, 1862, A&IGO, in RG 109, NA.

105 • "Annals of the War," Daughters of Charity Archives, p. 60.

106 • ELIZABETH STUART: Family Bible in possession of Mr. William Alexander Stuart, Jr., Rosedale, Virginia. Burial Records, Elizabeth Cemetery, Saltville, Smyth County, Virginia. The account of her sojourn at Florissant recorded in the Stuart Family Register is in the possession of Mr. Stuart B. Campbell, Jr., Wyethville, Virginia.

• ALEXANDER STUART: Stuart Family Register. Some biographical information, not all of which is accurate in Howard L. Conrad, *Encyclopedia of the History of Missouri* (4 vols.; New York: The Southern History Company, 1901), Vol. IV, p. 117.

• STUART-PANNILL FAMILY: *Stewart Clan Magazine*, XVII (1940), pp. 158-60. David H. Pannill, "The Genealogy of Gen. J.E.B. Stuart and of His Collateral Relations on His Mother's Side—Pannill, Strother, Banks, Bruce, Etc," *William & Mary Quarterly*, VI (1897), pp. 113-16. Maud Carter Clement, *History of Pittsylvania County, Virginia* (Lynchburg, Virginia: J.P. Bell, 1929), pp. 251-52. H.B. McClellan, *Life and Campaigns of Major-General J.E.B. Stuart* (Richmond, Virginia: J.W. Randolph & English, 1885), pp. 1-5.

• PHILIPPINE DUCHESNE: Louise Callan, R.S.C.J., *Philippine Duchesne: Frontier Missionary of the Sacred Heart, 1769-1851*. She was beatified by the Roman Catholic Church, May 12, 1940. For a brief history of the controversies between the Evangelical and Tractarian parties within the Episcopal Church in Virginia, see G. Maclaren Brydon, D.D., *From Highlights Along the Road of the Anglican Church: The Church of England in England and Her Oldest Daughter, the Protestant Episcopal Church of Virginia* (Richmond, Virginia: Virginia Diocesan Library, 1957), pp. 40-46.

107 • Ruth H. Early, *Campbell Chronicles and Family Sketches* (Lynchburg, Virginia: J.P. Bell & Co., 1937), pp. 221-222, 289. Martha Rivers Adams, "Old Winfree Home Once Served as Hospital During the Civil War," Lynchburg *Daily Advance*, April 5, 1960. "Works Progress Administration of Virginia: Historical Inventory, August 26, 1937," Virginia Room Collection, Jones Memorial Library, Lynchburg, Virginia. W. Harrison Daniel, "Old Lynchburg College, 1855-1869." Virginia Magazine of History and Biography, LXXX (1980), pp. 446-77.

108 • MARY DORRANCE: Marriage Book, Charles A. Dorrance—Mrs. Mary A. Mills, #45, May 20, 1835. Burial Book, #2280, March 23, 1875, Mobile Catholic Cathedral. She was a charter member of the "Military Aid Society of Mobile" which met for the first time, May 7, 1861, Temperance Hall, Mobile. "Women of the Confederacy," Loose papers and clippings from the

Mobile *Register* and *Advertiser* in the Mobile Public Library, Mobile, Alabama. *Deep South Genealogical Quarterly*, VI (1969), p. 168.

109 • ALEXANDER DIMITRY: Adelaide Stuart Dimitry, *War-Time Sketches: Historical & Otherwise* (New Orleans: Louisiana Printing Press, 1909), p. 63. Stanley Arthur & George C. Huchet de Kernion, *Old Families of Louisiana*, pp. 402-04. Thomas de Leon, *Belles, Beaux and Brains in the Sixties*, pp. 115. James S. Ruby, *Georgetown University and the Civil War*, p. 47.

110 • Michael Kenney, "Notes," p. 87.

111 • Cited in the article by William J. Kimball, "The Bread Riot in Richmond, 1863," *Civil War History*, VII (1961), pp. 149-54.

112 • The best history of the Daughters of Charity is in Alfred Milon, "Histoire de Filles de la Charité," *Annales de la Congregation de la Mission*, Vols. XCI-C (1926-30). For the controversies in Spain, see Ponciano Nieto, C.M., *Historia de las Hijas de la Caridad desde sus orígenes hasta el siglo* (XX vols., Madrid, Spain: Regina, 1932), Vol. I, pp. 125-47; 181-345.

113 • Payroll, September 1, 1864 (Lynchburg, Hospital #3) in Hospital Rolls, Virginia, Box #23, in RG 109, NA. City Directory for the City of Lynchburg, June 10, 1864 in *Lynchburg Historical Society Historical Papers* (Lynchburg: Lynchburg Historical Society, 1962), II, #6.

114 • "Report of the Sick and Wounded," (Lynchburg Hospital #3) in Hospital Rolls, Virginia, Box #23, in RG 109, NA.

115 • "Diuguid Funeral Directory Establishment-History," notes in the Virginia Room, Jones Memorial Library, Lynchbrugh, Virginia.

116 • JOHN DUFFEL: SH Register Book, II, p. 192, where his birth date is given as February 6, 1838. CSR (Louisiana) 8th; CSRO&M; Ch. I, Vol. 86, p. 313 (Appointment); Ch. VI, Vol. 147, p. 57 (Resignation); Ch. VI, Vol. 147, p. 141 (Assignment at Lynchburg), in RG 109, NA. Marriage to Angele Modeste Ayraud, May 22, 1866, Ascension Church, Donaldsonville, Louisiana, Vol. 15, p. 187. *New Orleans Genesis*, 4 (June 1965), pp. 227-28 contains some biographical information. Succession of John Duffel, Judicial District Court, Parish of Ascension, Louisiana, January 14, 1892, #196.

117 • JULES MAITRUGUES: Archives of the New Orleans Province of the Society of Jesus. "Historical Sketch of St. Charles College, Grand Coteau," *Woodstock Letters*, V (1875), pp. 27-29.

• EMMANUEL BRENANS: Michael Kenny, *Catholic Culture in Alabama*, p. 179.

• JAMES GRAVES: *Ibid.*, p. 227.

118 • FRANCIS NICHOLLS: Obit., New Orleans *Daily Picayune*, January 5, 1912; New Orleans *Times Democrat*. January 5, 1912; CSR (Louisiana) 8th & 15th; CSRO&M; Louisiana Militia, Ch. VIII, Vol. 170, p. 128 in RG 109, NA. Andrew Booth, *RLCS*, Vol. III, Bk. 1, p. 1280. *DAB*, XIII, pp. 487-88; Ezra Warner, *Generals in Gray*, p. 224. Alison Moore, *The Louisiana Tigers*, p. 166; Recommendation for Forno's appointment of the Louisiana Brigade, letter from Hill to Lee, May 15, 1863, CSRO&M (Forno), RG 109, NA.

119 • STANHOPE POSEY: "A Tribute to Capt. Stanhope Posey," a printed one page resume, no date, in possession of Mr. and Mrs. Harold C. Fisher, Yazoo City, Mississippi: Citations in text taken from this curriculum vitae. SH Register Book, III, p. 54: Date of baptism, April 5, 1857, Vice President's

Diary. CSR (Louisiana) 1st Special. CSRO&M, Ch. V, Vol. III, p. 382 (discharged from Dreux's). Ch. I, Vol. 94, p. 166 (assignment to Carnot Posey). Ch. I, Vol. 25, Part I p. 854 (wounded at Fredericksburg). James Barnwell Heyward, *The Genealogy of the Pendarvis-Bedon Families of South Carolina, 1670-1900* (Atlanta, Georgia: Foote & Davis Co., 1905), pp. 128, 189. Wedding, the Natchez Mississippi *Democrat*, June 16, 1866, p. 4.

• ELIZA WHYTE: Sixth Census, Virginia, City of Petersburg. Tombstone, Posey Section, Yazoo City Cemetery, Yazoo City, Mississippi.

120 • WILLIAM SIMS: Obit., New Orleans *Daily Picayune*, September 10, 1876, p. 4. SH Register Book, III p. 4. CSR (Louisiana) 8th. According to the company rolls he remained in the Lynchburg Hospital until after September 1, Prisoners, Old Capitol Prison, Washington, D.C., Register #304, Pt. 783, p. 488. Register of Johnson's Island, 2, p. 140, June 13, 1865, in RG 109, NA. Andrew Booth, *RLCS*, III, Bk. 2, p. 581. Napier Bartlett, *Military Record*, p. 35.

• ROBERT NICHOLLS SIMS: Obit., New Orleans *States* May 27, 1899, p. 1; SH Register Book, III, p. 5. CSR (Louisiana) 18th where the rolls list him as 1st lieutenant and adjutant (no date) in RG 109, NA. Andrew Booth *RLCS*, III, Bk. 2, p. 580. Known also as Nicholas Sims. In 1896 Judge Sims was elected a member of the Louisiana Senate, Sidney A. Marchand, "Forgotten Fighters, 1861-1865" (manuscript in Louisiana State Library), p. 160, #674.

• FRANCOIS SIMS: known also as Frank Sims. Obit., New Orleans *Daily Picayune*, November 8, 1901, p. 3; SH Register Book, III, p. 170. Records at the Archives of the Diocese of Baton Rouge give July 21, 1847 as the date of his birth, ASM 9. RCO (Louisiana) RG 109, NA. Andrew Booth, *RLCS*, III Bk. 2, p. 579.

• TREPAGNIER-SIMS family: Stanley Arthur & George Huchet de Kernion, *Old Families of Louisiana*, p. 288. Herman Seebold, *Old Louisiana Plantation Homes*, I pp. 92-93; 97-98.

121 • GUSTAVE BRUYÈRE: Obit., New Orleans *Daily Picayune*, August 4, 1864, p. 4. SH Register Book III, p. 68. CSR (Louisiana) 8th; Point Lookout, New Hampshire Register Book, I, p. 35 (prisoner of war), RG 109, NA. Andrew Booth, *RLCS*, II, p. 165.

122 • ALFRED LAFOREST: Obit., Versailles, Missouri *Leader*, May 12, 1911. Book of Baptisms 17 (1840-1842), St. Louis Cathedral Archives, New Orleans, Louisiana, p. 186, Act 585. SH Register Book, III, p. 38. CSR (Louisiana) 8th. List of killed, wounded and missing in Ewell's Division, August 22 to Sept. 20, 1862 (Manassas, August 29, 1862), Series I, Vol. 12, Pt. 1, p. 810. Point Lookout Register, I 269 (Rappahannock), I p. 276 (Spotsylvania); Charlottesville Hospital Rolls, VI, pp. 215, 282, in RG 109, NA; Andrew Booth, *RLCS*, III, Bk. 1, p. 620. Michael Kenny, *Catholic Culture in Alabama.*

123 • CELESTINE VALDES: CSR (Alabama) Pelham's Cadets, in RG 109, NA.

124 • JAMES A SCUDDAY: Obit., New Orleans *Daily States*, December 19, 1901, p. 1. SH Register Book, III, p. 22; CSR (Louisiana) Captain Green's Artillery; 1st Regiment (Nelligans'). Lynchburg Hospital, Ch. VI, Vol. 214, p. 107. Goode to Benjamin, January 25, 1862, A&IGO (citations in text

taken from this letter) in RG 109, NA. Marriage: James Aubert Scudday and Lelia Lee Walker, April 20, 1863, Corporation Court, Lynchburg, Virginia, pp. 72, 124.

- WILLIAM H. KINCKLE: Birth date information from Family Records of Kinckle Bible, Virginia Room, Jones Memorial Library, Lynchburg, Virginia; Obit., Lynchburg *Virginian*, March 4, 1867, p. 3.

125 • JOSEPH and FELIX HUCHET DE KERNION: Rufo Mendízabel, S.J., *Catalogus Defunctorum in renata Societate Iesu ab a. 1814 ad a. 1970*, (Romae: Apud Curiam P. #80, #28. Gen., 1972. Stanley Arthur, George Huchet de Kernion, *Old Families of Louisiana*, p. 201; *Woodstock Letters*, XXX (1902), p. 449.

126 • PAUL GUSMAN: Obit., New Orleans *Daily Picayune*, February 9, 1907, p. 12. SH Register Book, IV, p. 14. CSR (Louisiana) 5th & 10th: according to the rolls he was transferred to the 10th, November 2, 1864 (Ch. I, Vol. 82, p. 269), but Gache's letter shows this transfer took place at an earlier date. Ch. VI, Vol. 724, p. 298 (sick & wounded) RG 109, NA. Andrew Booth, *RLCS*, III, Bk. I, pp. 149-50.

127 • Michael Kenny, *Catholic Culture in Alabama*, pp. 156-57.

128 • BERNARD FOX: Obit., New Orleans *Daily Picayune*, December 7, 1898, p. 4. New Orleans *Times Democrat*, December 7, 1898, p. 2; New Orleans *States*, December 11, 1898, p. 5; SH Register Book, III, 19; CSR (Louisiana) 7th, Ch. I, Vol. 214, p. 82; Vol. 179 388 RG 109 in NA; Andrew Booth *RLCS*, III, Bk. I, p. 911; Michael Kenny, *Catholic Culture in Alabama*, pp. 156-57.

- FRANCIS LESPÈS: Michael Kenny, *Catholic Culture in Alabama*, pp. 256-57.

129 • JOSEPH DE JOCAS: Rufo Mendízabal, S.J., *Catalogus Defunctorum in renata Societate Iesu*, #73. Pierre Delattre, *Les Establissements des Jésuites en France*, I, p. 483.

- GUY GILLES: Walter H. Hill, "Some Reminiscences of St. Mary's College, Kentucky," *Woodstock Letters*, XX (1891), pp. 33-34. Anon., "Some Facts and Incidents Relating to St. Joseph's College, Bardstown, Kentucky;" *Ibid*., XXVI (1897), p. 101. H. Gache, "Our College at Baton Rouge," p. 5. Michael Kenny, *Catholic Culture in Alabama*, pp. 131-32, 155-57.
- PETER IMSAND: Michael Kenny, "Notes," p. 114-15; *Catholic Culture in Alabama*, pp. 207, 241.

130 • SIDNEY SMITH LEE: Edward Jennings Lee, M.D., *Lee of Virginia, 1642-1892. Biographical and Genealogical Sketches of the Descendants of Colonel Richard Lee* (Philadelphia: Edmund Jennings Lee, 1895), pp. 408-10.

- SISTER BLANCHE ROONEY: Biographical information in the Archives, Daughters of Charity, Emmitsburg, Maryland.

131 • Some biographical details about Lydia Johnston and her sisters are contained in John A. Monroe, *Louis McLane: Federalist and Jacksonian* (New Brunswick, New Jersey: Rutgers University Press, 1973).

- LYDIA MCLANE JOHNSTON: Obit., Washington, D.C. *Post*, February 23, 1887, p. 2; February 24, 1887, p. 3.
- JULIETTE MCLANE GARESCHÉ: Biographical sketches of the family are in Dorothy Garesché Holland, *The Garesché, de Bauduy, and Des Chapelles Families* (St. Louis: Schneider Printing Co., 1963), pp. 192-93;

246. Jeremiah J. O'Connell, *Catholicity in the Carolinas and Georgia*, p. 208.

• JEFFERSON DAVIS: The account of his stay at St. Thomas Aquinas College is given in Hudson Strode, *Jefferson Davis* (New York: Harcourt, 1964), Vol. I, pp. 14-16.

• VARINA HOWELL DAVIS: Gache's statement that the First Lady wanted a practicing Catholic as a governess for her children seems substantiated by Ishbel Ross, *First Lady of the South: The Life of Mrs. Jefferson Davis* (New York: Harper, 1958), pp. 145, 200, and by Hudson Strode *Jefferson Davis*, Vol. II, p. 259. Ishbel Ross gives Louisiana as the place of Mrs. Davis' birth in the *First Lady of the South*, p. 14. other references indicate that she was born in Natchez, Mississippi, see *DAB*, V, pp. 146-47.

• GEORGE WYTHE RANDOLPH: Ezra J. Warner, *Generals in Gray*, p. 252; *DAB* XV, pp. 358-59. In February 1978, Jonathan Daniels, the authority on the Randolph family and author of *The Randolphs of Virginia* (Garden City, New Jersey: Doubleday, 1972), offered his opinion in a private letter to the editor of this work that he knew of no Catholic marriages or Catholic converts within the Randolph family prior to 1864.

132 • Losses of the 10th: *Official Records*, 25, Pt. 1, p. 809. For fraudulant papers purporting to be bona fide discharges from the 10th which appeared after Chancellorsville: *Official Records*, Series IV, 2, p. 808. "Report of the Sick and Wounded," Hospital Rolls, Virginia (Lynchburg), Box 26, RG 109, NA.

• ANSELM USANNAZ: Obit., *Woodstock Letters*, XXIV (1895), pp. 484-5. There are some references to the work of Father Usannaz at Andersonville in Ovid L. Futch, *History of Andersonville* (Gainseville: University of Florida Press, 1968), p. 60. *Annales de la Propogation de la foi* 37 (1865) pp. 398-99.

133 • MAURICE LANGHORNE: Obit., Lynchburg *News*, March 29, 1908, p. 3; citations in text taken from this obituary. CSR (Virginia) 11th: Ch. I, Vol. 78, p. 200 (Register), also noted in Ch. I, Vol. 92, pp. 210 & 285 and Ch. I, Vol. 86, p. 66 (not reelected to 11th). Ch. I, Vol. 95, p. 219 (retired from 11th, December 20, 1864. Ch. VI, Vol. 724, p. 9 (wounded at Seven Pines; entered Lynchburg Hospital under treatment in private quarters) in RG 109, NA. Rosa Faulkner Yancy, *Lynchburg and its Neighbors* (Richmond, Virginia: J.W. Fergusson & Sons, 1935), pp. 356-57. Virgil A. Lewis, *Virginia and Virginians* (2 vols., Richmond, Virginia: H.H. Hardesty) Vol. II, pp. 574-75. Lyon Gardiner Tyler, *Encyclopedia of Virginia Biography* (5 vols., New York: Lewis, 1915), Vol. IV, pp. 398-99.

• JACOB MITCHELL: Obit., Lynchburg *News*, June 30, 1877, p. 3; Lynchburg *Daily Virginian*, June 30, 1877, p. 3: first citation in text taken from this obituary; second citation from: W. Asbury Christian, *Lynchburg and Its People* (Lynchburg: J.P. Bell Co., 1900) p. 196. See also pp. 104-05, 204. His obituary gives 1802 as the year of his birth but it is clear from other sources he was born in 1806. *Ministerial Directory of the Presbyterian Church: United States* (Southern). Dr. Mitchell's name is not listed in the Chaplain's Appointment Book, nor in Herman Norton, *Rebel Religion: the Story of Confederate Chaplains* (St. Louis: Bethany Press, 1961) nor is there a record of him in the Confederate Archives, although Colonel Langhorne identifies him in a memo to General Cooper, August 24, 1863, as "the Presbyterian chaplain at the Post and for the hospitals." Letters received A&IGO RG 109, NA.

134 • Langhorne to Cooper, August 3 and August 24, 1863, A&IGO in RG 109, NA. Nicholl's appointment in *Official Records*, XXIX, Pt. 2, p. 642.

135 • MICHAEL NOLAN: CSR (Louisiana) 1st; RCO in PACS, Ch. I, file 84, p. 375; Ch. I, pp. 76, 322 (succeeded James Nelligan). List of casualties in the 2nd (4th) Louisiana Brigade, in the Battles of Manassas, Virginia and Sharpsburg, Maryland, August 28 to 30 and September 17, 1862, Series I, Vol. 12, Pt. 2, p. 668, in RG 109, NA. Burial in New Orleans: New Orleans *Daily Picayune*, August 18, 1866, p. 4. Citation in text from Patrick Walsh, "The Irish in South Carolina, Georgia, Alabama, Louisiana and Tennessee," p. 103.

136 • SISTER ROSE NOYLAND: Sister Rose was the superior of the sisters at Lynchburg, having been one of the three sisters who moved from Manassas to Gordonsville and then to Danville in 1862. It was to her that Mrs. Stuart made the request to meet Gache. She entered the Daughters of Charity July 6, 1854. Archives of the Daughters of Charity, Emmitsburg. Payroll, September 1, 1864, Hospital Rolls, Virginia (Lynchburg), Box 26, in RG 109, NA.

• SISTER PACIFICA ULRICH: This sister entered the Daughters of Charity at Emmitsburg on August 22, 1861, and came to the Lynchburg hospital on July 1, 1863, less than one month before Gache went to South Carolina. Archives of the Daughters of Charity, Evansville, Indiana. Payroll, September 1, 1864, Hospital Rolls, Virginia (Lynchburg), Box 27, in RG 109, NA.

137 • ALBERT BLANCHARD: Obit., New Orleans *Daily Picayune*, June 22, 1891, p. 3. CSR (Louisiana) 1st; CSRO&M; Ch. VIII, Vol. 170, 11 (Louisiana Militia). File of letters received A&IGO: S.O. #138, June 18, 1862, Ch. I, Vol. 86, p. 6; relieved Blanchard from command of his brigade. On March 31, 1865 he wrote to Cooper: "I received order number 9, dropping me on the 11th of February 1865." in RG 109, NA. Andrew Booth, *RLCS*, II, p. 4. Ezra J. Werner, *Generals in Gray*, p. 27. St. Louis #2 Cemetery, New Orleans, Records.

138 • JAMES GERATY: Registre d'étudiants, no specific date c. 1861, where the name *Gerartry* also appears. Archives du College de Combrée, Maine-et-Loire, France.

139 • AMBLER WEED: Records, Archives and Historical Collections, Episcopal Church, Austin, Texas. Bishop William Meade, *Old Churches, Ministers and Families of Virginia* (2 vols.; Philadelphia: J.B. Lippincott, 1857) I, p. 269; *Sadlier's Catholic Directory* (New York: Sadlier, 1833-86, 1872, p. 43 gives Richmond as the place of his death, but this information is incorrect. *See* A. Bohmer Rudd (ed.) *Shockoe Hill Cemetery, Richmond, Virginia, Register of Interments*, April 10, 1822-December 30, 1950, (Washington: n.p. 1962) Vol. II, p. 94. Gache's account of his invitation to Charleston was substantiated in a letter by Weed to Sister Charles: "Tell the Mother Sup. that I have just sent Rev. F. Gache his furlough for 20 days from Aug. 1st," Richmond, July 21, 1863; and Sister Baptista Lynch to Patrick Lynch, July 11, 1863 and Hubert to Lynch, July 26, 1862 in Archdiocesan Archives, Charleston, South Carolina.

• SISTER CHARLES WEED: Mary Otis and Ambler were two of several children of Joseph (1785-1857), a Richmond merchant, and Mary George Weed (1798-1853). In October 1859 Mary entered the Ursuline Convent,

Columbia, South Carolina, and in 1866 she founded the Ursuline Convent, Tuscaloosa, Alabama. "Annals of the Ursulines, Columbia, South Carolina," manuscript in the Archives, Ursuline Sisters, Louisville, Kentucky. Hoffman's *Catholic Directory and Clergy List Quarterly* (Milwaukee: Hoffman Brothers, 1890), p. 35, hereinafter cited as Hoffman's *Catholic Directory*. A. Bohmer Rudd, (ed.) *Shockoe Hill Cemetery . . . Register of Interments*, Vol. II, 13, 32.

140 • MOTHER BAPTISTA LYNCH: "Archives of the Ursulines, Columbia, South Carolina," Hoffman's *Catholic Directory* (1888), p. 35; Mary Boykin Chesnut, *A Diary from Dixie*, ed. Ben Williams (Boston: Houghton-Mifflin, 1941), p. 181.

• PATRICK NEESON LYNCH: Joseph Cole, *DAHier*, p. 172.

• JOHN & ELIZABETH LYNCH: Biographical information on tombstone, St. Peter's Church Yard (cemetery), Columbia, South Carolina.

141 • JEREMIAH O'CONNELL: Obit., Hoffman's *Catholic Directory* (1895), p. 43; Jeremiah J. O'Connell, *Catholicity in the Carolinas and in Georgia*, pp. 138-39.

142 • HOWARD HAINE CALDWELL: Jeremiah O'Connell, *Catholicity in the Carolinas and in Georgia*, pp. 203, 245. George A. Wauchope, *The Writers of South Carolina* (Columbia, South Carolina: The State Co., 1910). John Belton O'Neall, *The Annals of Newberry, Historical, Biographical and Anecdotal* (Charleston, South Carolina: S.G. Courtenay & Co., 1859), pp. 156-57. Caldwell's published works were *Oliatta and Other Poems* (New York: Redfield, 1855) and *Poems* (Boston: Whittenmore, Niles and Hall, 1858). Schedule 3—"Persons who died during the Year ending 1st June, 1860 in Richland District, State of South Carolina," p.1, 20, South Carolina Department of Archives and History, Columbia, South Carolina.

• AGNES MONTAGUE CALDWELL: Jeremiah O'Connell, *Catholicity in the Carolinas and in Georgia*, p. 204. Date of birth: Baptism Records, St. Patrick's Church, Fayetteville, North Carolina. Certificate of death, File 81-13804, Richland County, South Carolina, Office of Vital Records, Columbia, S. C.

• CHARLES MONTAGUE, JR.: Baptism Records, St. Patrick's Church, Fayetteville, North Carolina; SH Register Book III, p. 125. CSR (Texas) 2nd (South Carolina), Aiken's Regiment Cavalry, subsequently, Co. B, 6th Cavalry. Ch. VI, Vol. 186, p. 436; Vol. 189, p. 71; Vol. 702, p. 59 in RG 109, NA. Citations in the text from "The Montagues in the United States," notes of John Montague, Special Collections, Academic Library, St. Mary's University of San Antonio, San Antonio, Texas, pp. 109-10.

• MONTAGUE-NEWTON FAMILY: "The Montagues in the United States," Jeremiah O'Connell, *Catholicity in the Carolinas and in Georgia*, pp. 204, 405.

143 • *Official Records of the Union and Confederate Navies in the War of the Rebellion* (30 vols.; Washington, D.C.: Government Printing Office, 1894-1922) hereinafter cited as *Official Records, Navies*, Ser. II, Vol. III, pp. 776, 793-95, 881-82, 971-73. *Correspondance Commerciale*, VII (1854-1865), "Charleston," #14, April 7, 1864 in the Archives du Ministre des Affaires Etrangères, Paris.

144 • JULIEN BAYOT: This man assumed command of the *Granade* April 10, 1863 and was relieved July 25, 1864. He was retired from service February

11, 1879. Biographical information and service record contained in "Dossier et des états de services de Julian-Sosthènes-Joseph Bayot," Service Historique de la Marine, Château de Vincennes, Paris. Unfortunately pension records for this period have not been classified at the Vincennes naval archives, and therefore it has not been possible to trace Captain Bayot's career after his retirement date. *Official Records*, Navies, XIV, p. 522.

145 • HENRI-LÉON FILLION: Biographical records in the Archives of the Diocese of Angers, France. J. Moreau, *Notice historique sur le College de Beaupreau*, (2 Vols.; Angers: 1903), I, pp. 74-75.

146 • DELPHIN BIENVENU: SH Register Book, I, 108; CSR (Louisiana) Sappers and Miners, Louisiana Militia; (South Carolina) 18th Artillery, in RG 109, NA; Andrew Booth, *RLCS*, I, 189. Herman Seebold, *Old Louisiana Plantation Homes*, I, pp. 67-8. *Vêritê sur l'affaire de Labadieville. Appel à la justice et a l'opinion publique* (n.p., n.d.). "Silence Monsieur!" Nouvelle Orléans *Dêmocrate française*, 19 aout 1882. Edward Tinker, *Les Ecrits de la langue française en Louisiane au XIXe siècle* (Paris: Honoré Champion, 1932), p. 39; Michael Kenny, *Catholic Culture in Alabama*, pp. 160, 192-3. Burial Records, St. Louis Cemetery #2, Lot #16, New Orleans.

• CYRILLE VILLERÉ: Obit. New Orleans *Daily Picayune*, January 29, 1886, p. 4. SH Register Book, I, p. 24. CSR (Louisiana) St. Bernard Horse Rifles, Louisiana Militia. (South Carolina) 18th Artillery, in RG 109, NA. Andrew Booth, *RLCS*, III Bk. 2, p. 935. Arthur Stanley & George Huchet de Kernion, *Old Families of Louisiana*, pp. 62-64, 398; Herman Seebold, *Old Louisiana Plantation Homes*, II, pp. 142-45.

147 • RAMON ORIEL: SH Register Book, III, p. 16. CSR (Louisiana) Points Coupee Artillery. Captured at Island #10, April 8, 1862, Roll of Prisoners of War, Camp Douglas, August 1, 1862, Roll 64, sheet 160. List of casualties of Herbert's Brigade at the siege of Vicksburg, Mississippi, May 17 to July 1863, Series I, Pt. 2 p. 374. Paroled July 10, 1863, Vicksburg, Mississippi. Andrew Booth, *RLCS* III, Bk. 1, p. 30. Vice President's Diary, July 26, 1863, noted that "R. Oriel graduate of Spring Hill, a prisoner on parole of Wisburg *[sic]* ... comes to spend some days with us."

• OCTAVE LEGIER: Obit., New Orleans *Daily Picayune*, February 12, 1905, p. 3; citations in text taken from this obituary. SH Register Book, III, p. 115. CSR (Louisiana) Bridges' Battery in RG 109, NA. Andrew Booth, *RLCS*, III, Bk. 1, p. 715.

148 • EDWARD BERMUDEZ: Obit., New Orleans *Daily Picayune*, August 23, 1892, p. 9; citation in text taken from this obituary. SH Register Book, I, p. 65. CSR (Louisiana) Orleans Guards. CSRO&M in RG 109, NA. Andrew Booth, *RLCS*, I, p. 175; Goodspeed, *BHML*, II, pp. 470-72. John S. Kendall, "The Humors of the Duello," *Louisiana Historical Quarterly*, XXIII (April 1940), pp. 449-51. Alcee Fortier, *Louisiana*, p. 85. Stanley Arthur & George Huchet de Kernion, *Old Families of Louisiana*, pp. 64-67. Herman Seebold, *Old Louisiana Plantation Homes*, II, pp. 19, 141. Michael Kenny, *Catholic Culture in Alabama*, pp. 148-49 et passim.

• OCTAVE DE ARMAS: Obit., New Orleans *Daily Picayune*, August 28, 1889, p. 4.

• ARTURO CHRISTOVAL LÉON DE ARMAS: Obit., New Orleans *Daily Picayune*, September 6, p. 10. Baptismal Book 10 (1822-1825), St. Louis Cathedral, New Orleans, Louisiana, p. 126, act 583.

• ARTHUR DE ARMAS, JR.: Obit., New Orleans *Daily Picayune*, April 27, 1903, p. 6; SH Register Book, IV, p. 91.

149 • Ruth H. Early, *Campbell Chronicle and Family Sketches*, p. 289. "Diuguid Funeral Directory Establishment—History," Manuscript on file in Virginia Room Collection, Jones Memorial Library, Lynchburg, Virginia.

150 • Herbert Bouldin Hawes, "Research on Families of Lynchburg, Virginia, and Surrounding Area," an alphabetized collection of manuscript notes compiled in 1965, in the Virginia Room Collection, Jones Memorial Library, Lynchburg, Virginia, #1800-G, #1800-T.

151 • "Autobiographical Sketch of Reverend George Washington Dame, of Danville, Virginia, 1812-1895," manuscript on file in Virginia Historical Society, Richmond, Virginia, D-1822a; *see* James I. Robertson, Jr., "Houses of Horror; Danville Civil War Prisoners," *Virginia Magazine of History and Biography*, LXIX (1961), p. 338.

152 • Vice President's Diary, July 10, 1863. The name of the student was: John Duggan (1847-1910) of Lynchburg, Virginia, SH Register Book, IV, p. 19. Lynchburg, Virginia, *City Directory* (1902), p. 251.

153 • Sister de Sales Brennan to Bishop Lynch, November 2, 1864, Lynch Papers. Sister Anne Francis Campbell, S.M., "Bishop England's Sisterhood, 1829-1929" (Ph.D. dissertation, St. Louis University, 1968). O'Connell had been reassigned in May 1863, and his place was taken by Rev. Charles Croghan (1822-80) also of South Carolina, and also a commissioned army chaplain. Aidan Germain, *Catholic Military and Naval Chaplains*, pp. 114-15, 125-26.

154 • Jacob Duche Mitchell: Ch. I, Vol, 86, p. 370, in RG 109, NA. Age was given as the reason for his resignation. At that date Rev. Mitchell was 58.

155 • WILLIAM MCGEE: Obit., *Minutes of the Annual Conferences of the Methodist Episcopal Church, South, for the Year 1891* (Nashville, Tennessee, Methodist Episcopal Church South, 1862), pp. 123-24. CSRO&M, Ch. I, Vol. 86, p. 520 (Appointment). Ch. I, Vol, 132, p. 264 (Indices). William McGee to Secretary of War, August 1, 1863 with endorsement from John Johnson, Letters Received, A&IGO, in RG 109, NA. Rev. John J. Lafferty, D.L., *Sketches of the Virginia Conference, Methodist Episcopal Church, South* (Richmond, Virginia: Christian Advocate, 1880), pp. 42-45.

156 • JOHN JOHNSON: Biographical information taken from John Lipscomb Johnson, *Autobiographical Notes* (n.p., 1958). CSR (Virginia) 17th and CSRO&M. Ch. I, Vol, 86, p. 51 (Appointment), September 26, 1861 in RG 109, NA. The best known of several of Dr. Johnson's books is one he edited: *The University Memorial: Biographical Sketches of Alumni of the University of Virginia who Fell in the Confederate War* (Baltimore, Maryland: Turnbull Brothers, 1971).

157 • WILLIAM WILSON: Obit., Lynchburg *News*, January 23, 1908, p. 6; CSRO&M; Ch. I, Vol, 86, p. 372 (Appointment), January 22, 1862, in RG 109, NA. Mary Elizabeth Kinnier Bratton, *Our Goodly Heritage: A History of the First Presbyterian Church of Lynchburg, Virginia, 1815-1940* (Lynchburg, Virginia: J.P. Bell Co., Inc., 1944) pp. 85, 104-05, 297. W. Asbury Christian, *Lynchburg and Its People*, p. 359.

158 • Lynchburg *Daily Virginian*, June 30, 1877, p. 3.

159 • THOMAS FISHER: CSRO&M; Ch. I, 86, p. 309 (Surgeon: date of appointment, September 1861) and Ch. I, 86, p. 266. Put in charge of the Post Hospital, Manassas, where the Daughters of Charity nursed, February 1862; Gordonsville, March 1862; Danville, April 1862, returns from Medical Director's Office, Army of the Potomac; assigned to Lynchburg, November 20, 1862. Medical Director and Inspector Office, Ch. VI, 724, 181; also Ch. VI, 147, 89; 386, 50, 68, in RG 109, NA. *Official Records*, Ser 2, II, 1495. The Census of 1860, Virginia, Fauquier County, gives the age of Thomas H. Fisher as 38, and his property assets are considerable, p. 140, RG 29, NA. This property in 1865, Clerk's Office, Circuit Court of Fauquier County, Warrington, Virginia, and after this date no further biographical data of Dr. Fisher has been found. An entry in the index of deeds, September 23, 1869, Fauquier County, suggests that Dr. Fisher's wife, Elmira Shackleford was a widow.

• FERGUSON FACTORY: *Diuguid Funeral Directory Establishment*; "Annals of the War," p. 61.

• SISTER ALOYSIUS: In the Lynchburg Hospital records she appears as "Sister Aloysia.' She entered the Emmitsburg convent, February 11, 1854. Archives of the Daughters of Charity, Emmitsburg. Payroll, September 1, 1864; Hospital Rolls, Virginia (Lynchburg), Box 26, in RG 109, NA.

• JOSEPH AKIN: (also known in many records as Aiken), Obit., Louisville, Kentucky, *Courier Journal*, June 20, 1904, p. 6. *Journal of the American Medical Association*, July 2, 1904, p. 61. CSR (Mississippi) 16th (Alabama) 15th. Ch. I, 86, 225 and Ch. I. 82, 313 (appointment and resignation from Mississippi 16th); name appears on the list of officers of Trimble's Brigade for the month of November 1862 and indicates that he was in the 15th Alabama, Box 59 #73; S.O. (not numbered); November 20, 1864 put in charge 2nd Division Hospital #3, Lynchburg in Ch. VI, file 724, p. 159. Dr. Akin did not practice medicine after the war but continued to be active in the Presbyterian Church where he served as an elder. Census of 1860, Mississippi, City of Natchez, RG 29, NA; Court Order Book, Green County, Kentucky, April 17, 1837, and Deed Book Green County, Kentucky, 25, December 1861 contain information about Dr. Akin and his family.

• FELIX MULDOON: Certificate of Death, District of Columbia, 154336; Vital Records Division, Washington D.C., CSR (Virginia) 4th Cavalry; Ch. VI, File 55, p. 107 and Ch. VI, file 724, p. 179, RG 109, NA.

160 • Smulders to Davis, October 16, 1864 in the Smulders file, CSRO&M, RG 109, NA.

161 • Davis' memo attached to the summary of Smulders' letter, October 15, 1864 (Richmond); Gardner's response, November 14, 1864 in Letters Received, A&IGO, Smulders' file, CSRO&M, RG 109, NA.

162 • Smulders to Kelly, March 1887 in Louisiana Collection 55C, Tulane University. In this letter Smulders put the number at 900 troops, but in his letter to his provincial he wrote 700 (September 26, 1865, Fort Jennings, Georgia, Redemptorist archives). This number corresponds to that given in the *Official Records*, Series 4, III, p. 1029. See also *Official Records*, *Ibid.*, p. 827 for York's work with the unnamed Smulders, and Series 2, VIII, 254 for the number of deaths at Salisbury.

163 • Smulders to Kelly, March 1887 in Special Collection Tulane University, 55-C.

164 • EDWARD ORD: Obit., San Francisco *Examiner*, November 13, 1905, p. 2; Ezra J. Warner, *Generals in Blue: Lives of Union Commanders* (Baton Rouge, Louisiana: Louisiana State Press, 1964), pp. 349-50. Joseph Ord Cresap and Bernard Cresap, *The History of the Cresaps* (McComb, Mississippi: The Cresap Society, 1937), p. 275.

• PLACIDUS ORD: Place of birth given in the marriage record of Placidus Ord and Julia Andre, July 7, 1846, St. Anne's Church, Detroit, Michigan. More biographical information in the pension application filed by Julia C. Ord (1822-1888), widow of Placidus, May 18, 1880. "Schedules Enumbering Union Veterans and Widows of Union Veterans of the Civil War," hereafter cited as "Schedules, Union Veterans," #265, 466 in RG 15, NA; *Official Records* 46, p.1164.

• JAMES ORD: Bounty Land Warrants and Pensions #6229 in RG 15, NA contains the war record and subsequent history of this man. Day of birth, entrance and departure from the Society of Jesus, Jesuit Archives, Maryland Province, Baltimore, Maryland. Shane Leslie, *George the Fourth* (London: Bouverie House, 1926), pp. 198-203. According to his pension records he was born in 1787; Jesuit Records, 1789.

• JOHN COUGHLIN: *Liber Baptismorum*, St. Mary's Church, Burlington, Vermont, gives the day of baptism October 6, 1837 of John Coughlin, p. 46 #254, Archives of the Diocese of Burlington, Vermont. Civil War record of John Coughlin gives the place of birth, Division of Records and Archives, State of New Hampshire, Concord, New Hampshire. Biographical information given in Pension Record, #164, 884 in RG 15, NA. *Official Records* 51, p. 1210 (Commanding Officer of 10th Regiment, New Hampshire is made provost marshall of the Dept. of Virginia).

165 • Sister Angela Heath, "Annals of the Civil War," p. 98; Fisher, Ch. VI, File 724, p. 181; Akin, Ch. VI, File 724, p. 313. Muldoon, "Return of Hospital Stewards serving at Stuart Hospital," March 20, 1865, indicated that this man was "indispensable," in RG 109, NA.

• WILLIAM H. PALMER: Pension Record, Department of the Interior, #1087254, in RG 15, NA.

166 • ANGELO PARESCE: Obit., *Woodstock Letters* VIII (1879), p. 186-91.

• ALOYSIUS ROCCOFFORT: *Ibid.*, IXX (1890), p. 92.

• HENRY DURANQUET: Obituary, Ibid., XXII (1893), pp. 133-37.

• ISADORE DAUBRESSE: Sketch, *Ibid.*, XXVI (1897), pp. 114-117.

• JEREMIAH O'CONNOR: *Catalogus Provinciae Marylandiae* lists this man as *Mag. caer.* (Master of Ceremonies) at Loyola College, Baltimore, and therefore he was the trainer of the altar boys' sketch, *Woodstock Letters* XXI (1892), pp. 117-19.

• CHARLES DOIZÉ: Rufo Mendízabal, *Catalogus Defunctorum*, p. 75.

• JEROME DAUGHERTY: Obit., *Woodstock Letters* XLIII (1914), pp. 385-88; citation in the text from *Ibid.*, LVI (1927), p. 136.

• HENRY SHANDELLE: Obit., *Ibid.*, LV (1925), pp. 277-79; citation in text from *Ibid.*, LVI (1927), p. 136.

167 • MARTIN SPALDING: Joseph Bernard Code, *DAHier*, p. 275.

• JOHN MOORE: *Ibid.*, p. 207. Jeremiah O'Connell, *Catholicity in the Carolinas and in Georgia*, p. 126.

• PATRICK O'NEILL: *Ibid.*, pp. 151-33. Spalding to Odin, May 29, 1865 in Odin Papers. Quotation in text describing Hubert, taken from Hubert File CSR (Louisiana) 1st, RG 109, NA.

168 • Hudson Strode, *Jefferson Davis*, III, p. 520; Louisiana Collection, Tulane University, 55-c.

169 • *William and Mary Quarterly Historical Magazine*, 2nd series, III (1923), pp. 222-24; Gache to Elizabeth Ewell, August 29, 1867, Ewell Papers.

170 • Moore to Spalding, June 23, 1865 in Spalding Papers.

171 • Annals of the Ursulines, 18, pp. 57-58. Robert Labrely, *Le vieux Bourg-Saint-Andéol*, p. 2.

172 • John Moore to Spalding, October 4, 1865 in Spalding Papers.

173 • Baptista Lynch to Odin, January 14, 1866 in Odin Paper; Obit. H. Gache.

174 • Laurence Kelly, S.J., *The History of Holy Trinity Parish, Washington, D.C.*, 1795-1945 (Baltimore, Maryland: John D. Lucas Printing Co., 1945), p. 74.

175 • Georges Pettit, S.J. to Marie Boisson, November 24, 1907 in Laffont family collection.

BIBLIOGRAPHY

Primary Sources

Archives and Manuscript Depositories

Archives du Collège de Combrée. Maine-et-Loire, France.
"Registre d'étudiants" 1850-70.

Archives du Grand Séminaire d' Angers. Maine-et-Loire, France.
"Registres d'étudiants."

Archives du Ministre des Affaires Etrangères. Paris, France.
Correspondance Commerciale, VII (1854-65), "Charleston."

Archives of All Hallows College, Dublin, Ireland.
Register of Students.

Archives of Notre Dame University, New Orleans Collection. Notre Dame, Indiana.
Blanc, Bishop Anthony. Papers.
Odin, Archbishop John Mary. Papers.

Archives of St. Louis Cathedral, New Orleans, Louisiana.
Book of Baptisms 17 (1840-42).

Archives of Spring Hill College, Mobile, Alabama.
"Register Books of the Prefect of Classes and Studies," (4 volumes).

Archives of the Archdiocese of Baltimore, Baltimore, Maryland.
Archbishop Martin J. Spalding Papers.

Archives of the Archdiocese of Charleston, Charleston, South Carolina.
Gache and Hubert letters.

Archives of the Archdiocese of Cincinnati, Cincinnati, Ohio.
Elder Papers.

Archives of the Convent of the Sacred Heart, Grand Coteau, Louisiana.
House Journal, 1847.
Biographical Information of Religious of the Sacred Heart who served in Louisiana.

Archives of the Daughters of Charity, St. Joseph's Provincial House, Emmitsburg, Maryland.
"Annals of the (Civil) War."
Biographical information.

Archives of the Diocese of Baton Rouge, Baton Rouge, Louisiana.
Indices: Baptisms and Marriages.

Archives of the Diocese of Burlington, Burlington, Vermont.
Liber Baptismorum, St. Mary's Church, 1830-40.

Archives of the Diocese of Nashville, Nashville, Tennessee.
Biographical information of priests who have served in the diocese.

Archives of the Diocese of Richmond, Richmond, Virginia.
Bishop John McGill Papers.

Archives of the Franciscan Institute, St. Bonaventure University, St. Bonaventure, New York.
Personal notes of Reverend Cherubino Viola, O.F.M., manuscript.

Archives of the Georgetown Visitation Convent, Washington, D.C.
Student Records, 1843-60.

Archives of the Maryland Province of the Society of Jesus, Baltimore, Maryland.
"Dimissi" notebook.

Personal Records.
Archives of the New Orleans Province of the Society of Jesus, Grand Coteau, Louisiana.
Michael Kenny, "Jesuits in the Southland," notes.
Archives of the Religious of the Sacred Heart, St. Louis Province, St. Louis, Missouri.
Register, Eden Hall, Philadelphia.
Archives of the Ursuline Sisters, Louisville, Kentucky.
"Annals of the Ursulines, Columbia, South Carolina" manuscript.
Archives, United States Military Academy, West Point, New York.
"Cadet Records"
Archives, Virginia Military Institute, Lexington, Virginia.
Letter from Murray F. Taylor to Joseph R. Anderson.
Archivi del Istituto del Sacro Cuore, Rome.
Biographical information of the Religious of the Sacred Heart.
Baptist Historical Society Library, Richmond, Virginia.
Unpublished minutes of the 76th and 77th meetings of the Dover Baptist Association.
College of William and Mary, Williamsburg, Virginia, Swem Library.
Ewell Papers.
Episcopal Church Historical Society Library, Austin, Texas.
Records, Archives and Historical Collections.
Historical Pensacola Preservation Board, Pensacola, Florida.
LeBaron file.
Jones Memorial Library, Lynchburg, Virginia, Virginia Room Collection.
"Works Progress Administration of Virginia: Historical Inventory, August 26, 1937," manuscript.
"Diuguid Funeral Directory Establishment—History," manuscript.
Kinckle family Bible.
"Research on Families of Lynchburg, Virginia and surrounding Area," manuscript notes compiled by Herbert Bouldin Hawes, (1965), 1800-G, 1800-T.
Medical University of South Carolina, Waring Library.
Waddy Thompson file.
National Archives, Washington, D.C.
Record Group 15—Schedules enumerating Union Veterans and widows of Union Veterans of the Civil War.
Bounty Land Warrants and Pensions.
Record Group 29—Seventh Census (1850): Virginia, City of Petersburg.
—Eighth Census (1860):
Alabama, City of Mobile, Southern Division, 4th Ward.
Virginia, City of Williamsburg; Gaines City.
Virginia, Warwick County, York County, Fauquier County.
Louisiana, Calcasieu Parish.
Mississippi, City of Natchez.
—Ninth Census (1870): Virginia, City of Williamsburg.
Record Group 36—Quarterly Abstracts of Passenger Lists of Vessels Arriving at New Orleans, 1820-75.

Alphabetical Card Index to ships arriving at New Orleans before 1900.
Record Group 109—Compiled Service Records of Confederate soldiers who served in organizations from the states of: Alabama; Florida; Louisiana; North Carolina; South Carolina; Texas; Virginia. (CGSO)
Record Group 109—Register of the appointment of chaplains (Chaplain Book), Ch. I. Vol. 132.
Indices, Entries pertaining to chaplains' appointments. (Indices), Ch. I. Vol. 86.
Compiled Service Records of Confederate generals & staff officers, and nonregimental enlisted men.

New Jersey Historical Society Library, Newark, New Jersey.
Baldwin file.

Pensacola Historical Museum, Pensacola, Florida.
LeBaron file.

Redemptorist Provincial Archives, Brooklyn, New York.
Giles Smulders, C.SS.R. letters and records.

St. Mary's University of San Antonio, San Antonio, Texas.
"The Montagues in the United States," manuscript, Special Collections, Academic Library.

Service Historique de la Marine, Chatèau de Vincennes, Paris, France.
"Dossier et des états de services de Julien-Sosthènes-Joseph Bayot."

South Carolina Department of Archives and History, Columbia, South Carolina.
Schedule 3 "Persons who died during the Year ending 1 June 1860 in Richland District."

State of Alabama, Department of Archives and History, Montgomery, Alabama.
Record rolls of Alabama military personnel (1861-65).
Final Statement by John J. Huggins, Captain, 3rd Alabama, March 1, 1865.

State of New Hampshire, Records and Archives, Concord, New Hampshire.

Tulane University, Louisiana Historical Association Collection, Howard-Tilton Memorial Library, New Orleans, Louisiana.
55-B. Civil War Papers, 1861-63.
55-C. Confederate Personnel, 1861-1955.
55-V. Association of the Army of Northern Virginia Papers, 1870-1954.
Typescript of Tablet Inscription on Tombs, (Girot Cemetery, New Orleans.) Prepared by D.A.R., Chapter "Spirit of '76."

University of California, Berkeley, California, Bancroft Library.
Phoebe Apperson Hearst Papers.

University of Virginia, Alderman Library, Manuscripts Department.
Z. Lee Gilmer Diary.

University of West Florida Library.
Panton-Forbes-Innerarity-Hulse Papers.

Books

Battle-fields of the South, from Bull Run to Fredericksburg, with Sketches of Confederate Commanders, and Gossip of the Camps. By an English Combatant (lieutenant of artillery on the field staff). London: Smith, Elder & Co., 1863, 2 vols.

Bienvenu, Delphin. *Vérité sur l'affaire de Labadieville. Appel à la justice et à l'opinion publique*. n.p. n.d.

Burnichon, Joseph. *La Vie du Père François-Xavier Gautrelet*. Paris: Retaux, 1896.

Caldwell, Howard Haine. *Oliatta and Other Poems*. New York: Redfield, 1855.

_______. *Poems*. Boston: Whittenmore, Niles and Hall, 1858.

Chesnut, Mary Boykin. *A Diary from Dixie*. Edited by Ben Ames Williams. Boston: Houghton Mifflin Co., 1941.

Clark, George A. *A Glance Backward; or Some Events in the Past History of My Life*. Houston, Texas: Rein & Sons Co., 1920.

Cumming, Kate. *The Journal of a Confederate Nurse*. Edited by Richard Barksdale Harwell. Baton Rouge: Louisiana State University Press, 1959.

De Leon, Thomas C. *Belles, Beaux and Brains in the Sixties*. New York: G.W. Dillingham, 1907.

Dimitry, Adelaide Stuart. *War-Time Sketches; Historical & Otherwise*. New Orleans: Louisiana Printing Press, 1909.

Exercises et Manoeuvres de l'Infanterie: Ecole du Soldat, Ecole du Peloton, Ecole des Guides, Service de Places, Service en Campagne. Nouvelle-Orleans: L. Marchaud, Imprimateur, 1861.

Guerzoni, Giuseppi. *La Vita di Nino Bixio*. Firenze: G. Barberá, editore, 1875.

Hamlin, Percy Gatling, ed. *The Making of a Soldier: Letters of General R.S. Ewell*. Richmond: Whittet & Shepperson, 1935.

Hotze, Henry. *Three Months in the Confederate Army*. Edited by Richard Barksdale Harweck. Tuscaloosa: University of Alabama Press, 1952.

Jewell, Edwin L. (ed. & comp.), *Crescent City Illustrated*. New Orleans: Printed privately, 1874.

Johnson, John Lipscomb, editor. *The University Memorial: Biographical Sketches of Alumni of the University of Virginia who Fell in the Confederate War*. Baltimore, Maryland: Turnbull Brothers, 1871.

Jones, John B. *A Rebel War Clerk's Diary*. New York: Old Hickory Bookshop, 1935. 2 vols.

Meade, Bishop William. *Old Churches, Ministers and Families of Virginia*. Philadelphia: J. B. Lippincott, 1857. 2 vols.

Meynier, Arthur, Jr. *Life and Military Service of Colonel Charles D. Dreux*. New Orleans: E. A. Brandas & Co., 1883.

Minutes of the Annual Conference of the Methodist Episcopal Church, South, for the Year 1895. Nashville, Tennessee: Methodist Episcopal Church, South, 1862.

Sheeran, C.SS.R., James B. *Confederate Chaplain War Journal*. Edited by Joseph T. Durkin, S.J. Milwaukee: Bruce, 1960.

Spring Hill College, 1830-1905, Mobile, Alabama: Commercial Printing, 1906.

Private Papers and Family Bibles

De Villier, Jorge. Pensacola, Florida.

Fisher, Mr. and Mrs. Harld C., Yazoo City, Mississippi.
"A Tribute to Captain Stanhope Posey," (resumé, n.p., n.d.)

Gache, Hippolyte. Letters. Ms. in possession of Madame Roselyne Laffont, Salindres (Ardèche) France.

Innerarity, H. Edmund, Oklahoma. Genealogical chart of the Innerarity family.

Jones, Mary Fisk Southall. Family Bible in possession of Mrs. James H. Stone, Richmond, Virginia.

Pettit, George, S.J. Letter. Ms. in possession of Madame Roselyne Laffont, Salindres (Ardèche) France.
Stuart, Elizabeth Letcher (Pannill). Family Bible in possession of Mr. William Alexander Stuart, Jr., Rosedale, Virginia.
Stuart Family Register. Manuscript in possession of Mr. Stuart B. Campbell, Jr., Wytheville, Virginia.
Thompson, Mary Ellen Hinton. Family Bible in possession of Mrs. Norma Thompson, Shreveport, Louisiana.
Turner, Elizabeth Bouche Southall. Family Bible in possession of Mr. C.B. League, Tampa, Florida.

Unpublished Documents

Ascension Church, Donaldsonville, Louisiana.
Marriage Records.
Ascension Parish, Louisiana, Judicial District Court.
Succession of John Duffel, manuscript.
Blandford Cemetery, Petersburg, Virginia.
Burial Records.
Monuments.
Bruton Parish, Williamsburg, Virginia.
Marriage and Birth Records, 1868-1907.
Catholic Cemetery, Stone Street, Mobile, Alabama.
Burial Records.
Children of the Confederacy: Stars and Bars Chapter 69, Mobile, Alabama.
Chapter Book 43.
Christ Episcopal Church, Mobile, Alabama.
Baptismal Records.
Elizabeth Cemetery, Saltville, Smyth County, Virginia.
Burial Records.
Fauquier County, Virginia Circuit Court.
Land Office Records 1860.
Green County, Kentucky Circuit Court.
Deed Book, 1861.
Court Order Book, 1837.
Hancock County, Mississippi.
Certificates of Death.
Holy Spirit Catholic Church, Tuscaloosa, Alabama.
Marriage Records.
Immaculate Conception Catholic Cathedral, Mobile, Alabama.
Baptismal Records.
Marriage Records.
Burial Records.
Lynchburg, Virginia.
Corporation Court Marriage Records, 1863.
Maryland State Department of Health and Mental Hygiene, Baltimore, Maryland.
Certificate of Death: Michael O'Keefe.
Mobile, Alabama.
Circuit Court Minutes, 1837-40.
Mobile County Alabama Probate Court.
Record of Deed, 1845-81.

Record of Wills, 1847-73.
Mobile Public Library, Mobile, Alabama.
"Naturalization Entries, City Court Minutes, Mobile, Alabama," abstract made by a W.P.A. Project (n.d.).
Newport, Virginia, Warwick County Circuit Court.
Book of Wills.
Petersburg, Virginia, Hustings Court.
Index to Marriage Register, 1784-1865.
Register of Marriages, 1854-1900.
Prince of Peace Catholic Church (formerly St. Vincent's). Mobile, Alabama.
Marriage Records.
Baptismal Records.
Richmond, Virginia, Hustings Court.
Record of Marriages, 1880.
Schockoe Cemetery, Richmond, Virginia.
Index to Interments, 1822-1955.
St. Anne's Catholic Church, Detroit, Michigan.
Marriage Records, 1840-50.
St. Louis Cemetery #1, New Orleans, Louisiana.
Records.
St. Louis Cemetery #2, New Orleans, Louisiana.
Cemetery Records.
St. Patrick's Church, Fayetteville, North Carolina.
Baptism Records, 1830-60.
St. Peter's Roman Catholic Church, Richmond, Virginia.
Baptismal Records, 1830-40.
Marriage Records, 1880-90.
Trinity Episcopal Church, Mobile, Alabama.
Marriage Records, 1865-85.
Vital Records Division, District of Columbia.
York County, Virginia.
Deed Book 15, 1849-54.
Deed Book 16, 1854-66.

Magazine Articles

Gache, Hippolyte. "Our College at Baton Rouge, Louisiana." *Woodstock Letters*, 27, (1898), 1-5.

Gazeau, F. "L'Apostolat catholique aux Etats-Unis Pendant la guerre." *Etudes*, VII (1862), 813-28.

Grene, John. "A Contribution Towards a History of the Irish Province of the Society of Jesus." *Woodstock Letters*, XVI (1887), 217-25.

Obituary: P. Hippolytus Gache. *Letterae annuae Provinciae Lugdunensis, S.J., a die 1 octobris 1907 ad diem 15 Augusti 1908*. Bruxellis: typis Josephi Polleunis, 1909.

Nash, Michael, S.J. "Letters of a Civil War Chaplain." *Woodstock Letters*, XVI (1887), 20-31; 144-156; 238-260. XXVII (1888).

Maitrugues, Jules. "St. Charles College, Grand Coteau, Louisiana." *Woodstock Letters*. V (1876), 17-19.

Schmandt, Raymond B. and Josephene H. Schulte. "Civil War Chaplains: A Document from a Jesuit Community." *Records of the American Historical Society of Philadelphia*, X (1962), 58-64.

______. Editors "Spring Hill College Diary, 1861-1865." *Alabama Review*, XV (1962), 213-35.

"A Southern Teaching Order: The Sisters of Mercy of Charleston, S.C. 1829-1904." *Records of the American Catholic Historical Society*, XV (1904), 249-65.

Tissot, Peter. "Lettre d'un autre Père de la Compagnie de Jésus." *Annales de la Propagation de la foi*, XXXV (1863), 284.

______. "A Year in the Army of the Potomac" *Historical Records & Studies* III (1904), 42-87.

Toulemont, P. "L'Apostolat catholique aux Etats-Unis pendant la guerre." *Etudes*, VIII (1863), 863-86.

Non-Published Materials

Alabama Society of the D.A.R. (comps.). Index to Alabama Wills, 1808-70. Ann Arbor, Michigan, 1955.

Campbell, Sister Anne Francis, S.M. "Bishop England's Sisterhood, 1829-1929." Ph.D. dissertation, St. Louis University, 1968.

Hitzman, Reverend Lyle F. "St. Joseph's Church, Baton Rouge (1792-1893): The First One Hundred Years." M.A. thesis, Notre Dame Seminary, New Orleans, Louisiana, 1973.

Louisiana State Library, Baton Rouge, Louisiana. Sidney A. Marchand, "Forgotten Fighters, 1861-1865."

Virginia State Library, Richmond, Virginia. Mrs. Robert A. Ryland. "Family History of Ewell-Ford-Gulick-Hixon-Humphrey-Hutchison-Ish-Marks-Purcell." Genealogical Records Committee, N.S.D.A.R, 1949.

Secondary Sources

Guides

Annual Report to the Adjutant General of the State of Louisiana for the Year Ending December 31, 1894 to the Governor. Baton Rouge: The Advocate, Official Journal of Louisiana, 1895.

Bartlett, Napier. (ed. & comp.) *Military Record of Louisiana; Including Biographical and Historical Papers Relating to the Military Organizations of the State.* New Orleans: L. Graham & Co., 1875.

Bates, Samuel P. *History of the Pennsylvania Volunteers, 1861-1865. Prepared in Compliance with Acts of the Legislature.* Harrisburg, Pennsylvania: B. Singerly, State Printer, 1869. (4 vols.)

Beers, Henry P. *Guide to the Archives of the Government of the Confederate States of America.* Washington: U.S. Government Printing Office, 1968.

Biographical and Historical Memoires of Louisiana Embracing an Authentic and Comprehensive Account of the Chief Events in the History of the State, A Special Sketch of Every Parish and Record of the Lives of Many of the Most Worthy and Illustrious Families and Individuals. Chicago: Goodspeed Publishing Co., 1892. (2 Vols.)

Biographical and Historical Memoires of Mississippi Embracing an Authentic and Comprehensive Account of the Chief Events in the History of the State, A

Special Sketch of Every Parish and Record of the Lives of Many of the Most Worthy and Illustrious Families and Individuals. Chicago: Goodspeed Publishing Co., 1891. (2 Vols.)

Biographical Souvenir of the State of Texas. Chicago: F.A. Battey Co., 1889.

Blanton, Wyndham B. *Medicine in Virginia in the Nineteenth Century.* Richmond: Garrett & Massie, Inc., 1933.

Booth, Andrew B. (comp.) *Records of Louisiana Confederate Soldiers and Louisiana Commands.* New Orleans: n.p., 1920. (3 Vols.)

Branda, Eldon Stephen, editor. *The Handbook of Texas.* Austin: Texas State Historical Association, 1976. (3 vols. and supplement)

Burnichon S.J., Joseph. *La Compagnie de Jésus en France: Histoire d'un Siècle,* 1814-1914. Paris: Beauchesne, 1916. (4 vols.)

The Catholic Directory, Almanac and Clergy List, 1900-05. New York: J. P. Kennedy, 1900-1905. (5 Vols.)

Catholic Biblical Association of America, translators. *The New American Bible.* New York: J.P. Kennedy, 1970.

Catalogus Sociorum et Officiorum Provinciae Lugdunensis. n.p. 1849.

Code, Joseph Bernard. *Dictionary of the American Hierarchy, 1789-1964.* New York: Joseph F. Wagner, 1964.

Conrad, Howard L. *Encyclopedia of the History of Missouri.* New York: The Southern History Co., 1901. (4 Vols.)

Cullum, Bvt. Major-General George W. *Biographical Register of the Officers and Graduates of the U.S. Military Academy at West Point, N.Y., from its Establishment, March 16, 1802 to the Army Re-Organization of 1866-67.* New York: D. Van Nostrand, 1868. (4 Vols.)

Delattre, Pierre, S.J., *Les Etablissements des Jésuites en France depuis quatre siècles.* Wetteren, Belgium: De Meestre, 1949-57. (5 Vols.)

Dictionary of American Biography. New York: Scribner & Sons, 1935. (21 Vols.)

Dunigan's American Catholic Almanac and list of the clergy. New York: James R. Kirker 1858-60. (3 Vols.)

Evans, Clement A, editor. *Confederate Military History.* Atlanta: Confederate Press, 1899. (12 Vols.)

Fairclough, Henry Rushton. *Virgil, with an English Translation.* Cambridge, Massachusetts: Harvard University Press, 1966.

Fox, William F. *Regimental Losses in the American Civil War, 1861-1865.* Albany, New York: Albany Publishing Co., 1889.

Ghisalberti, Alberto, editor. *Dizionario biografio delli Italiana.* Roma: Istituto della Enciclopedia italiana, 1960-to date. (20 Vols.)

Gandrud, Pauline Jones. *Marriage Records of Tuscaloosa County, Alabama, 1823-1860.* Memphis, Tennessee: Milestone Press, 1968.

Germain, Don Aidan Henry. *Catholic Military and Naval Chaplains, 1776-1917: A Dissertation Submitted to the Faculty of Philosophy in partial fulfillment of the requirements for the Degree of Doctor of Philosophy.* Upper Darby, Pennsylvania: Dougherty Printing Company, 1929.

Hebert, Donald. *Southwest Louisiana Records.* Eunice, Louisiana: n.p., 1974-to date. (7 Vols.)

Heitman, Francis B. *Historical Register and Dictionary of the United States Army from its Organization, September 29, 1789 to March 2, 1903* Washington, D.C.: Government Printing Office. (2 Vols.)

Hoffmann's Catholic Directory, Almanac and Clergy List. New York: Hoffman, 1886-89.

Humphreys, General A.A., compiler. *Campaign Maps. Army of the Potomac Prepared by Command of Major General George B. McClellan,* U.S.A., Bureau of Topographical Engineers, April, 1862.

Litterae Annuae Provinciae Lugdunensis, Soc. Jésu a 1 octobris 1840 ad 1 octobris 1841. n.p., n.d.

Litterae annuae Provinciae Lugdunensis, S.J., a die 1 Octobris 1907 ad diem 15 Augusti, 1908. Bruxellis: typis Josephi Polleunis, 1909.

Massachusetts Adjutant General's Office, *Massachusetts Soldiers, Sailors and Marines in the Civil War.* Norwood, Mass.: Norwood Press, 1931. (8 Vols.)

Matthews, James Moscoe, editor. *Confederate States of America. Laws, Statutes, etc... the Statutes at large of the provisional government, February 8, 1861, to its termination, February 18, 1862...* Richmond: R.M. Smith, 1864.

Mendízabal, Rufo, S.J. *Catalogus Defunctorum in renata Societate Iseu ab a. 1814 ad a. 1970.* Romae: Apud Curiam P. Gen., 1972.

The Metropolitan Catholic Almanac and Laity's Directory. Baltimore: John Murphy & Company, 1859-61. (3 Vols.) 135-149; 269-288. XVIII (1889), 2-32; 153-168; 319-333. XIX (1890), 22-41; 154-163.

Ministerial Directory of the Ministers in "The Presbyterian Church in the United States" (Southern) and in "The Presbyterian Church in the United States of America" (Northern). Oxford, Ohio: n.p., 1898.

National Cyclopedia of American Biography. New York: White, 1893-to date.

Official Records of the Union and Confederate Navies in the War of the Rebellion. Washington, D.C.: Government Printing Office, 1894-1922. (30 Vols.)

The Official Catholic Directory. New York: P.K. Kennedy, 1886-1900. (14 Vols.)

Owen, Thomas M. *History of Alabama and Dictionary of Alabama History.* Chicago: S.J. Clarke Publishing Co., 1921. (4 Vols.)

Portraits and Bibliographical Record of Orange County, New York, Containing Portraits and Biographical Sketches of Prominent and Representative Citizens of the County Together with Biographies and Portraits of all of the Presidents of the United States. New York: Chapman Publishing Company, 1895.

Register of the Commissioned and Warrant Officers of the Navy of the Confederate States to January 1, 1863. Richmond: MacFarlane & Fergusson, 1862.

Ruby, James S., editor. *Georgetown University and the Civil War.* Washington, D.C.: Georgetown Alumni Association, 1961.

Rudd A. Bohmer, editor, *Shockoe Hill Cemetery, Richmond, Virginia, Register of Interments, April 10, 1822-December 31, 1950.* Washington, D.C.: n.p., 1962. (2 Vols.)

Sadlier's Catholic Almanac and Ordo. New York: Sadlier, 1864-66. (2 Vols.)

Sadlier's Catholic Directory and Ordo. New York: Sadlier, 1880-1896. (16 Vols.)

Sprague, William Buell. *Annals of the American Pulpit.* New York: Robert Carter & Brothers, 1866. (9 Vols.)

Thompson, Helen A. *Magnolia Cemetery, 1828-1971.* New Orleans: Polyanthos, 1974.

Thompson, James M., editor. *Louisiana Today: An Illustrated Description of the Advantages & Opportunities of the State of Louisiana and the Progress that Has Here Been Achieved, With a Biographical Record of those Citizens Whose Endeavour Has Produced the Superb Structure—Commercial, Industrial,*

Agricultural & Political which Comprises the Strength of this Great State. Baton Rouge: The James O. Jones Company, 1939.
Tyler, Lyon Gardiner, editor. *Encyclopedia of Virginia Biography.* New York: Lewis, 1915. (15 Vols.)
Wakelyn, John L. *Biographical Dictionary of the Confederacy.* Westport, Connecticut: Greenwood Press, 1977.
The War of the Rebellion: A Compilation of the Official Records of the Union and Confederate Armies. Washington, D.C.: Government Printing Office, 1894-1927. (130 Vols.)
Wauchope, George A. *The Writers of South Carolina.* Columbia: The University Press, 1910.
Werner, Ezra J. *Generals in Gray: Lives of Confederate Commanders.* Baton Rouge, Louisiana: State University Press, 1959.
Wyatt, Edward A. IV, editor and compiler. *Checklist for Petersburg, 1786-1876.* Richmond: Virginia State Library, 1949.

Newspapers

Commercial Register. Mobile, Alabama.
Daily Register. Mobile, Alabama.
Advertiser. Montgomery, Alabama.
Examiner. San Francisco, California.
Courier Journal. Louisville, Kentucky.
Daily Crescent. New Orleans, Louisiana.
Daily Picayune. New Orleans, Louisiana.
Daily States. New Orleans, Louisiana.
Deutsche Zeitung. New Orleans, Louisiana.
State. New Orleans, Louisiana.
States. New Orleans, Louisiana.
Times Democrat. New Orleans, Louisiana.
Evening Journal. Boston, Massachusetts.
Pilot. Boston, Massachusetts.
Sea Coast Echo. Bay St. Louis, Mississippi.
Democrat. Natchez, Mississippi.
Daily Advance. Lynchburg, Virginia.
Daily Virginian. Lynchburg, Virginia.
News. Lynchburg, Virginia.
Virginian. Lynchburg, Virginia.
Daily Express. Petersburg, Virginia.
Daily Index-Appeal. Petersburg, Virginia.
Progress-Index. Petersburg, Virginia.
South-Side Daily Democrat, Petersburg, Virginia.
Daily Dispatch. Richmond, Virginia.
Times Dispatch. Richmond, Virginia.
Religious Herald. Richmond, Virginia.
Virginia Gazette. Williamsburg, Virginia.
Post. Washington, D.C.

Books

Arthur, Stanley C. and George C. Huchet de Kernion. *Old Families of Louisiana.* New Orleans: Harmanson, 1931.

Bailey, James H. *A Century of Catholicism in Historic Petersburg: A History of St. Joseph's Parish*. Richmond, Virginia: The Catholic Historical Society of the Diocese of Richmond, 1942.

________. *A History of the Diocese of Richmond: The Formative Years*. Richmond: Chancery Office, 1956.

________. *Jubilee, 1842-1942: St. Joseph's Church, Petersburg, Virginia*. Petersburg: (n.p.) 1942.

Barton, George. *Angels of the Battlefield*. Philadelphia: Catholic Art Publishing Co., 1898.

Baudier, Roger. *The Catholic Church in Louisiana*. New Orleans: A. W. Hyatt, Stationery, 1939.

Biever, S.J., Albert H. *The Jesuits in New Orleans and the Mississippi Valley: Jubilee Memorial*. New Orleans: Hauser Printing, 1924.

Bill, Alfred Hoyt. *The Beleagured City, Richmond, 1861-1865*. New York: Alfred Knopf, 1946.

Blied, Benjamin J. *Catholics and the Civil War*. Milwaukee: n.p., 1945.

Bratton, Mary Elizabeth. *Our Goodly Heritage: A History of the First Presbyterian Church of Lynchburg, Virginia, 1815-1940*. Lynchburg: J.P. Bell Co., Inc., 1944.

Brydon, G. Maclaren. *From Highlights Along the Road of the Anglican Church: The Church of England in England and Her Oldest Daughter, the Protestant Episcopal Church of Virginia*. Richmond, Virginia: Virginia Diocesan Library, 1957.

Burns, S.J., Robert Ignatius. *The Jesuits and the Indian Wars in the Northwest*. New Haven: Yale University Press, 1966.

Burton, Katherine. *Difficult Star: The Life of Pauline Jaricot*. New York: Longmans, Green & Co., 1947.

Callan, RSCJ., Louise. *Philippine Duchesne: Frontier Missionary of the Sacred Heart, 1769-1851*. Westminister, Maryland: Newman, 1957.

Carlson, Oliver & Ernest Sutherland Bates. *Hearst, Lord of San Simeon*. New York: Viking, 1936.

Carne, Richard L. *A Brief Sketch of the History of St. Mary's Church, Alexandria, Virginia*. Alexandria, Virginia: J.M. Hill & Co., 1874.

Carwile, John B. *Reminiscences of Newberry, embracing Important Occurrences, brief biographies of prominent citizens and historical sketches of Churches: To which is appended an Historical Account of Newberry College*. Charleston: Walker, Evans & Cogswell Co., Printers, 1890.

Chamberlain, Samuel. *Behold Williamsburg: A Pictoral Tour of Virginia's Colonial Capital*. New York: Hasting's House, 1947.

Christian, W. Asbury. *Lynchburg and its People*. Lynchburg, Virginia: J.P. Bell, 1900.

Clement, Maud Carter. *History of Pittsylvania County, Virginia*. Lynchburg, Virginia: J.P. Bell, 1929.

Cooper, J. Wesley. *A Treasury of Louisiana Plantation Homes*. Natchez, Mississippi: Southern Historical Publications, Inc., 1961.

Cresap, Joseph Ord and Bernard Cresap. *The History of the Cresaps*. McComb, Mississippi: The Cresap Society, 1937.

Cunningham, H.H. *Doctors in Gray: The Confederate Medical Service*. Baton Rouge, Louisiana: Louisiana State University Press, 1958.

Daniels, Jonathan. *The Randolphs of Virginia*. New York: Doubleday, 1972.

Dumas, Alexandre, editor. *The Memoirs of Garibaldi* (translated by R.S. Garnett). London: E. Benn, 1931.

Early, Ruth H. *Campbell Chronicles and Family Sketches*. Lynchburg, Virginia: J.P. Bell & Co., 1937.

Futch, Orvil L. *History of Andersonville*. Gainesville, Florida: University of Florida Press, 1968.

Gannon, Michael V. *Rebel Bishop: The Life and Era of Augustin Verot*. Milwaukee: Bruce, 1944.

Goodwin, Mary Frances, editor. *The Record of Bruton Parish by Rev. William Rutherford Goodwin*. Richmond, Virginia: Dietz Press, 1941.

Hayden, Horace Edwin. *Virginia Genealogies*. Wilkes-Barre, Pennsylvania: E.B. Yordy Printers, 1891.

Hogan, Thomas J. *The Golden Jubilee of the Church of St. Mary's of the Immaculate Conception With a Resumê of Catholic History of the City of Norfolk, Virginia*. Norfolk: Burke & Gregory, 1909.

Holland, Dorothy Garesché. *The Garesché, de Bauduy, and Des Chapelles Families: History and Genealogy*. St. Louis: Schneider Printing Co., 1963.

Jolly, Ellen Ryan. *The Nuns of the Battlefield*. Providence, Rhode Island: Visitor Press, 1927.

Kane, Harnett T. *Deep Delta Country*. New York: Duell, Sloan & Pearce, 1944.

Keily, Anthony M. *Memoranda of the History of the Catholic Church, Richmond, Virginia*. Norfolk, Virginia: Virginia Book and Job Print, 1874.

Kelly, Dayton, editor. *The Handbook of Waco and McLennan County, Texas*. Waco Texas, Texan Press, 1972.

Kelly, Laurence, S.J. *The History of Holy Trinity Parish, Washington, D.C., 1795-1945*. Baltimore, Maryland: John D. Lucas Printing Co., 1945.

Kenny, S.J., Michael. *Catholic Culture in Alabama*. New York: The America Press, 1931.

King, Grace. *Creole Families of Old New Orleans*. New York: Macmillan, 1921.

Labrèly, Robert. *Le vieux Bourg-Saint-Andéol*. Viviers, France: Largentieré, 1960.

Lafferty, Rev. John J. *Sketches of the Virginia Conference, Methodist Episcopal Church, South*. Richmond: Christian Advocate, 1880.

Lamott, John. *History of the Archdiocese of Cincinnati*. New York: Pustet, 1921.

Lee, Edward Jennings. *Lee of Virginia, 1642-1892: Biographical and Genealogical Sketches of the Descendants of Colonel Richard Lee*. Philadelphia: Franklin Printing Co., 1895.

Leslie, Shane. *George the Fourth*. London: Bouverie House, 1926.

Lewis, Clifford M., S.J., & Albert J. Loomie, S.J. *The First Spanish Mission in Virginia, 1570-1572*. Chapel Hill: University of North Carolina Press, 1953.

Lewis, Virgin A., editor. *Virginia and Virginians*. Richmond: H.H. Hardesty, 1880. (2 Vols.)

Lonn, Ella. *Foreigners in the Confederacy*. Gloucester, Mass.: Peter Smith, 1965.

Lord, Robert H., et. al. *The History of the Archdiocese of Boston*. Boston: Pilot Publishing Co., 1944. (3 Vols.)

Lynchburg Historical Society Historical Papers II, Lynchburg, Virginia: Lynchburg Historical Society, 1962.

McClellan, H.B. *Life and Campaigns of Major-General J.E.B. Stuart*. Richmond, Virginia: J.W. Randolph & English, 1885.

McMillan, Malcom C. *The Alabama Confederate Reader*. Tuscaloosa, Alabama: University of Alabama Press, 1963.

Mallon, Lucille and Rochelle Ferris, compilers. *Burial Records: Mobile County Alabama*. Mobile, Alabama: Mobile Genealogical Society, Inc., 1971. (2 Vols.)

Marchand, Sidney A. *The Story of Ascension Parish*. Baton Rouge: G.E. Ortlieb, Printer, 1931.

Margi, Francis Joseph. *The Catholic Church in the City and Diocese of Richmond*. Richmond, Virginia: Whittet and Shepperson, 1906.

Moore, Alison. *Louisiana Tigers, or the Two Louisiana Brigades of the Army of Northern Virginia*, 1861-65. Baton Rouge: Ortlich Press, 1961.

Munroe, John A. *Louis McLane: Federalist and Jacksonian*. New Brunswick, New Jersey: Rutgers University Press, 1973.

Newman, Harvey Wright. *The Maryland Semmes and Kindred Families*. Baltimore, Maryland: Maryland Historical Society, 1956.

Nieto Asensio, Ponciano. *Historia de las Hijas de la caridad desde sus origenes hasta el siglo XX*. Madrid: Regina, 1932.

Norton, Herman. *Rebel Religion: The Story of Confederate Chaplains*. St. Louis: Bethany Press, 1961.

Older, Fremont. *George Hearst: California Pioneer*. Los Angeles: Westernlore, 1966.

O'Brien, Joseph L., *A Chronicle of St. Patrick's Parish. Charleston, S.C.*, Charleston: Private Printing, 1937.

O'Neall, John Barton. *The Annals of Newberry, Historical, Biographical and Anecdotal*. Charleston: S.G. Courtenay & Co., 1859.

Padberg, John W. *Colleges in Controversy: The Jesuit Schools in France from Revival to Suppression*, 1815-80. Cambridge: Harvard University Press, 1969.

Peyton, J. Lewis. *History of Augusta County, Virginia*. Staunton, Virginia: S.M. Yost & Sons, 1882.

Ramière, Henry, S.J. *The Apostleship of Prayer*. New York: The Apostleship of Prayer Press, 1898.

Ross, Ishbel. *First Lady of the South: The Life of Mrs. Jefferson Davis*. New York, 1958.

Seebold, Herman de Bachellé. *Old Louisiana Plantation Homes and Family Trees*. New Orleans: Publication Prints, 1941. (2 Vols.)

Shea, John G. *History of the Catholic Church in the United States*. New York: Galin G. Shea, 1892.

Strode, Hudson. *Jefferson Davis*. New York: Harcourt, 1959. (3 Vols.)

Taylor, George Braxton. *Virginia Baptist Ministers: Fourth Series*. Lynchburg, Virginia: J.P. Bell, Inc., 1913.

Tinker, Edward Larocque. *Les Ecrites de la langue française en Louisiane au XIX siècle*. Paris: Honore Champion, 1932.

Travis, Robert J. *The Travis (Travers) Family and its Allies: Darracott, Lewis, Livingston, Nicholson, McLaughlin, Pharr, Smith and Terrell*. Savannah, Georgia: Publication private, 1954.

Walsh, Grace. *The Catholic Church in Lynchburg, 1829-1936*. Lynchburg: Coleman & Bradley, Printers.

Webb, Alexander S. *The Peninsula: McClellan's Campaign of 1862*. New York: Scribners, 1882.

Wiley, Bell Irvin. " 'Holy Joes' of the Sixties: A Study of Civil War Chaplains." *The Huntington Library Quarterly*. XVI, 1953.

Williams, T. Harry. *P.G.T. Beauregard: Napoleon in Gray*. Baton Rouge: Louisiana State University Press, 1955.

Wright, Marcus J. and Colonel Harold B. Simpson. *Texas in the War, 1861-1865.* Hillsboro, Texas: Hillsboro Press, 1965.

Wuest, Joseph, C.SS.R. *Rev. Giles Smulders, C.SS.R.* Ilchester, Maryland: St. Mary's College, 1901.

Yancy, Rosa Faulkner. *Lynchburg and its Neighbors.* Richmond: J.W. Fergusson & Sons, 1935.

Magazine Articles

Adams, Martha Rivers. "Old Winfree Home Once Served as Hospital During the Civil War." Lynchburg *Daily Advance,* April 5, 1960.

Ambrose, Stephen E. "The Bread Riots in Richmond." *Virginia Magazine of History and Biography,* LXXI.

Annales de la Congregation de la Mission. (periodical)

Annales de la Propagation de la foi. (journal)

Bailey, James H. "Anthony M. Keiley and the 'Keiley Incident'." *Virginia Magazine of History and Biography,* LXVII (1959), 65-81.

Bearss, Edwin C. "Civil War Operations in and Around Pensacola." *Florida Historical Quarterly.* XXXVI (1957), 125-65.

Civil War History. (periodical)

Confederate Veteran. (journal)

Conlan, C.S.C., Alfonso. "A Study of the Trustee Problem in the St. Louis Cathedral of New Orleans, Louisiana, 1842-1844." *Louisiana Quarterly,* XXXI (1948).

Daniel, W. Harrison. "The Christian Association: A Religious Society in the Army of Northern Virginia." *Virginia Magazine of History and Biography,* LXIX (1961), 93-100.

Daniel, W. Harrison. "Old Lynchburg College, 1855-1869." *Virginia Magazine of History and Biography* LXXX (1980), 446-477.

Daniel, W. Harrison. *"Southern Protestantism and Army Missions in the Confederacy."* Mississippi Quarterly, XVII (1964), 179-191.

Deep South Genealogical Quarterly. (periodical)

Etudes. (journal)

Giblin, Gerald F. "American Jesuits as Chaplains: 1775-1917." *Woodstock Letters,* XCI, (1962), 101-12.

Greenslade, Marie Taylor. "John Innerarity, 1783-1845." *Florida Historical Quarterly,* IX (1930), 90-95.

Hill, Walter H. "Some Reminiscences of St. Mary's College, Kentucky," *Woodstock Letters,* XX (1891), 25-38.

_______. "Some Facts and Incidents Relating to St. Joseph's College, Bardstown, Kentucky." *Woodstock Letters,* XXVI (1897), 90-105.

Jones, John E. *Florida During the Civil War.* Gainesville: University of Florida Press, 1963

Journal of the American Medical Association.

Journal of the One Hundred and Twelfth Annual Council of the Diocese of Virginia. Richmond: Medical Journal, 1907.

Kay, William Kennon. "Drewy's Bluff or Fort Darling." *Virginia Magazine of History and Biography,* LXXVII (1969), 191-200.

Kimball, William J. "The Bread Riot in Richmond, 1863." *Civil War History,* VII (1961), 149-154.

King, T.S. "Letters of Civil War Chaplains." *Woodstock Letters*, XLIII (1914), 24-34; 168-80.

Lenoir, Chambers. "Notes on Life in Occupied Norfolk, 1862-1865." *Virginia Magazine of History and Biography*, LXXII (1965), 131-44.

Louisiana Historical Quarterly. (journal)

Lucy, William L., Rev. "The Diary of Joseph B. O'Hagan, S.J., Chaplain of the Excelsior Brigade." *Civil War History*, VI (1960), 402-09.

Lipscomb, Oscar Hugh. "Catholics in Alabama, 1861-1865." *Alabama Review*, XX (1967), 278-88.

_______. "The Administration of John Quinlan, Second Bishop of Mobile, 1859-1883." *Records of the American Catholic Historical Society of Philadelphia*, LXXVIII (1967), 1-163.

Maioriello, George Theodore. "History of Tidewater Catholicism." *The Catholic Virginian*, February 29, 1952.

Maitrugues, Jules, S.J. "Historical Sketch of St. Charles College, Grand Coteau." *Woodstock Letters*, V (1875), 27-29.

Mississippi Quarterly. (periodical)

Musser, Benjamin Francis. "The Lion of Winsted." *The Provincial Annals*, V (1945-56), 260-73.

Milon, Alfred. "Histoire de Filles de la Charite." *Annales de la Congregation de la Mission*, XCI-C (1926-30).

New Orleans Genesis. (periodical)

Owen, Thomas M. "Brief Memoranda Concerning a Southern Line of the Sands Family." *The Gulf States Historical Magazine*, I (March 1903), 353.

Prachensky, Joseph. "Emigrants Refuge and Hospital, Ward's Island, N.Y." *Woodstock Letters*, I (1872), 57-63.

Price, Beulah M. d'Olive. "The Reverend John-Baptist Mouton: Confederate Chaplain." *Journal of Mississippi History*, XXIV (1962).

The Provincial Annals. (periodical)

Quimbly, Rollin W. "The Chaplain's Predicament." *Civil War History*, VIII (1962), 25-37.

Rice, Philip Morrison. "The Know-Nothing Party in Virginia, 1854-1856." *Virginia Magazine of History and Biography*, LV (1947), 6675; 159-69.

Robertson, James I., Jr. "Houses of Horror: Danville Civil War Prisoners." *Virginia Magazine of History and Biography*, LIX (1961), 329-45.

Robertson, William M., Jr. "Drewry's Bluff: Naval Defense of Richmond, 1862." *Civil War History*, VII (1961), 167-75.

Romero, Sidney J. "The Confederate Chaplain." *Civil War History*, I (1955), 127-40.

_______. "Louisiana Clergy and the Confederate Army." *Louisiana History*, II (1961), 277-300.

Seabourne, J. Gay. "The Battle of Cedar Mountain." *Civil War Times Illustrated*, V, No. 8, (1966), 29-41

South Carolina Historical Magazine. (periodical)

Southern Churchman. (journal)

Stewart Clan Magazine (periodical)

Stock, Leo F. "Catholic Participation in the Diplomacy of the Southern Confederacy." *Catholic Historical Review*, XVI (1930), 1-18.

Turner, Charles W., editor. "Major Charles A. Davidson: Letters of a Virginia Soldier." *Civil War History*, XXII (1976), 16-40.

Virginia Magazine of History and Biography. (periodical)

Wallace, Lee A., Jr. "Coppens' Louisiana Zouaves." *Civil War History*, VIII (1962), 269-82.

Walker, Arthur, Jr. "Three Alabama Baptist Chaplains, 1861-65." *Alabama Review*, XVI (1963), 174-84.

Walsh, Patrick. "The Irish in South Carolina, Georgia, Alabama, Louisiana, and Tennessee." *Journal of the American-Irish Historical Society*, III (1900), 95-109.

Welles, Gideon. "Fort Pickens. Facts in Relation to Reinforcement of Fort Pickens, in the Spring of 1861." *Galaxy*, XI (January 1871).

Widman, C.M. "Spring Hill College, 1830-1898." *Woodstock Letters*, XXVII (1898), 267-76.

______. "Grand Coteau College in War Times, 1860-1866." *Woodstock Letters*, XXX (1901), 34-49.

William and Mary College Quarterly Historical Magazine.

Williamson, Edward C., Jr. "Francis P. Flemming in the War for Southern Independence, Soldiering with the 2nd Florida Regiment." *Florida Historical Quarterly*. XXVIII (July 1949), 143-55; 205-10.

Woodstock Letters (1872-1951), 80 Vols.

Wright, Willard, "Bishop Elder and the Civil War." *Catholic Historical Review*, XLIV (1958), 290-306.

______. "The Bishop of Natchez and the Confederate Chaplaincy." *Mid America*, XXXIX (1957), 67-72.

______. "Some War Time Letters of Bishop Lynch." *Catholic Historical Review*, XLIII (1957), 20-37.

INDEX